Jo Jo Famous

From Tears to Laughter
the Life Story of Jo Jo the Clown

Joann M. Jordan
aka Jo Jo the Clown

PublishAmerica
Baltimore

© 2004 by Joann M. Jordan.
All rights reserved. No part of this book may be reproduced, stored in a retrieval system or transmitted in any form or by any means without the prior written permission of the publishers, except by a reviewer who may quote brief passages in a review to be printed in a newspaper, magazine or journal.

First printing

ISBN: 1-4137-3475-8
PUBLISHED BY PUBLISHAMERICA, LLLP
www.publishamerica.com
Baltimore

Printed in the United States of America

I dedicate this book to my beloved husband, Dennis, who understands me, believes in me, and who is always there for me. For enduring grease paint fingerprints on doorknobs, furniture and drinking glasses. For birthday cake batter and icing bowls on the kitchen table and counters. For glitter, sparkling all over the house, including…himself! For all the long, lonely, crazy hours he patiently awaited my return home, while I spread love and joy to…OTHERS! For putting up with my down moods when I felt like I had lost my touch and I was old, fat, ugly and my hair looked like weeds! Total elation and maybe a little *too* much…pride, after receiving high reviews from the television and newspaper media, receiving cards, letters, phone calls and e-mails of praise from children and parents, making me feel like, as one little child put it, "the goodist clown in the world!" For putting him through all of this and he loves me anyway!

Also to my children, Mary Ann, Dominic, Catherine and Joseph (Danny).

Sometimes they thought I'd lost my mind and many times would try to hide the fact that their mother was a real clown! Their home life may not have always been too normal, while their mother sang and danced all over the house, and forced them put to on plays and skits. For understanding that sometimes they had an "absentee" mom, because she was spending time entertaining…"other people's kids!"

To my baby sister, Mary Jane… who always looked up to me as her "Big Sissy." Who always had a positive effect in my life, both growing up and now. Someone who is not just a sister, but a great friend and after all these years, still makes me feel…needed!

To my dearest friend, Ann Murnock, who lovingly sews all my costumes. Not only does she make "Jo Jo" look beautiful, but the only fee she ever charges is friendship!

To my godparents, Aunt Rose and Uncle Johnny and my Aunt Annie, who always made me feel like their very own daughter.

To my mother and father, who raised me the best that they could with what little they had.

Most importantly to Almighty God… for all the gifts and talents He has blessed me with. And for "calling" me to make this world a happier, better place through laughter, joy and love!

Prologue

My immediate family consisted of four people: my father, Dominick Anthony; my mother, Carmella Rose, who was better known as Molly; my baby sister, Mary Jane; and of course myself, Joann Marie. We were poor, but proud and hardworking people of Italian descent, known as "The Scorzafava Family."

Both sets of my grandparents came directly from Europe. My father's parents came from Calabria, Italy and my mother's family immigrated from around Venice and Naples, Italy.

It is said I received my "hard head" and cute chubby little legs from my father's family and my sense of humor, fair skin, red hair and "fiery temper," from my mother's. My kind loving nature, honesty and faith in God came from both!

We were proud of both our nationality and American citizenship and were strong, faithful Roman Catholics.

I was born on a hot Summer day, August 22, 1949, about 3:30 AM, at the State General Hospital in Scranton, Pennsylvania. My mother said, "Boom! You came flying right out, showering Doctor Lavelle!" Everyone in the delivery room was laughing over my very surprisingly quick birth, as the nurse showed my mother her baby for the very first time, she said, "Wow ! Molly, this little redhead of yours just couldn't wait to come out and join the rest of the world!"

I guess I was destined to make "grand entrances" and "clown around" in life! Well, that is how I came into the picture... but God only knows HOW I stayed in the frame!

JOANN M. JORDAN

(HERE'S... JO JO!)

I paint my face white... A symbol of the Purity and Goodness of God.

Above my eyes... I draw green triangles, representing the Trinity: Father, Son and Holy Spirit.

On my cheeks I add a blue star and a moon. The star on the left, the moon on the right, for the universe... "God is the Creator of Heaven and Earth and all things." (Genesis 1:1)

My nose is bright pink, on which I sprinkle glitter... We are to be "The light of the world." (Matt. 5:14-16)

Next I paint a red heart on my chin for Love! We are commanded to: "Love one another, as I have loved you!" (John 15:12)

I print three letters on my face... JMJ. The first J is in the middle of my forehead; the M is below the left temple; and the other J is below the right. These letters represent the "Holy Family," Jesus, Mary and Joseph.

Lastly, I place a red dot on the side of my star. A red dot painted anywhere on a clown's face is the universal symbol of a "Christian Clown."

My name is Joann.
My patron saint is St. Joseph.
Thus the name "Jo Jo."

I have finished painting my face and as I gaze in the mirror I say my usual prayer, "Lord, please cover me and my celebrations with your holy and precious blood. Fill me with your Holy Spirit, so that others will see YOU, in me! Let me do a fantastic job, earning my money rightly. Most importantly, allow me to bring love, peace and happiness to all I meet and bring about your Kingdom through my work. Amen."

I had the honor and pleasure of becoming an entrepreneur in 1982. As an entertainer, I am well known throughout northeastern & central Pennsylvania as "Jo Jo the Clown."

All through the many years, the joy that children and adults have brought me is far greater than any happiness I may have given them! I wish I could thank each and every one of them personally. I know this is practically impossible, for I have met thousands and thousands of people since I started my career. Hopefully, many will read my book so they can know how much they mean to me and how much they have enriched my life!

Each individual is so different and wonderful in their own way. I have learned from them, delighted in their stories, smiles and hugs, and fell in love with all of them!

Through my volunteer work and "Christian Clown Ministry," I have become a much better human being and have gained far more "riches" than any price that could have ever been paid to me!

I love my job and take pride in what I do! How blessed I am to be able to earn a living doing something so fantastic, that it not only pays my bills, it fills my heart and soul to the brim, not only with a feeling of accomplishment, but also with every positive emotion anyone could ever have... all at once!

My belief is that each and every one of us is given unique gifts and talents and is called by God to use them in His plan for our lives to "bring about His Kingdom," through the work we do, and we will all have plenty of opportunities to do so. All we need to do is believe, listen and... go for it!

It does not matter if you are a king, housewife, or trash collector, each job is valuable and important! I also firmly believe that He calls us from childhood and that the situations that occur, positive, or negative are setting the stage for the "Big Show."

My life growing up was filled with many things: joy, sorrow, heartache, love, pain, regrets and happiness. I have certainly made my share of mistakes! However, we all grow from our life experiences. Hopefully, we can learn from the bad ones and prosper from the good.

I have written this book to share my experiences with you, not merely so you can get to know the "Real Jo Jo," but that others may be helped, find comfort, inspiration, faith and trust in God, and in...themselves.

"Clowning is not just a job to me, but my personal commitment to make this world a happier, better place to live, through laughter, joy and most of all love!"

*Jo Jo is a member of the World Clown Association

Introduction

Jo Jo Famous

Entering Osprey Ridge Nursing Home, located on Scott Street in Carbondale, Pennsylvania, I notice how the sunlight reflects upon the sequins of my costume, casting sparkling rainbows of light which dance upon the wall as I move. I am greeted with a big smile by Mary, the receptionist. As I walk, the halls echo with the merry sounds of jingle bells hidden beneath the layers of taffeta, and my flowing, colorful skirt. The staff and residents alerted by my entrance smile, and I hear a familiar welcome: "Look! It's Jo Jo Famous!" I am making my daily visit to my Mother. She suffered a stroke when she was only forty-two years old. Mommy lived with me for almost twenty-eight years, until she had another stroke and needed the skilled care the facility provided. She celebrated her seventy-seventh birthday this past August. Her whole right side is paralyzed and although she knows who and where she is, her memory is failing. My mother can only speak few words and she has a difficult time communicating, which causes much frustration for her and the staff. However, everyone can understand what she is saying when Jo Jo comes to visit.

As I approach the nurses' desk, I greet and hug several of the elderly people I meet along the way. "Your mother will be so happy to see you! She sure loves it when you visit in costume!" states Sandy, the hospitality aid.

Roger, the head nurse, comes around the corner. Smiling, he jokingly announces, "Why, it's Miss Jo Jo Famous!" He then opens the door to my mother's room and says, "Molly, look who's here!"

As I enter her room, she pulls herself up with her good arm; a huge, toothless grin crosses her still beautiful face. Filled with joy and pride she shouts out, "Praise the Lord! JOJO...FAMOUS!"

My mother is so excited... yelling to everyone in the hall, "Hurry! Jo Jo...Famous! Jo Jo... FAMOUS! Hurry!"

Some of the staff take a moment from their busy schedule to peek into the room. "Molly is sure proud of you! We have no trouble knowing what she is saying when you come!" states Nicole, one of the nurses.

Although I am only well known in this area, in my mother's mind I am "FAMOUS" throughout the whole world! Sitting in the chair next to her bed, I can't keep from smiling as I listen to her brag about her firstborn daughter! I am thankful that the staff indulge her and share in her joy. They truly make her feel important! "After all, Molly, if it wasn't for *you*, Jo Jo wouldn't be here!" states Roger. Her green eyes fill up and she smiles from ear to ear. Nodding her head and raising her good arm towards heaven, she shouts, "Praise the Lord... Jo Jo Famous!"

My eyes begin to wander the bulletin board hanging over her dresser across from her bed. It is filled with newspaper clippings and photos of her costume-clad, firstborn child that the employees have put up for her to see. The thought crosses my mind that everyone knows my mother is filled with pride over my accomplishments, however, how could they possibly know why she is so proud? Even in my mother's fragile state of mind, I am sure there are stored the memories of my humble childhood and the heartaches we have endured together.

Closing my eyes, I thank God that my mother will never know the pain and sorrow her child had endured without her. Mentally, I leave the room and travel back in time to my childhood. I see two little girls, and memories of my daddy, a coal miner, fill my heart.

I have named this book "Jo Jo Famous" as a tribute to my mother, who was called home to the Lord, on October 20, 2003.

Chapter 1

118 Moosic Road
The Front Cellar

I grew up in a small coal mining town, nestled between the Allegheny and Pocono Mountains of northeastern Pennsylvania called Old Forge, the…"Pizza capital of the World!"

My first thoughts of my father… I find myself and my little sister Mary Jane sitting outside, in front of a large glass window of a butcher shop. It was part of a two story house that had been painted white long ago, but had faded, the paint cracking and peeling due to the hot summers and long freezing snowy winters. We rented it for twenty-two dollars a month. Our house was located at 118 Moosic Road, just one block off Main Street. The street was so named because it was the principle way to the next town of Moosic. The butcher shop, owned by our landlady, had been out of business for many years. My mother would refer to it as "the front cellar"… to my sister and me, it was a personal, magical playhouse! I can still see the large room, with light green shelves lining two sides of the walls. Once they displayed groceries, but now held our dolls and other treasures so important to little girls! We possessed many items which cost little or no money, but gave us hours of enjoyment and allowed our imaginations to soar, so we could be anything or anyone we felt like being! There was a glass mason jar that we filled with old fancy buttons, stones and small pieces of coal that we would find in different shapes and shades of black, which we thought were beautiful! Another shelf held a lovely pink satin cloth bag. It was trimmed with golden fringe, and had a picture of a large red seven with a gold crown on top. It once held a bottle of whisky, with a similar name. Happily, I rescued this fancy pouch from our next door neighbor's trash, filling it with about three dollars in pennies. Each time one of Daddy's buddies would come to visit, they would usually give us a few coins for us to save in our bag. But it was a fortune to me in those days! I would open the gold drawstring and carefully count and stack the copper coins, playing "The Queen" as I beheld riches from the treasury! There was also a basket filled with necklaces and bracelets which we proudly made all by ourselves, cutting holes through chestnuts from the tree in the back yard, and threading them with yarn.

Then there was "the Chalice," an old chipped wine glass, covered with silver paper (aluminum foil). It was used when we were lucky enough to receive a nickel to buy "Necco" candy from Cherry's Book Shop, located up on Main Street. I would pick out all the white candy wafers from the roll pretending I was Father Guriox, our pastor from St. Mary's Church, giving out Holy Communion to Mary Jane and our dolls. That is, until the day I was surprised by my angry and shocked grandmother, who pulled me by the ear and yelled at me Italian, that I was committing a great big… mortal sin, and if I ever did such a terrible thing again, I was headed straight for…HELL! Frightened out of my wits, I carefully peeled away the foil from the glass, praying "Our Father's" and "Hail Mary's," begging God to forgive me! After that, it became a mold to make perfect mud "cupcakes."

The floor of the butcher shop was made of concrete. It was unpainted, so cool to bare feet. It had a long crack curving a little to the right leading up to double glass front doors. There was a little brass bell hanging above the door, suspended on a spring-like gadget. The bell would ring when the door was opened to alert the butcher when a customer entered, if he was busy in the back storage room. I learned the reason for the bell the hard way! Because the doors were so old, we were absolutely forbidden to open them. In fact, they had not been opened for many years and were kept locked by an rusty old skeleton key having a place of honor on an equally rusty nail on the right upper corner of the door… up high, away from little children's hands. One day I was feeling a little bored and particularly brave, knowing that my mother was out in the back yard hanging clothes, I dared to touch the forbidden key!

Standing on an old, shaky crate that contained small pieces of wood to start a fire in the stove, I carefully lifted the key off the nail and took it into my hands. I can still remember the rusty odor and the way it stained my fingers. I shall never forget the awestruck look three-year-old Mary Jane had given me as she watched in amazement! I slowly slid the key into the lock and turned it…there was a click, slowly the door creaked open and then it hit than darn bell! I tried to shut the door quickly only to hit the bell again, as it slammed shut…glass shattering about my feet. It was too late…there stood my mother, her left hand on her hip, her right hand opened, shaking it up and down in front of her, saying, in a much too angry voice, "WAIT…WAIT, YOU'RE GONNA GIT IT!"

Needless to say, I never, ever opened…or even thought about opening, those doors with that darn bell ever again!

In the middle of the cement floor with the long crack stood a huge piece of a tree trunk. It was oak, a little more than three feet high, and so big around that Mary Jane could stand on one side, and I on the other, and no matter how hard we tried, or how far we stretched our arms, we could never even touch each other's fingertips! This was used as the chopping block, to cut the meat in the butcher shop's heyday.

So there we sat each evening outside, under the window, in front of the old butcher shop, anxiously awaiting our daddy's return home from work in the coal mines—or should I say, one of our daddies?

Our Kitchen Stove

About an hour or so before my father was to come home, my mother would fill large pots with water that she heated on the huge cast iron kitchen coal stove. It was so mysterious, almost scary to a little girl, yet beautiful in a way, all black, white and chrome. The stove was huge, almost three times the size of today's modern stoves, and stood in the middle of the back wall. On top it featured a large shelf running the whole length of the stove. It had a cover that rolled down, enclosing the salt and spices. This made them within easy reach for my Mother as she cooked. The top of the stove was flat and black, with round circles cut into the metal which a person could lift away from the stove with a silver lever-like tool to reveal the red hot burning coals beneath.

I remember how the large oven right in front, always reminded me of *Hansel and Gretel*! My Mother would open the large, heavy door to place food or cakes to bake on the metal racks. I can remember feeling the intense heat which radiated from the burning coals. She would always chase me away in a threatening voice: "Get away! You will get burnt and your hands will melt to the stove!" However, I would always manage to get a good look and see how big the space inside the oven was and how easily a little girl or boy could fit in there!

The entire stove was held up by four ornately curved legs. On front of the oven door was an emblem that boldly stated "Dickson Stove Company." On the side of the stove was a pail, always filled with black shiny nuggets of coal and a shovel. Sometimes I would take a piece when no one was looking to draw outside on the sidewalk. My hand would become so black I had a hard time removing the stain, even washing them with Octagon soap!

The kitchen was my most favorite place in the whole house! I could almost smell the chestnuts that were placed in a pie tin to slowly roast on top of the stove! They were a special Christmas treat! The sweet aroma would fill the house. We would watch and listen to them sizzle, popping open when they were ready to eat! There were many other wonderful smells that came from our kitchen stove: pots of soup simmering all day, rich pasta sauce that Mom made from tomatoes that my father grew in his garden, potatoes we would wrap in silver paper and roast on top of the coals! So every day my mother would do the strange ritual of boiling large pots of water about an hour or so before one of my daddies would come home from the mines.

Chapter 2

I Had Two Daddies!

My Black Daddy

Mary Jane and I would faithfully man our post outside the butcher shop, after Mom would start to fill the pots to boil awaiting our father's return. As the sun was going down I could hear the sounds of horses hoofs and the creaking of iron wheels on the cobblestones of Main Street, a block up the road. There was a silence for a moment, then the horses and creaking wheels would once again make their special sounds as they continued their journey. Then slowly, there emerged this dark figure, the last of the sunlight behind his head… my DADDY! He was covered with coal dust from head to toe—his skin, hair, face and clothes were literally black as coal! We might be terrified that he was a monster, if not for the only white, familiar thing that showed out from all that darkness—his smile. We were safe, our beloved daddy was finally home—well, one of them anyway!

My sister and I were never allowed to hug or even touch this daddy, but we knew that he loved us so very much by the big smile on his face and the look of pride in his eyes as he would always say, "There's my girls… Daddy is home!" Being the oldest, I would always get to take his black lunch pail and open it to see what little treat he saved for us! Sometimes, it was part of a bologna sandwich, or maybe half a cookie, or a piece of orange or apple. Once in a while he would save us sips of coffee from his black and red thermos. It was always such a wonderful special part of the day. How I looked forward to greeting my daddy and seeing what goodie he would save for us!

I didn't understand that we couldn't hug him because we would get all dirty and black from the coal dust. I never even got a hint when he would sometimes tap us on the nose and we would get a black smudge on top. Mary Jane and I would look at ourselves in the reflection between the red and blue lettering of the butcher shop window and laugh. I would always say, "Oh, Daddy... you made me look like a clown!" Could it have been nothing more than a little joke between a father and his child, or did my daddy have a little insight about my future?

We would walk Daddy down the side of the house, a narrow sidewalk between the hedges that separated our house and our neighbors', The Calvittis. The path led us to an opening underneath a grape arbor. There were wooden benches that Daddy had made for us to sit on. My father always took time to talk with us for a while. He would ask about our day, sometimes with funny questions like: "Ya mean to tell me, yer husband still ain't home yet!" or "What ya think about that big polka dotted cow in the sky about noon?" He would always make us giggle with his funny questions! We couldn't wait to hear about the exciting things that happened in the mines that day. Then finally, he'd stand up, blow us kisses saying, "I love you!" and disappear into the house.

We did not know why, but were not allowed to enter the house at this time, unless it was too cold in winter, then we would wait in the front cellar. Of course, it was because my mother would then pour the pots of boiling water into a galvanized tub, right there in front of the kitchen stove, for my father's bath.

My White Daddy

So there Mary Jane and I sat, underneath the grape arbor, to await the appearance of our other daddy! As I close my eyes, I can smell the aroma from the fresh, ripe grapes hanging in purple clusters above our head. It was always so nice and cool under there, protecting us from the hot summers.

A shady, cozy tunnel, about twelve feet long and eight feet wide, with the benches my daddy built to rest on. The fragrance was wonderful and just sitting there could be so entertaining! We would watch birds hopping about, reaching for a grape for their supper. Sometimes, they would even build their nests between the branches. In the winter, we would pretend we were in Alaska, inside an igloo. In those days we had some very severe winters, with huge snow storms. Sometimes times the snow would be several feet high. Everyone would get snowed in.

Since the arbor was right off our kitchen, all we had to do was open the door and walk right under the rafters that held up the grapevines, that sheltered us from the snow. What more could you ask for with all the intriguing places to play any season of the year!

As Mary Jane and I sat under the grapevine watching the door, soon it would open and our "other daddy" would appear! At first, he would peek out the door just a bit and say the exact thing our first daddy always said, with the exact same voice: "There's my girls!" Then the door would fly open, and we would run into his open arms. At last, our "white daddy" was home—we were safe once more! Inside the house, my mother would be busy in the kitchen emptying out the tub. The kitchen was large, but cozy. The only other rooms downstairs were the front cellar and another large room that was used for storage.

Between the storage room and the kitchen was a staircase leading up to the parlor and bedrooms. I see myself walking up the steps. On top of the landing was a window. To the right was my mother and father's bedroom. The room was large, the walls covered in white wallpaper, with large red roses. My mother would always have white starched lacey curtains on the windows. I remember how we used to help her put the wet curtains on a curtain stretcher. It was a large wooden frame, with what seemed like a million little nails all around it, and we would help her stick the edges of the curtains on each and every nail, then pull it open until they were real tight. When they dried they would be stiff, without a wrinkle and ready to hang.

They had a bedroom suite that any antique dealer would die for. I especially loved the beautiful dressing table; it featured a large round mirror with intricate carvings all around it. I could see my whole body in it. How many times had I sung into a brush handle pretending I was a singing star. Or would put a black apron upon my head and rosary beads around my neck, making myself a nun, or put on my mother's makeup and old costume jewelry beads, becoming a famous movie star?

On each side were drawers with built in jewelry boxes. The knobs were ruby red. A space between the drawers fit a fancy bench covered with shiny red satin. There was a double bed and a matching dresser and chest. The wood was shiny and smelled like lemon oil.

On one side of the large room was a single bed, that had a head and foot board made out of fancy wrought iron; it was painted green. This was my daddy's bed. He would sleep there on the long, cold winter nights so Mary Jane and I could sleep in the big bed with my mother to keep warm.

I used to love to sleep in their room, sharing the bed with my mother. She used to sing us to sleep; not with the usual lullabies—she'd sing: "South of the Border Down Mexico Way," "All Day, All Night, Mary Ann," and my favorite, "My Little Buckaroo."

In the center of the room was a floor vent, directly over the large stove downstairs in the kitchen. The warm air would radiate up from the burning coals would come up through the vent. This was our only source of heat in the bedroom.

Across the landing to the left, on top of the stairs, was the parlor. It was furnished with a maroon mohair couch and two matching maroon and green chairs. They were placed around the heater. It was a tall tan colored stove, and like the kitchen stove, it too was ornate and burned coal. The stove stood on top of a metal sheet that was placed on the floor for protection from the heat. In front of the stove was a door. My parents would open it to shovel in the coal. I can still remember the sound of the shovel digging into the hard, black fuel. The smell of the sulfur, as the coal was thrown on top of the hot, burning coals; the snapping and crackling as the new coal burned. Daddy would slide open a slot when the coals were burning real good. There were about four spaces which would allow the heat to flow through. When the lights were out, it looked like a huge jack-o'-lantern smiling at you! On top of the stove was a hole for a basin to sit inside, my mother would pour water into the basin, adding moisture into the room.

My parents' bedroom, the parlor suite and kitchen set were purchased when they first got married as a three room special. My father's cousin owned a store and allowed them to purchase the furniture and make payments when they first got married. It took many years for them to pay for the furniture. I remember a man from the store would come around every month for a payment. My mother was very fussy with everything, she would say, "It's taking me forever to pay off this furniture. I don't want you kids ruining it before it's even paid for!"

There was a wall in back of the stove, with a door to the left of it and one on the right. This was facing the front of the house. The door on the right led to my bedroom. It was painted light blue and was about medium in size. It had odds and ends for furniture, a double bed for Mary Jane and me. We also had a dresser drawer and huge old chiffonier where my mother kept her sheets, pillowcases and curtains. Many of the sheets and pillowcases were made by her and my grandmother, from King Midas flour bags. Sometimes, they would even let me help embroider flowers on the edges! None of the furniture matched, however, they served their purpose. Anyway, we would much rather sleep with my mother so she could rock and sing us to sleep. Especially in the winter, when she could keep us nice and warm, since there was no source of heat in my room.

There was an outside door in the room; it was nailed shut. This door led to an old porch that was directly above the butcher shop windows. The porch was all rotted and held up by four rusty pillars. Looking out the window, you could see the holes in the floor. My mother's voice still rings in my ears, "Don't ever climb out that window and get on the porch, or else you'll fall through the holes in the floor and kill yourself, and you'll be dead! Then you'll really be in BIG trouble!" She would always place one hand on her hip, and shake her other opened hand at us and say, "Then you'll get this!"

The door on the other side of the stove led to another bedroom. It was always locked and all our landlady's stuff was in there. Every once in a while, she would come over. She was very old and mysterious and the grumpiest person I ever knew! She would come over and let herself in our house and go up into the bedroom. Our family was never allowed in that room. We would look through the keyhole and could see a huge trunk, and cardboard boxes filled with papers and letters. The furniture was covered with sheets giving the appearance of ghosts! The room was a mystery to Mary Jane and me. We would play guessing games—what was hidden in the boxes and what did the furniture look like?

The landlady was real crabby and always angry with my mother about one thing or another. We were glad she usually only came around once a month to collect the rent.

I never told anybody, but at that time I was sure I knew the secret of the room! I was positive that there was a secret passageway, and every night my white daddy would come home, and my black daddy would go through the room to go back to the mines after all, where else did he go? Besides, just where did my white daddy come from? I looked in each and every corner of the house and I could never find them anywhere! So I imagined that they had a special key the old landlady didn't know about. Each evening they would tip their hats as they passed each other in this secret passageway.

What a wonderful black daddy we had. He loved us so very much that he would come home from work every night just as the sun was setting, smile at us and bring us treats from his lunch pail. He would tell us exciting stories about the cold dark mines. My father was a great storyteller; his tales would make us laugh and frighten us at the same time. How I loved him! We couldn't wait for him to come home from the mines each day. My parents never knew that I thought I had two different fathers. They just figured that I was out in the front playing. The memory that is so clear in my mind, and especially in my heart, is when the coal mines closed due to the tragic Knox Mine Disaster. Naturally, my father no longer went to toil there.

I find myself sitting outside under the butcher shop window, waiting for my black daddy to come home. The sun would go down and no matter how I strained my ears, I could no longer hear the sound of horses on the cobblestones of the Main Street. Tears would well up in my eyes, my heart would sink, my black daddy was not coming home today but, he will come… he will come tomorrow, I just know he will! He just has to come home! I am waiting for him!

How many days, or weeks, did I wait for him to come home only to be disappointed; I do not know. However, I do know that one day it hit me, my black daddy was not coming home! Nobody even talks about him anymore, that means…He was NEVER, EVER coming home again! I felt an awful emptiness in my soul and pit of my stomach, and I filled up with fear. My heart, my poor little heart was breaking. My entire being was experiencing pain and every kind of negative emotion, that any little girl could ever fear in her life. Never had I felt so confused and alone.

Then, from deep within, I started to cry… cry so hard and loud that I was sure that I could never stop. Throwing myself on the sidewalk in front of the butcher shop windows, so many tears pouring down my face that the front of my dress became wet. Just when my heart felt as if it would break in two suddenly, I felt strong, warm arms surround me, it was my white daddy!

He lifted me up from the ground, and held me so tight and close to him saying, "Tell Daddy what's the matter. Don't cry…Daddy is here! Tell me why my little girl is cryin' so hard!" But how could I tell him, how could I ever tell him that my heart was breaking for my black daddy! The daddy who didn't even say goodbye! The daddy who was never, ever coming home again! I loved my white daddy very much too, so how could I hurt him by telling him I was crying so hard, and hurting so much, over the other daddy? This daddy would think I didn't love him as much as I loved the other daddy and I loved them both!

After he calmed me down a little, I did the only thing I could think of, so I wouldn't hurt his feelings…with tears streaming down my cheeks, I told a lie! "Daddy," I sobbed, "I got so scared by a great, big, ugly doggy! He was all black, with shiny red eyes and he growled at me with big long teeth, just like the big, bad wolf. I thought he was going to eat me all up!"

Daddy carried me around the house, and set me under the grape arbor, telling me to stay right there. "Don't you worry!" he said, as he went into the house. Soon, he came out with his shotgun, that he used for hunting, and yelled, "There he goes... in the back yard!" Then Daddy ran around the house and fired two shots into his garden, kicking the dirt around with his foot, he yelled to me, "There... Daddy took care of him! Joining me under the grapevine, my father put his arm around me and stated, "That big, bad wolf will never scare you again! I killed him and buried him under the tomatoes!"

I honestly do not remember when it was that I finally realized that my two daddies, were really one and the same man. Or how long I mourned the loss of my black daddy. Or when I got over the pain and stopped missing him, or even stopped hoping and praying he would come home. But now I know the answer... yes, after all these years, I finally know the answer. I never stopped missing him. I still miss him, and have pain in my heart. Although I'm grown up and my mind tells me there was really no black or white daddy, he was the same person... my childlike heart never believed it. Underneath, there is still that little girl who can't understand why he never returned. There was never any closure; we never said goodbye. Now, I have finally come to terms with this heartache... it will never, ever leave, and will remain with me all the days of my life.

How often I think of my black daddy walking down the road with the sun setting behind him, all covered with coal dust from head to toe. I can still smell the musty odor from his clothes, and see him smiling at me with that incredible smile, love shining from his eyes...longing, once again to hear his voice: "There's my girls... Daddy is home!"

The Anthracite Coal Region

As a child, when my father worked in the coal mines, I was too young to comprehend the reason why he would return home black from the top of his head to the soles of his feet. It was due to the coal dust that smothered the air and covered everything and everyone, as he extracted the coal from the earth.

There were many coal mining towns in northeastern Pennsylvania. We lived a few miles from Scranton, boasting the third largest city at the time.

Carbondale and Honesdale, east of us, were the first mining towns to introduce the Gravity Railway. At first mules, then later steam engines would pull the coal cars up the high tracks to the mines. When the cars were filled with chunks of coal, then gravity took over and allowed the heavy cars to flow freely down the tracks to be transported to other destinations.

To the south, lower in the valley, active coal mines were located in the Pittston and Wilkes Barre areas and surrounding towns and boroughs of northeastern Pennsylvania.

Actually, Old Forge is a borough, although it is commonly referred to as a town. It is situated in Lackawanna County, on the Lackawanna River and was settled in 1789 then incorporated as a borough in 1899. An old, long-forgotten forge was found along the river, thus the name…Old Forge. It now has a population of 8,800 and the current mayor is my dear friend, His Honor Anthony Torquato.

Coal at the time, was just as important as air, water and the soil. The black matter was formed in the earth, hundreds of millions of years ago, by dense vegetation. Each piece has a vast store of energy drawn by the sun. The better the grade, the more carbon it contained; it burned hot, clean, and efficiently. There are several types of coal… lignite, bituminous and anthracite. The mines in our area are most commonly mined for the anthracite coal. It is the hardest, longest burning and most sought after of the several kinds. Anthracite coal was the first to be mined in the United States in the region of Carbondale, Pennsylvania about 1745. Although there are many coal mines throughout the United States and other countries.

Coal mining towns were a booming business. It was very difficult and hard work. Anthracite coal is the hardest of the three types of coal. It is located very deep within the earth. Men had to travel down a long shaft on a car pulled by cables. They usually traveled hundreds of feet to reach their destination. It was cold and damp and of course very, very dark! There were two shafts in the mines, one to transport the miners and the coal, the other to allow air and oxygen to flow down into the mines.

The coal was extracted in a planned pattern. Sections of coal were picked and blasted out of an area, thereby leaving columns of coal that actually held up the ceiling. One of the greatest dangers was this ceiling caving in on top of the minors. Many miners were trapped and killed in tragedies throughout the area. It was always a dangerous task to explode sections to loosen the coal from the cave walls.

Another problem was the presence of methane gas. It is highly inflammable. So due to the danger of a gas explosion, no open flame was allowed in the mines.

Many times I recall stories told by my father. He told of the rats being the miners' best friends. They actually fed them, wanting them around, knowing that if they would scurry away quickly, present danger was upon them! Also, he would tell of the foreman keeping a canary bird in a cage. If the bird was dead when he came to work he knew that methane gas was present in the mines. Sometimes, my father had to crawl on his stomach into narrow veins no more than two feet high, and use a pick to break the coal away from the wall! He had to fill a large railway car with heavy chunks of coal, each piece sometimes weighing up to fifty pounds, and he had to pile it higher than the car itself before he could call it a day and come home. No light was able to reach the mines because they were so deep in the earth. My father had to wear a hard hat with a lantern attached, that cast only a narrow beam of light upon the immediate area where he was working. One time, when he was working in an area all by himself, he sat down to take a short rest. Closing his eyes, he reached up and turned off his lantern to save the batteries. He said that he must have dozed off for a few moments, when he opened his eyes again, it was so black, and quiet, that he actually thought he was dead!

I think the most dangerous of all was the coal dust. At the time, it was only considered an inconvenience. Black soot would permeate their clothes, hair, fingernails, nostrils and unknown to them, their lungs. All that fine dust would be inhaled, filling up all their breathing passages and bodies. A terrible condition that eventually plagued most of the miners was a debilitating disease… "black lung."

Later on, years after the mines closed, I would hear my father coughing and gasping for air. He would cough up the black coal dust that had imbedded itself in his lungs. Sometimes, more often than not, he would also spit up blood. It is so painful to remember him struggling just to breathe, with the dreaded condition the old timers called "miners' asthma."

The miners earned very little income for this strenuous and dangerous job. They had to purchase their own explosives from the company store and also hire and pay their own helpers. Many miners who came to America were from European countries. They lived in small, cramped shack-like houses, owned by the coal companies. They were charged high rents, and also had to purchase their food and other essentials from these company stores, so more often than not, they owed the coal company more than they were paid. I remember a song that was sung on the radio by Tennessee Ernie Ford, called, "Sixteen Tons."

The popular song stated, "Sixteen tons, what do I get, another day older and deeper in debt... St. Peter don't ya call me cause I can't go... I owe my soul to the company store!"

Our family, and the families and friends around us, were blessed. We came from an established town, and although we were poor, we had a decent roof over our heads that was not owned by the coal company, and we had food on the table. Most importantly... we had faith in God, love and family!

On January 22, 1959, while coal was being extracted at the Knox Coal Mine, near Pittston, the Susquehanna River broke through, trapping and killing many coalminers. This disaster caused permanent flooding to all the connecting coal mines, and marked an end to deep coal mining in this area of Pennsylvania. It was such a tragedy, not only for the lives that were lost, but also because it was the major source of work, causing thousands of men to lose their livelihoods! The last coalmine to close was the Lackawanna Valley Coalmine. It is now a National Historic site, featuring a "Coalmine Tour," which is located in McDade Park, Scranton, Pennsylvania.

Note... references about coal mining was taken from the 1960 edition of the *Encyclopedia Britannica*. Some references about Old Forge and surrounding areas, was taken from the Centennial Celebration book of Old Forge, May 2, 1999 edition, Anthony Pann, editor. Much of the information was from memory, and stories told to me by my father.

Chapter 3

The Back Yard

Our house had a large back yard. It extended so deep that it merged into a large field, which made the yard look even bigger.

What memories I keep locked in my heart of my friends—Shirley Augustini, Pat Sabetta, Nicky Calvitti and other kids from the neighborhood. We didn't have money for fancy toys, but that never bothered us! We would all meet and play such exciting games as tag, baseball, hide and go seek, and even made up a few of our own along the way! The fun times we spent in this playground—laughing, playing and, of course, fighting! Now, it is a little sad to me that the place where I spent some of the happiest hours of my childhood is covered with pavement. Somehow, I thought that everything would always remain the same; little children would always play, laugh and of course fight in this special place. But, the only thing that never changes is change itself, so our playground was changed into the parking lot for the Old Forge Bank.

My Daddy's Garden

My father's garden was a paradise in my eyes. I remember the peach, mulberry and chestnut trees. How beautiful and fragrant they were in the spring, and in the summer, the sweet tasting mulberries and peaches were incredible!

Daddy had a green thumb. He would take out his garden fork and turn over the soil, pulling out the many rocks that lay below. Then he would plant rows of corn that would tower so high. Mary Jane and I would run between the rows and no one could even see us! We would make up stories pretending that we were soldiers fighting the enemy, or that we were being invaded by giant creatures from outer space! My favorite was playing "Dorothy" and the pathway between the rows of corn, was "The Yellow Brick Road" and we were on our way to Oz!

It is May of 1957. Joann and Mary Jane are standing in the back yard with their faithful dog "Daisy Mae." Notice the shanties and outhouse in the background.

He also planted lettuce and tomatoes; his green beans would grow extra long, and we would love to snap them in half and eat them raw. Daddy would get out his fork and dig up new potatoes; we would help pull the green bushy plants that produced bright, orange carrots from the soil. I still love the feel and smell of the freshly dug earth! The bell peppers looked like little green and red lanterns hanging from their branches. Every day, my father would pull up some green scallions. He'd dip them in olive oil, and pour salt across the top, eating them just like that, or he would put them on a piece of Italian bread. Sometimes even enjoying them with a glass of homemade wine. "Man, what good eatin'!" he'd say. But the most fun job was splitting open the pea pods and using our thumb to pop out the peas into bowl!

At the end of each season, my father would always save seeds from the garden. He would dry them in paper bags. Then, he would plant them in the spring. This way he was always assured a fine harvest without spending too much money for seeds and new plants.

We would love to go with him to Wimpy's Market located down Main Street. He would buy a tray of little tiny tomato plants and some other garden items also. But most of the seeds came from last year's garden. There would always be large, wooden barrels of imported olives in front. When I would think no one was looking, I would always pop one of the shiny, black morsels into my mouth! The hard part was getting rid of the pit. Sometimes, I would just hold it under my tongue until we left the store, or I would just use slight of hand, and pretend I was blowing my nose and pop it into my handkerchief. Once, some lady spoke to me and I swallowed the pit so I could answer her. All day I prayed that I didn't get punished for stealing and that an olive tree didn't start to grow in my stomach!

Some situations from our past will always remain in our minds. Every time I hear the expression, "I got a funny feeling in the pit of my stomach," I chuckle thinking of that day!

The place always had a distinctive, funny odor, since there was always a display of fresh fish across the front of the store all packed in crushed ice. I recall a joke my father used to always tell about the smell, that went right over my head at the time, but I would laugh and laugh anyway! Everyone else would laugh too. I don't know if it was because the joke was actually that funny (in fact, it was downright degrading to women), or because they knew that I had absolutely no idea what I was laughing at, so they found my innocence humorous. Daddy would say to his friends, "What did the blind man say as he was passing Wimpy's Fish Market?" His buddies would wink at my father, and say, "Gee, I don't know." Then my father would look at me and scratch his head saying, "Why I can't remember… do you know, Joann?"

Standing tall, and speaking in a loud, clear voice, I would proudly proclaim, "Good morning, ladies!" Well, everyone would laugh so hard, and slap their hands on the bar…as if I'd told the world's most funniest joke!

Laughing right along with them I would think, "What a silly person I must be…just like Lucille Ball! Just look at how my joke made them all laugh! When I grow up, I will get on television!" It was fairly new at that time, and every program was in black and white. Very few people had one, because only "rich" people could afford such a luxury and only "famous" people could be a guest on one. We used to watch *The Lucy Show* and *Red Skelton* on the television in one of the taverns. I used to daydream, "I bet I am so silly, I could tell jokes and get on one of their shows! Why, I could even could even sing and dance just like Shirley Temple!" It wasn't until I was much older that I realized that the big joke my father told, was on me!

It was almost two thirty in the morning, and I couldn't sleep. It was only days after my forty-fifth birthday…I felt OLD! Maybe too OLD to Clown around! "Maybe I am losing my touch! Maybe no one likes me anymore! Maybe I need plastic surgery…I can't afford plastic surgery! Maybe I'm getting FAT! Oh God…I'm OLD and FAT!"

I put on the television but, all I see are infomercials with beautiful young thin girls telling me I should buy their wrinkle cream, or exercise machine so I won't look so FAT and OLD! Now I don't only feel OLD and FAT, I'm depressed! I want to cry!

I slip in a videotape of a recently televised show.

The camera man counts down, the musical theme plays, and a gentleman in a tuxedo speaks into a microphone: "Hi, everyone, this is your host, Sam LaSante, and welcome to Spotlight Talent Showcase*! We have a great show lined up for you this week. Once again ladies & gentlemen, our favorite clown, Jo Jo, with us today!"*

I perform my song and dance with several local children, the audience applauds! Sam steps up to me stating, "Jo Jo, what a wonderful, wonderful job you did, as usual! You look great! Is that a new costume?" Turning to the camera he says, "Jo Jo has been a regular on our program for the past six years, and she has been on other television programs as well: Real to Reel, Hatchy Malatchy, *and she even co-hosted* PM Magazine. *Jo Jo was a guest several times on my dear friend's program, The* Jan Lewan Polka Show, *and she has been seen many, many times on our local public broadcasting station, WVIA. Jo Jo, you have even been a guest on nationwide TV—The* 700 Club—*for your Clown Ministry, haven't you?"* I nod in agreement. *"I hear you will be entertaining at the mall, where they will be televising the* Jerry Lewis Telethon*! What a great talent you have! Jo Jo, everyone just loves you!"* I smile and lower my eyes, but not before the camera catches a glimpse of them filling up.

"Jo Jo, who are these wonderful talented children?"

I say, "Sam, they are wonderful, aren't they!" I introduce each one of them. "You know, Sam, the best part is that all the children I bring on your show never had singing or dancing lessons, and they learned this song in only a few practices. I am so proud of them!"

Sam says, "You're absolutely right, Jo Jo! Most of the people appearing on our show have been singing and dancing for quite some time. If it wasn't for you, these children and all the other children you have taken on our show over the past years probably would never have a chance to get on TV. You truly have a gift!"

I tease saying, "Oh, come on, Sam, you say that to all the clowns!"

Putting his arm around me Sam states, "No clowning around...I tell you, we receive many, many letters about you. The people especially love the songs you do in sign language; you have even taught some children to sign songs on past shows. Viewers also love that you usually have a Christian theme. No wonder you are northeast Pennsylvania's most favorite clown!"

Once again, I smile softly and lower my eyes, as I hug a little girl, saying, "Thank you Sam, but it's not me, it's these beautiful little children, and my talents...they come from the good Lord above!"

All the other children rush towards me and we engage in a group hug. The emotional audience stands and applauds.

Turning off the VCR, I sit in the darkened, quiet room for a little while smiling. *"Thank you, God... I needed that!"* I whisper. *"Maybe I still have a few good years left in me yet!"* Walking down the hall to my bedroom, I feel very peaceful, knowing I finally will be able to sleep.

*(*I actually made my television debut on a show called *Party Time*. The show featured real birthday kids. It opened with children coming down a sliding board while the theme song played. The MC would then talk to each child, asking them the date of their birthday. When he asked me what I received for my birthday I stated, "I got a dolly from my Aunt Rosie.")

In my father's garden, vegetables were his specialty, however, he also grew beautiful, colorful flowers. Red and pink hollyhocks, yellow daisies, red roses, and blue belles that would spread the aroma of perfume about the air. The flowers also drew honeybees, butterflies and my favorite—hummingbirds.

One sunny afternoon I watched in amazement as a little robin flew into the rows of corn, picking up little pieces of husk with its tiny beak, then flying up into the grapevine, beginning to build a nest. Back and forth she flew, never tiring. Then, another robin joined in to assist her. Together they took turns, intertwining the husks and pieces of grass, forming a perfect home for the new eggs she was soon to lay.

All of a sudden, the peace was broken when a tom cat peered out from under the green pepper plants and, quick as a wink, he pounced and jumped up to catch the robin. I screamed! But before I could take another breath to yell at the cat, my father ran out of nowhere and grabbed the bird right out of the cat's mouth before he could hurt it. The poor robin was scared half to death, panting and shaking, making an awful, pitiful noise. My father brought her under the shade of the grapevine, and held her ever so gently. Softly, he petted the top of her head. He bent down so close to the bird, his lips almost touched her, and started to hum! In a little while, the bird calmed down and closed its eyes, as if to show she was no longer afraid and settled down in my father's hands, actually making herself comfortable. Soon, her breathing was normal. Daddy slowly opened his hands, and in a little while the robin flew up to the rafters, where the other robin anxiously awaited her return. That robin turned around and chirped out to my father, and you would swear it sounded like "Thank you!"

A few days later, there were three tiny blue eggs in the nest! The robins took turns sitting on them, until one day we awoke to the sounds of her babies chirping.

My father always kept watch for that old tom cat. Several times he would chase it away. One day, my daddy became so angry that he tossed a pail of water at him and that pesky cat very seldom came around after that! Daddy would sit under the grapevine and talk to the birds. He would sing and whistle out to them, and they would actually whistle back to him. They even began to take crumbs of bread right out of his from his hands.

Later on, while attending St. Mary's School, I learned about St. Francis of Assisi. He was a very holy man and so close to God that he could talk to the animals, and the animals would talk back. The birds were never afraid of St. Francis and they would even land on his shoulders.

Walking home from school that day, I asked some of my classmates if any of their fathers ever talked to the animals and did any animals ever talked back to their fathers. They all laughed and made fun of me saying, "You're crazy! What a stupid thing to ask! Nobody's father can talk to the animals; only saints can do that!" That night as we lay in bed, after saying our prayers, I whispered to Mary Jane, "Promise you won't ever tell anyone I told you this. I have a big secret. Our daddy is a…SAINT!"

Needing a break, I went out on my deck this afternoon. I was relaxing on the lounge chair, enjoying the lovely spring day, taking in the fresh air and the beauty that surrounded me. The large maple tree across the road, which was estimated to be about three hundred years old, gave wonderful shade. Many of the flowers and bushes I had planted were in full bloom, rich with color and the sweet aroma of perfume. Butterflies and honey bees flitted about and I was watching out for the hummingbirds that would come to drink form the feeders we hung from the roof of the deck. The wind chimes made soft music as they swayed in a gentle breeze. How blessed I felt! Then, something caught my eye. I noticed that several birds were flying in and about my grape arbor that I had planted in 1991, the year we moved to Carbondale, into this lovely old house on the corner of Chestnut and Cemetery Streets ten years prior. I got up to investigate and to my joy, two robins were building a nest up high, in between the branches of the grapevine. Waving to my husband Dennis, I whispered, "Look, they are building a nest!" Dennis carefully walked over. We stood there, his arm around me, and watched in amazement. I suddenly felt chills crawling up the back of my neck, and I tried to stop the tear threatening to spill over, but I couldn't. "Dennis." I said, "I don't know if this is a coincidence or what, but don't you think it is so ironic that the same day I am writing in my book about the robins building a nest in my father's grape arbor, I come out here to find two robins building a nest in my grapevines? I feel like my father is still watching over me!"

Looking at my husband, I saw he too was a little emotional, and he said, "What I think is even more impressive is that the statue of St. Francis standing in the corner looks as if he is overseeing the whole thing!"

Not only did birds enjoy my father's garden, everyone did! He always shared his bounty with others. He would wrap up tomatoes, squash and other produce in old newspapers, giving them to friends and neighbors, saying, "The more ya give away, the more God blesses ya with the next year!" My mother would can the vegetables so we all could enjoy them in the winter. We had little money to splurge on store bought food, except for a chicken once in a while from Nick Caroccia's up the street. There he kept live chickens in back of his store. If you wanted a fresh chicken, he'd go in the back and kill one for you.

My mother would also have a grocery tab at Birnbuams. She would ask me to run up the Main Street and get a few things and to tell Harry to mark it on the bill. He would save all the leftover ends from cold cuts, and sell them to us for a few cents.

We loved going to Augustini's Bakery! You could smell the wonderful aroma of the fresh baked bread even before you entered the shop. I would always have to ask for the two-day-old bread. It was real cheap—sometimes, it didn't even cost a cent, when it was hard as a rock! Every once in a while, the lady behind the counter would pretend she didn't realize it, and slip a fresh, soft roll in the bag. Mary Jane and I couldn't wait to pull it in half, and eat it on the way home. My mother would use the hard bread mostly for bread crumbs to make meat loaf, or meatballs—however, I remember times when there was hardly anything to eat. So she would make spaghetti sauce, or just make a salad with vinegar, oil and dandelion greens and we would dip the hard bread into it, eating only this for supper, but we thought it was so delicious!

On payday, the day my father received his "relief" check, my mother would always go up to the A&P. She would buy a pound of round steak, whiting fish, hamburger, coffee, sliced bread and maybe a treat. When she came home, you could smell the aroma of the fresh ground Eight o'Clock coffee coming from the brown paper grocery bag. The rest of the time we depended on things from his garden and what he caught hunting and fishing. My mother always managed, even without much money to make a meal for her family.

So my mother would boil glass, mason jars in big pots, on top of the stove. She'd prepare for this event, which took up a whole day. I would help her clean, cut and cook the food, but she would always chase us away when it came time to fill the hot, steaming jars. "Get over there, away from the stove, or else you'll get scalded, and then your skin will get all red and cooked, and your hands and face will fall off!"

She would also make grape jelly, with the fresh grapes we would pick right off the vine. The whole house would smell delicious. We would watch as she washed the grapes, and then we would help her pull them off the branches. A large pot would be set on top of the coal stove for the grapes to boil.

The windows would steam up and I would draw pictures on the panes of glass. I would always draw the sun and a figure of a stick man with a big, wide smile, holding a lunch pail; he would be coming home from the mines. It would always be the same picture, even long after the mines closed and the real coal miner no longer returned home.

Sometimes, even after all these years on a cool, crisp autumn day, I find myself drawing a picture of a stick man on the window pane and the ache in my heart deepens as I draw his great big smile I say, "There's my girls…Daddy is home!"

The Outhouse

From the kitchen door led a path that was made out of flat stones, which my father had placed in the ground to make a walkway. He did this so our feet wouldn't sink in the mud when it rained. This path led past the beautiful flowers, past the garden, past everything, to one of the most important rooms of the house. Although it wasn't exactly in the house—it was as far away from the house as one can get…"the outhouse." It was a shack-like structure, about a five by five square, and around eight feet tall, with a tin roof. Along the back wall was a long bench with two holes cut into the seats. This was our toilet. The door was hung on rusty hinges. It was connected to a spring, so it slammed shut on its own. But it didn't bother us, it was normal since everyone else had one too!

Some of the richer neighbors would whitewash the outside. Some people would even decorate theirs, painting flowers and stars; however, ours was just a plain old thing, we needed to use our money for more important things. Daddy told us we could decorate it on the inside. When he was little, he used to decorate the inside of his, with posters from the Holland Movie Theater, which was located up on Main Street. The movie ushers would put up posters of the Coming Attractions in the theater windows. After the movie played for a week they would get rid of the posters. So my father and his brothers and sisters would take the posters out of the trash and nail them to the inside of the walls. So Mary Jane and I proudly drew and colored pictures of all sorts of things: flowers, trees, rainbows, people, even our dog, Daisy Mae! I would try to print words under the pictures telling a story about each drawing. Daddy nailed them up and said, "Good readin'…it gives ya something a do while yer just sittin' there, and if ya can't read, ya can enjoy lookin at the pictures!"

We were never alone in there, no matter how many times my mother would sweep it out, and Daddy would spray it with some awful smelling stuff. Many times as I was sitting there a huge spider would scurry across my foot! There were always ants and other bugs; once, even a frog that visited me in there.

This arrangement was just fine in the spring and summer months, but come the winter—that was another story! How I used to dread getting all dressed up in my heavy clothes, especially early in the morning, and running down the pathway in the freezing cold. My teeth would be chattering, and I could see my breath steaming before me. What was even worse was the thought of taking off some of my clothes when I reached the outhouse and making it in time!

The Toilet Paper Box

I continued my effort to beautify the inside of our outhouse. In the corner, on the ledge of a wooden board, sat a cigar box. This held a place of honor for something very important, our toilet paper.

Several times, I had been in other people's outhouses, but none was as special as ours. We had the most beautiful toilet paper box in the whole neighborhood! My mother always covered ours with silver paper. Mary Jane and I had covered it with sea shell and elbow macaroni, and painted them with our watercolors. It was truly a work of art, and Daddy said that even the Queen of England didn't have one so beautiful!

All day we worked on the cigar box to make it as fancy as we could. My father had been away at Camp Deer Head, where he went each summer. He was due home that day, and I couldn't wait to show him this beautiful creation.

As he entered the house we rushed up to him with our usual hugs & kisses, telling him how much we missed him and asking the big question, "What did you bring us?" He would open his duffel bag and old suitcase, pulling out all sorts of trinkets, from Indian bracelets to pine cones, and bird feathers that he found on the ground.

This year I had a present to give him! "Daddy," I said, "Close your eyes, and hold out your hands. I got something to show you!" Carefully, I placed the toilet paper box in his hands. Excitedly, I couldn't wait for his reaction!

He opened his eyes, and made a loud sound of surprise, "Where did you get this?" As he turned the box this way and that, pretending to inspect the quality of the thing, he stated, "This is so beautiful, it must have cost a lot of money! You can't keep this; you have to bring it back to the store! We can't afford something so expensive, how are we gonna pay the rent?"

All the while I was trying to tell him that we made it, but he pretended to act as if he was so taken up with the beauty and expense of the box that he didn't hear me. Finally, I shouted very loud, "No Daddy, we didn't buy it...we made it!"

He sat down with a look of awe upon his face, and said, "I can't believe you made this; even the Queen of England don't have a beautiful toilet paper box like this!"

I said, "Daddy, you're fooling me...you don't know the Queen of England!"

"Oh yes, I do!" he said, "I know all kinds of important people, and saw many things, when I was in the World War II, fightin' for our country. And once, when I was flyin' over England, I had to go—really, really bad—so I landed my airplane in England. I knocked on the palace door, and asked the Queen if I could use her outhouse. And the Queen said, 'Of course you can; why you just go right ahead, since you're doing such a fine job fightin' to keep yer country free!'" My father said that hers was lovely, all right, but still not as beautiful as ours! So naturally, I received a lot of strange looks, as I went all over the neighborhood proclaiming that we had a more beautiful toilet paper box than the Queen of England!

To be honest, it wasn't really my idea to make the box so fancy. My mother was reading *Good Housekeeping* magazine that our neighbor, Ruthie, had given her, and she got the idea from an article. A lady, dressed like a movie star, was covering a basket with the macaroni; so my mother decided to try it out. We made paste with flour and water to glue the shell macaroni on top of the box in the shape of a heart, and the elbow macaroni around the other spaces. But it was MY idea to cover it with silver paper first and it was MY idea to paint them with watercolors...and sprinkle glitter on top!

Mary Jane and I had an important job; we would sit down at the kitchen table and cut magazines, and any other kind of paper we could find, into little four inch squares. I made them perfect, because I would always measure them with my wooden ruler. Then when they were all done, we would wad the papers up in our hands, roll them into a ball, and open them up again...we would do this to each piece about five or six times to make the pieces nice and soft. When they were all finished, we were so proud to present the finished product, brand new toilet paper! We would make a big ceremony of carrying the box up the path, filling it with our homemade goods, then returning it back inside the outhouse. I bet even the Queen of Anywhere didn't have such a fine celebration!

Sometimes, even now after all these years, dressed as my alter ego, "Jo Jo the Clown," using my "watercolors" to paint cartoon images on little children's faces and putting glitter on their noses, my mind still wanders back to that big kitchen table. I see a little girl, so proudly coloring elbow and shell macaroni with brightly colored paints...then putting glitter on top!

Disappearing Water Trick

One day, when I was about eight years old, we heard a loud knocking on the door. It was so early in the morning, that I didn't even have my school uniform on yet. There stood these two workmen proclaiming that the landlord sent them.

All day in school I couldn't even concentrate on my books, wondering about the work that was going on at my house. Finally school was over, and I ran home just as fast as my feet would take me. Huffing and puffing, I flew up the steps...and there it was, in the far left hand corner of the parlor.

Mary Jane pulled on the skirt of my uniform and said, "JA, look we got a new, shiny, white chair!"

I looked down at her, and thinking that she was such a child…me, on the other hand, I was older, and much wiser, going to school and all! In fact, we had a whole row of them in school, so I quickly corrected her and stated in my most sophisticated voice, "No, Mary Jane, it is not a chair, it is LABORATORY!"

The workmen continued, and with my father's help, it only took a few days to finish. They built a little room, about five by six, around it, and added a door. We still had to wait for the plumber to connect some pipes. I waited for the carpenters to return, and when they didn't I asked my mother when they were coming back. I was surprised when she said they were all finished, so I asked her, "Well, is it the girls' laboratory, or the boys' laboratory?"

The way she looked at me, you would have thought I asked her if the aliens had landed yet! In an aggravated voice she said, "What in the hell is the matter with you, Joann…it doesn't make any difference if you're a boy or girl; it's for everybody!"

Now, I know that your parents were supposed to always be right, and I hated to think it, but for a while, anyway, I was sure she had made a mistake! Especially the next day in school, when the girls' line was a little long, and I had to go very badly! There was only one boy left on the boys' line, so I simply said to Sister Rose, "Sister, I have to pee so bad, I'm going to go to the boys' laboratory, ok?" Well, you would have thought I hit her with a pie by the look she gave me! Grabbing me by the arm, mumbling under her breath, she dragged me down to Mother Pious, the principal. It was bad enough the other kids were laughing at me, but if the principal's office didn't have a restroom I would have wet my pants!

So there I was, in trouble again, and as usual, I had no idea what in the world I did wrong.

At home, we still had to use the outhouse for a week or so, until the big day when the plumber finally arrived from Weinburger's. On this Saturday, all of us waited with excitement, as he did his work—banging and welding. Then in the late afternoon, he called us upstairs to demonstrate his handiwork. "See here, there's water in the bowl, after you do yer duty, all ya hafta do is push down on this little handle, and it empties the water and the waste down the drain. Ya don't hafta do anything else, it fills right back up for ya again, all ready for the next time!"

Why, I never even thought about where it all went in school. All we did was step on a lever, then walk to the sink, and wash our hands. So where did it all go? As the plumber flushed, we could hear the water running down the pipe. I became a little worried. Since we weren't educated on the fine skills of plumbing, I was sure that all the water and everything else would fall downstairs, all over everything! Why weren't my mother and father troubled? In fact they looked happy about the whole thing. They probably didn't even realize that all that water must be, all over—quickly figuring it out in my mind—the ice box.

Taking my sister by the hand, I whispered, "Boy, are they going to be mad, all the water is falling all over downstairs!"

The plumber was saying to my mother, "Come on, you try; just press the handle, and it will flush."

As she reached for the lever, I said to Mary Jane, "Hurry!" As we ran down the steps, I thought maybe we could catch the water in something. We heard it flowing and ran right to the very spot where the water would be falling, but there was no water anywhere. We heard the flushing sound again. I said to Mary Jane, "Watch out, the water will fall on your head!" We scooted into the front cellar, and watched for the flood. Still no water! I thought, "This is weird, where did it go?"

I just knew that my little sister was thinking I was crazy or something. There I stood, expecting her to laugh and say I was dumb, instead, she looked up at me in awe, and in her sweet, little voice she simply stated, "Wow, JA, you're magic…you made all the water disappear!"

Joann's mother & father were married on June 29, 1946, at St. Anthony of Padua Church, on Smith Street, in Dunmore, Pennsylvania.

In the summer of 1996, I was celebrating at little Amanda's birthday party at Arcaros' and Genells'. The children were seated on the floor, while I stood before them, performing my "Magic Coloring Book" illusion, when I heard this sweet, little voice in the back of the group of children say, "Wow, Jo Jo, you're magic; you made all the colors disappear!" I looked up, and there was this sweet, little girl, with blond hair and big, blue eyes, looking up at me in awe. Instantly, I was transported back in time, standing next to the icebox, looking for the water to fall on our heads.

I stood frozen for a moment, and then jokingly said, "Your name wouldn't happen to be Mary Jane, would it?"

She smiled, and put her head down, not speaking. Her mother then came up to me and whispered, "I can't believe she even spoke to you, JoJo...she is so shy! By the way, her name isn't Mary Jane, but you're very close—it's Mary Jean!"

Swallowing the lump in my throat , I said, "That's ok...it's close enough!

His New Tool Shed

It was wonderful not having to run outside to go. That is of course, unless you were outside playing, then you had to run inside to go—then I used to wish it was back outside!

The best was we didn't have to go in that pot with the lid in the middle of the night. And in the morning, I didn't have to be the one to carry it out by the handle, holding my nose, hoping not to spill any of it—ever again!

It took several weeks, but my father, his friend, and my Uncle Tommy made trips with the wheelbarrow each day, filling the hole in the outhouse with rocks and dirt, from the woods. Soon, it was all filled in. My daddy got out his Bugler tobacco and rolling paper. As he rolled a cigarette for himself and his brother, Tommy, he happily stated, "This old outhouse will make me a dandy tool shed!"

My father then bought a bag of cement, mixing it with water in a big tub, and skillfully he poured the cement over the spot and smoothed it out with a flat board. Before it dried completely, he told me and Mary Jane to put our handprints in the cement.

Daddy said, "Now my girls are just like movie stars! Ya know, that's just what they do when yer a star, make ya stick yer hands in the sidewalk, right there in front of the 'Grumpy Chinese Theater!'"

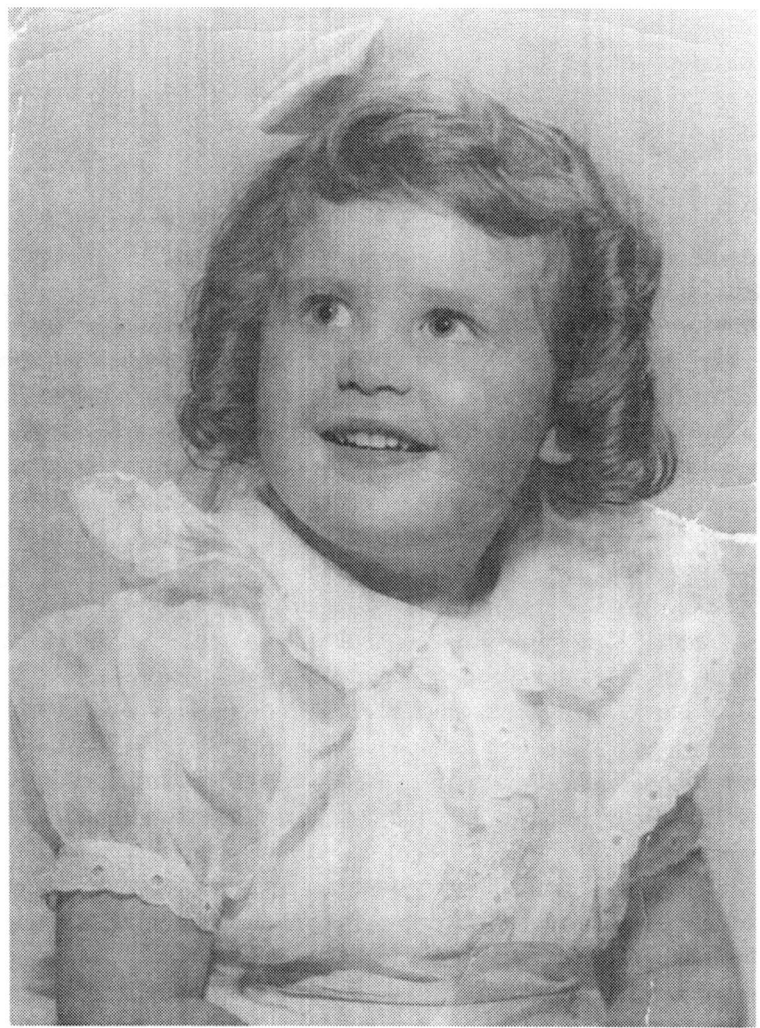

Photo taken when Joann was 3 years old. It was taken at "The Scranton Dry Goods Store." This picture won the "Children's National Photograph Award." Joann's dress was handmade by her Grandma Scorzafava..

Chapter 4

The Icebox

Of course, no one had a refrigerator, but we had our own special way to keep our food cold. We would put our milk and other perishables outside, or on the window sills in the winter. In the summer, we would keep them in a tub of cold water under the grapevine. When the water started to get warm, we would simply add more cold water. One day, there was a lot of excitement; some of my father's friends were carrying this big "thing" into our house. They placed it in the hallway between the front cellar and the kitchen. Daddy proudly stated that it was our new icebox. One of the places where he tended bar got some new fancy icebox that kept the food cold without any ice. All one had to do was plug it into the wall! My father called it a "Frigerator," and they gave him the old one.

It was a large plain, green metal box, which stood on legs with two doors and silver handles. My mother would place milk and other food inside to keep them fresh. On top was a compartment which held a huge piece of ice that the ice man would deliver each morning. He would blow his horn and and yell, "Ice man!" In he would come, carrying this massive block of ice, held by iron tongs, over his shoulder, placing it on top of the icebox. This would keep the inside cold. As the ice melted during the day, it would trickle down the back into a tray underneath.

The block of ice would only cost about ten cents—however, I do remember times when my mother had to turn him away because we didn't even have that small amount, or we didn't have food to put in it.

One of my chores was to empty the tray from the bottom of the icebox. How I hated to do it! Getting on my knees, I would look under and slide the tray out; that was the easy part. Next, I would have to lift this tray and carry it to the sink to empty it. Not that it was very heavy, but trying to carry a flat tray filled with water, across the kitchen was a balancing act.

My mother would say, "Be careful, you're so clumsy, and don't spill anything, you'll slip and fall and kill yourself!" So there I was holding the tray, holding my breath, trying not to spill the water!

Mary Jane would just sit there at the kitchen table. Once in a while, I would see her squinting those big, blue eyes, and holding her hands up to her face. That would make me angry, and even more determined to make it to the sink. I knew she was just waiting for me to mess up and get hollered at.

Most of the time I would make it, only spilling a few drops, that I would quickly wipe up with my dress, before my mother saw them. This one day, for some reason, there seemed to be a lot more water in the tray. There shouldn't have been, because the blocks of ice were always the same size. As I struggled, I began to use my imagination. While my sister watched, I said out loud, "Ladies and gentlemen, welcome to the circus! Look in the center ring and you will see the best tightrope walker in the world—Miss Joann the Great! She will walk the tightrope hundreds of feet above the crowd, carrying a tray of—hot, boiling oil!" Slowly, I imagined the tightrope; carefully, I placed one foot in front of the other, getting closer to my goal. I could hear the roar of the crowd. Mary Jane started to clap and cheer!

I was almost there, and just about the time I was about to dump my tray of hot, boiling oil, my mother came into the kitchen, and yelled, "Joann! Stop your foolin' around; you're gonna get it!"

It wasn't my fault—why, she scared me half to death! I jumped up, the tray of water flying across the room, the water pouring all over the kitchen, most of it, on my mother! Was she ever mad, and boy, I did get it!

That night, I could hear my mother and father laughing as she related to him what had happened! Mary Jane and I giggled too, under the covers, but we didn't want them to hear us, because she would get mad again!

Drifting off to sleep, Mary Jane whispered, "JA, you were so silly today, maybe someday you will join a real circus, and make everybody laugh!"

That night I dreamed that I was on a stage taking a bow, and all the people stood and cheered. I was dressed as a sparkling clown.

Chapter 5

Mary Jane's Solo

My mother was a very faithful woman. She made us go to church for every Mass, Holiday, confession, Novena & Rosary. Of course, if she didn't make us go, the nuns would—telling us we would go to *Hell* if we didn't! But I would have gone anyway, without all their threats. Sitting there in the church, I was always intrigued by the mystery and beauty of all the paintings on the walls and ceilings. The smell and sight of the candles burning and the statues of Jesus, Our Blessed Mother, and all the Saints. I would feel a little frightened, yet peaceful and safe in such a holy place. Somehow, even at a very young age, I understood the love God had for us and I knew that He was always with me.

One May evening my mother, Aunt Annie, Mary Jane and I all walked down to St. Mary's church for the Rosary Devotion. We were dressed in our summer dresses and white shoes.

The church would always be filled with people carrying their rosary beads. I used to look around to see what color other people would have. Mine were white; I received them with a little prayer book for my First Holy Communion. The priest would come out and we all said the rosary. Then we would have Benediction and Adoration of the Blessed Sacrament. How I loved the aroma from the incense that the priest would burn. I would think that it must smell like that in Heaven.

Then we would sing: "Immaculate Mary," "Gentle Woman,","Holy God we Praise Thy Name," and my favorite…"Good Night Sweet Jesus." Well, we were sitting right in front and I was singing away, along with everyone else. Mary Jane pulled on my dress and whispered, "JA, can I sing?"

I whispered back, "Yes, you could sing," which surprised me since she was so shy. She would never sing even with everybody else.

Again, she pulled on my dress and said, "JA, can I really sing too?"

Again, I whispered, "Yes, you could sing too."

Finally she pulled a little harder and repeated her question, "JA, are you sure I can sing?"

This time I became a little annoyed, and whispered loudly, "Mary Jane, how many times do I have to tell you...YES, YOU COULD SING TOO!"

Would you believe after all that, she just SAT there and didn't make a sound! So everyone finished singing all our beautiful songs and sat down. Then, just as Father Guriox was about to give the final blessing, Mary Jane stood up and started singing...just as loud as she possibly could, "HAPPY BIRTHDAY TO YOU, HAPPY BIRTHDAY TO YOU!"

Oh my God! I wanted to die of embarrassment as everyone in the church started to roar with laughter! The priest said, "Let's give the little lady a big hand!"

I was so mortified, and angry with my sister! I couldn't wait to get out of the church! I wanted to bop her on the head for doing something so dumb, especially in front of all my schoolmates; everyone was staring at us and laughing. Now they would have something else to make fun of me about.

Looking over at my mother and Aunt Annie, I saw they were also laughing! What was wrong with them; weren't they embarrassed? It seemed like it took forever to get to the back of the church. Finally, we made it and I was just about to tell my sister a thing or two, when Mary Jane pulled on my dress and whispered so proudly, "JA, did I sing good?"

I looked down at her big, blue eyes looking up at me, so filled with pride, and my anger just melted. I couldn't help but whisper back, "Yes, Mary Jane, you sang good...you sang very good!" She pulled on my dress again and whispered, "JA, that was a special song, I sanged...just for you!"

As I reflect on that summer's evening, I often think...even until this very day, that was Mary Jane's one and only solo in public! What possessed her to ask me if she could sing, and sing not just any song, but THAT song? Could it be that somehow God gave her some insight; maybe she knew that someday her "Big Sissy" would sing to thousands of little children that very same, special song..."Happy Birthday!"

Chapter 6

Making His Rounds

After the mines closed my father had a lot of time on his hands. Although he only made it up to third grade in school and he had no special training, he was a gifted carpenter. Amazed, we would watch him as he carefully handled his tools. My favorite was his plane. He would skillfully slide it across a piece of board, the wooden shavings falling to the ground in curls. He would make tables and cabinets for my mother, and other people too, earning a few dollars. In the summer he had his garden to tend, but he also loved to attend "The Beer Gardens."

Each day he would dress in a white shirt and putting on his Fedora hat, he would say, "Well, I'm off to make my rounds." We didn't own an automobile—in fact, hardly anyone did—so we had to walk everywhere. Up the road he would go, his first place to visit was Ciuccio's Bar. It was located on the corner of Main Street and Moosic Road. He had many friends—old co-workers from the mines and service buddies from the war. They would greet each other with a hug and a slap on the shoulder. He would always order the same thing, "Give me a shot and a beer!" Then he would have a glass of port wine as a chaser. The bartender would always pour the Stegmier beer in a tall glass, fresh from the tap. White foam would form at the top of the glass, and it always looked so refreshing with all those little bubbles rolling up the glass from the brew…sometimes my father would let us take a sip, but we really didn't get much of the actual beer, mostly the foam, which would tickle my nose.

He and his friends would talk, and maybe play shuffleboard or cards. After a while, he'd head for his next stop, Salerino's, and then a few other places, like The Shifting Shanty. It was truly an appropriate name; all the miners would go there to wet their whistle between shifts at the coal mine.

After "having a few" and "shooting the breeze" for a while he would travel to the VFW, there he would sometimes tend bar.

I think this was the main reason he made his rounds each day—to reminisce with people who could understand the horrors of war. He shared with me, when I was older, that he drank to forget the terrible things he saw and had to do in the war! Once when my mother was so upset with him for drinking homemade wine after he just came home from the bars, he simply looked at her, his eyes swelling with tears and said, "Molly, if you were forced to kill another human being, you'd drink too!"

During the coal mine days, they went to the beer gardens to "wash the dust down." After it closed, they would share stories about the mines. It was hard, backbreaking and very dangerous work, but it gave them a sense of pride. After the mines closed, many men like my father had no training. They were unable to find a decent job, and if they did find work it was usually in another state. As the years passed he and many of his friends would not be able to work even if they had a steady job, due to the black lung disease they contracted from the mines.

I know both of these things bothered my father's spirit, and haunted him all the days of his life.

The VFW was my father's favorite place; he was so proud to be an American! I would never tire hearing his old war stories, over and over again. He would get dressed in his Army uniform, along with his drinking buddies from the service and march in all the parades. I remember feeling such pride, as my father carried the American flag. I would shout and wave, "There's my daddy. There's my daddy!" He would always salute us and wink as he passed us by, while we stood on the sidewalk watching all the festivities.

One of my most touching memorie is the way he would always stand up with his hand over his heart, and tears streaming down his cheek, every time he heard "The National Anthem."

I remember the day of my father's funeral; all his buddies were dressed in their uniforms at the Cathedral Cemetery in Scranton. They gave him a twenty-one gun salute. As they shot off their riffles, a loud booming sound rang in the air, then there was a haunting silence. A moment later, his best friend started to play "Taps" on the bugle. It sounded flat and out of tune. Everyone was upset with him, until they realized that he loved my father so much and the pain of losing his friend made him cry so hard he couldn't play!

So each day my father made his rounds. By the afternoon, he would be "feeling good" and he'd come back home. He would usually bring us back Hershey Bars and orange Crystal soda, if he tended bar. He would barter for these treats for his girls and free drinks for himself, in exchange for the service.

Many times he would come in singing, "Just Molly and Me and Baby makes three…" and go over and try to hug and kiss my mother. But she would chase him away, saying, "Get, get… go sleep it off, you old drunk!"

Mostly, my father would laugh it off and continue to tease my mother, "Come on, Molly…give us a little kiss!" while chasing her around, making loud kissing noises. He would also tell tall tales and silly stories about such fictitious people as "John, Slap Her Ass Sky," "Harry, See More Hair" and "Dick, Do To Do." My mother would always yell at him to keep quiet and go to bed. Mary Jane and I didn't even understand all of his stories, but he made us laugh anyway.

However, there were other days when he came home and he wasn't in such a good mood, especially when my mother would argue with him. Instead of teasing her, they would get into a big fight, yelling, cursing and calling each other awful names. There were times that they even threw things at each other. My sister would start to cry, and I would take her outside and go for a walk. If it was late at night, we would go in our bedroom and I would put clothes under the door, trying to block out the noise. Then we'd scoot into bed and put the covers over our heads. I'd hold her tight, and sing her songs that I learned in school about Jesus.

In the morning, no matter how big the fight was, or how scared we were the night before, we would awake to the sounds of my father singing. He used to sing silly songs, with words that made no sense. He'd claim that he was singing in another language, "I used to be an alter boy when I was yer age, so I'm singin' in Latin!"

My mother would say, "Latin, my ass… Pig Latin is more like it!"

My mother always hated my father's drinking, and they had many fights about it, but somehow, they would always laugh in the morning about the mean things they said and did to each other the night before.

Our parents had a strange relationship; they had a very deep love—and dislike—for each other at the same time!

We'd come downstairs and he'd be sitting at the table with his shaving kit. He would take the shaving brush and make a thick lather, rubbing it all over his face. What comical faces he would make to position the straight-edged razor under his nose and chin. We would mimic him, making the same faces right along with him. He would tease, "Ya otta be glad yer not old enough to shave yet... it tires yer arms doing this every day!" It never failed; he would always dab a bit of shaving cream on our faces just when we were not expecting it!

In a little while, he'd fool around in the garden, or maybe tinker with some shelf that he was working on, then he'd say, "Well, it's time for me to make my rounds!"

I used to think, "When I get married, I will marry a rich, handsome, man. We will always have lots of money to pay our bills and buy anything we want. He would never get drunk and we would never, ever fight. Our children would never cry and be afraid, no matter what."

How sad it was for that little girl, the things that she feared the most came true, and her hopes and dreams for a wonderful life almost took a lifetime!

I was about thirteen years old when I met John, however I looked about eighteen. Several of my friends and I would walk miles to the next town of Moosic, to our final destination, Rocky Glen Amusement Park.

This place was a big attraction in those days. It wasn't a huge park, but it featured many rides, including, The Million Dollar Roller Coaster, which boasted that it was the largest in the world.

There was a beautiful lake where we could swim, or take a ferry boat ride. It also had the usual: games, food, a fortune teller, picnic ground, and a stage, were famous bands and singers, would entertain. Each year the owner, Ben Sterling, would hold "Warm Day" that was hosted by a local radio station...WARM. Thousands of people would crowd the few acres of the park.

We decided to take a ride on the merry-go-round; it was very ornate, brightly colored and beautiful! All the horses were hand carved and imported from Germany. It was so finely detailed, with realistic looking glass eyes. In fact, years later, when the park closed down, it is said that Disney bought the huge antique carousel for Disneyland.

My friends Ann Jo, Barbara and I sat on the horses; a man came around to collect the tickets. I was startled...how my young heart started racing! "Wow! Is he cute, or what!" I whispered to my friends. We all agreed that this tall, rugged, "older" man, who was a combination of Jack Palance, Jack Nickalson, and the boy next door, was indeed cute!

Several times a week, we would make our venture to Rocky Glen, always visiting the carousel, not so much to ride, but to see the man we all had a crush on and whom we dubbed, "Johnny on the Merry-go-

Round."

It was hard to believe that this charming, handsome ride operator—who, not too many years later became my husband—not only drank and was physically and sexually abusive, but broke my heart and wounded my spirit, turning a little girl's sweet dreams for a better life into a living nightmare.

The Movie Star

Going to the "Beer Gardens" was, in a way, a part of life for many men and their families. They were not just a place to have a drink, they were places for neighbors and families to socialize. The tavern owners were also our friends. Their beer, wine and homemade food was inexpensive and everyone always ran up a tab, so most everyone in town owed them money. One of the arguments my parents would always have was over money. Since my father only received a very small Welfare check each month, this could barely pay our rent and other bills. So not to take away more than just a few dollars from his check, Daddy would tend bar, paint, do carpentry and odds and ends around the taverns to lower his bar tab. So very little money was actually exchanged.

There were times when my father would take our family with him because one place or another was having a chicken barbecue, tripe, or spaghetti dinner. Since he tended bar, he would exchange the job for a meal for us. We would always meet some of our neighbors there. I loved to play with the pinball machine, and my favorite—shuffleboard. It was such a challenge trying to slide the round, silver pucks across a long board dusted with saw dust. One had to try to hit the puck at the very end, knocking it off the board. I really never made it to the end, my puck always slid off somewhere in the middle of the board, however it was fun trying.

Mary Jane was a short, little, tiny thing, with big blue eyes and long blond hair. Her face was like a cherub. But what good did it do her…she was so shy, if a stranger just asked her name, she would either start to cry or bury her head in my lap! If anyone she knew asked her a question, she'd whisper to me, "JA, you tell them!" So feeling like a translator… she would whisper to me and I would have to relate it to them.

Now, me on the other hand, I was a big ham! In fact, sometimes I would never shut up, talking to everybody, whether they spoke back to me or not. I was tall for my age, and unlike my skinny little sibling, I was just a wee bit chubby. My mother would refer to my size as "pleasingly plump." I was blessed, because my grandmother used to make my dresses when I was real young, before her eyesight started to go. Sometimes they were made out of pieces of material she had left over from the clothing and wedding gowns she would make for others on her Singer sewing machine.

What a gift my father's mother had! She usually needed no pattern. A person would stand there, and Grandma would just look and measure, then set her foot peddling away on her machine and the clothing would turn out beautiful! Because she was so talented her homemade clothing could even pass for store bought.

At night, my mother would wrap our long tresses of hair with strips of cloth. We looked real weird with long white things hanging from our heads. They were so uncomfortable to sleep on, so I was happy that she usually only did this on Saturday nights, so we would look nice for church, on a holiday or special occasion. The next day my mother would unwrap us, and down would fall this perfect "bologna" curl.

One day my mother took us to a grocery store on Oak Street. This sweet old lady who owned it called Grandma Pann told my mother that I looked a little like Shirley Temple with my red curls and big bow in my hair. Boy, did I eat that all up! I would practice all her songs, pretending that I was on a stage. Quite often my father would take me and Mary Jane with him as he made his rounds. We had a game plan. He'd tell everyone, "Are you ready for the show!" He would lift me up on the bar, as everyone cheered me on. I would sing "On the Good Ship Lollipop" and "Animal Crackers in My Soup" while dancing and doing all kinds of actions…just as loud as I could! All the while I would be peeking at my reflection in the mirror, on the wall behind the bar. Big, exciting thoughts would spin around in my little head: "Someday, I will go far away from here and become very famous and make lots of money, and all the world will know my name! I am so talented and pretty. Why, I really do look like Shirley Temple, don't I?"

As I took my final bow, everyone would clap and whistle, saying I was so cute! Then I would go sit at a table and all my father's friends would buy me candy bars, potato chips and soda, which I always shared with Mary Jane, even if she didn't DO anything to DESERVE some. The owner would always say, "Nick, sit a spell…yer drinks are on the house!" Daddy would wink at me and smile from ear to ear. I would wink back. "We did it!" I'd whisper to Mary Jane, "We got free everything!"

My father knew I really didn't really look *that* much like Shirley Temple, and that I couldn't really sing or dance very good…but he was proud of me anyway. His love for us shined from his twinkling blue eyes. We were his little girls.

When my show was over, he would always cheer the loudest and say, "My Joann is going to be a movie star someday—just you wait and see!"

I am standing in front of the train station in Moscow, Pennsylvania in 1995 dressed like a passenger of the 1940 era. The director shouts, "ACTION!" The camera man, riding on a portable track, follows me as my scene opens. I pose as an passenger walking with a Red Cap as he carries my luggage towards the train. As we continue to converse, you can see the excitement in my face as we reach the entrance. The porter asks me if this was my first trip to Chicago. Smiling I say, "Why yes it is!" while handing him my ticket. Searching through my purse, I finally pull out some coins, and hand them a tip. I then say, "Please be careful of the bags…I don't want them lost or damaged."

He states with confidence, "Don't you worry none, miss; I'll take real good care of them for you!"

As I climb up the steps of the huge rail car, I pause for a second and turn back to look at him. I then state, "Oh, porter, please wake me at 7:00 AM." He nods in agreement, and I say, "Now, don't be late." And I disappear into the train. The name of the movie is Steel and Steam.

As I sit inside coach, I look out the window and watch all the other actors doing their parts. I can't help but laugh to myself over my "big" part. The movie is only about a half hour long, featuring several local people as extras, including my friends Cindy Wilces, Joe Vargo, and my husband Dennis. Most of the people are just walking to and fro, giving the illusion of a busy station. My part was obtained through Ed Curry, one of my entertainment agents. I had one of the few speaking rolls in the whole movie. It is a beautiful, heartwarming movie about the railroad. It will be shown for the next twenty years at the Steamtown National Historic Museum in Scranton.

Looking out the window, I notice all the beauty around the area. It is autumn and the leaves are dressed in full color. With the aura of the movie, I was transformed back in time, and I imagined myself really

heading to Chicago.
August 6, 2004

Trains were a way of life back then, and the movie reflects their heyday. It explains not only how important they were, but it also portrays how wonderful, beautiful and clean the cars were. It is said that a woman named Phoebe Snow would dare to ride the railway dressed in pure white, thus, proving that the steam engines produced no soot, allowing her outfit to remain spotless. Trains not only provided transportation, they provided sleeping cars, and had elegant dining rooms. The movie also, sadly explains the passenger train's demise, with the invention of the automobile and airplane.

The Steamtown Museum has several working trains and engines including the "Big Boy," a huge, black steam engine. One could spend hours looking at the museum's photos and information about the railroad, preserving an important part of our heritage. They even hold seasonal train excursions to Honesdale, a quaint town where the "Gravity Railroad" actually began. In the fall you can enjoy the majestic mountains and breathtaking, colorful foliage. At Christmas time, you can enjoy the beauty of the trees, covered in glistening, white snow. And the children of all ages will love the special guest...Santa.

I think about my ancestors and what a big part of their lives the railway must have been to them. A working railway still passes through the area, although the cars are no longer used for passengers; they carry goods to manufacturers.

So there I sat in the train car, my mind pondering all these things, when I was brought back to the present by the director shouting that practice was over. We had a fifteen minute break before shooting the real scene. I still had to laugh at all the long, long hours of practice ensuring that I got my "important" part just right; I would be on the screen for all of about three minutes! I waited in my seat, watching the others exit the train, when my heart leaped! A man passed me by and I thought I'd seen a ghost! From the back, he looked just like my father! I could not believe my eyes...his height, his walk, his after shave, even the fedora hat on his head. My pulse raced and I felt flushed. I wanted to run up to him and say, "Daddy, Daddy...It's me!" I started to feel a little faint so I closed my eyes, just for a few seconds, and then I heard his voice, strong and clear, "I told you, someday you will be a movie star! Daddy sure is proud of you!" I almost jumped out of the seat as I opened my eyes...but he was gone.

Tears welled up in my eyes as I rushed from the train, looking for the man...my father? I don't know...WHO! It was too late; he was lost in the crowd, or was he? Was it my father; did his spirit come back to let me know he was watching over me and the length of my role didn't matter, I was a movie star and he was proud of me! Was my mind playing tricks on me since I was all caught up in the past, or was it just wishful thinking, and he was nothing more than a stranger who resembled my father? Could it be that while my eyes were closed, just for those few seconds, that the man said those wonderful words to his own child, who was an extra in the movie with him? Who knows...stranger things have been known to happen.

I find comfort in the fact that God sometimes sends us messages through other people, and that day He sent me a message. It could have been through a stranger who I never saw again. Then again, God can do all things...maybe, just maybe, the man wasn't a stranger at all!

Photo taken in front of "The Big Boy" locomotive, at the movie set of "Steel and Steam," in Moscow, Pennsylvania. Left to right, cast members...Bob Haynes, Cindy (Wilce) Killhullen, Dennis Jordan, Joann Jordan and Joe Vargo.

Chapter 7

Grandma Scorzafava...I Think?

A little further down the street from our house, at 620 Moosic Road, lived my grandmother. She was not only my father's mother, but a mother to five girls and four boys, and she even adopted another little girl. Not only did they have different first names—Dominick, Sammy, Tommy (Teemy), Ralph, Angeline, Rosie, Annie & Mary (twins), Pauline (Parmie), and little Marie, the adopted child—they all had different last names. No, my grandmother didn't marry nine different men, nor did she have any out of wedlock. This situation was all to blame on the midwives and doctors!

I love my maiden name—Scorzafava; it has character! It sounds romantic, intriguing and musical. Even if it does mean "Peel of the Bean" in Italian!

This name is not only long, but was probably hard to pronounce in English, especially since my grandparents only spoke Italian. Children were usually born at home, with the aid of a midwife, or local doctor, if they got there on time! So as each child was born, whoever delivered the baby would spell it, and register the birth in Harrisburg, like they thought it should be spelled: Scorzafava, Scazafavo, Scazzafavo, Scavafabo—whatever!

My Grandmother was the holiest person alive. Each and every morning she would walk six long blocks up to Main Street, then several more blocks to get to Grace Street. At Grace Street she still had to walk another block, to reach St. Mary's Church for daily Mass. After Mass she would sometimes visit for a cup of tea. She did this until she was almost ninety!

Some of my fondest memories were walking down to her house. Grandma would always make us feel welcomed and loved. Mary Jane and I would pick her Blue bells and dandelions along the way, and faithfully deliver them to her—bugs and all! She used to make a big fuss about them and put them in a glass of water. Then we would go outside and place them in front of the statue of the Blessed Virgin Mary.

Her bedroom was like a shrine. All four walls were decorated with religious pictures from top to bottom. She must have had every Angel and Saint in Heaven in her room! Each picture was large and framed with thick, ornate, dark wooden frames. On her dresser, she had quite an assortment of statues and little glass cups that held water and oil, in which she placed floating wicks that were perpetually lit. The candles would cast moving shadows upon the walls. When I went into her bedroom, I would always find myself speaking in a whisper. For I would get the exact same reverent, awesome feeling that I got when I entered a church.

There were little shrines all about Grandma's house. One was on a little kitchen shelf with statues and floating candles. Even outside, the statue of the Blessed Mother reflected her strong faith. My father and Uncle Tommy built a grotto from cinder blocks right around her. We would plant flowers with my Aunt Annie, who lived at home. Grandma always had a large candle lit right in front of the statue.

Of course, Grandma also had her rosary beads and numerous prayer books. They were written in Italian, so I couldn't read the prayers. However, I knew that they were sacred, containing the Word of God. I feel truly blessed to have inherited one of her prayer books and, although I still can't read Italian, it is so precious to my heart!

Grandma would sit in the living room chair for hours, her eyesight failing, reading her holy books and prayer cards with pictures of Jesus, through a magnifying glass. I would sit at her feet, my head resting on her leg, while she'd softly pet my hair. Sometimes I would doze off to the sounds of her whispers…"pssh, pssh, pssh!"

Once again, I find myself sitting in the choir loft of St. Rose's church, singing God's praises dressed as —Jo Jo the Clown. Our choir director, Doreen, looks so beautiful as she conducts. I love to watch her smooth, sweeping motions, and the look of pride upon her face.

Since Sundays are one of my busy days to entertain at birthday parties, I sometimes had to get made up so I could leave for my engagements straight from Mass.

Everyone in town is so used to seeing me in my costume at doctors' offices, grocery stores and church, that no one even bats an eye—well, except for an occasional child who happens to turn around and look up in the choir loft and yell, "Mommy, Mommy there's Jo Jo upstairs!"

Well things were fine, until I reached that age when I was unable to read without glasses. Since Jo Jo has really long, long eyelashes, she can't wear my glasses. Someone jokingly mentioned that maybe a magnifying glass would help...and she was right!

So there I am singing God's praises, not only dressed like a clown, but I'm holding a large magnifying glass. I get a chuckle from the other choir members. One friend turned around and asked me if I felt just like Sherlock Holmes. I was about to whisper back, in jest, "Yes I do...and I'm so PROUD of it!" But all of a sudden I smiled, as a wonderful, warm, loving memory came into my heart. Instead, I softly said, "No I feel just like my grandmother...and I'm SO PROUD of it!"

Grandma also had a "gift." People were always coming to my grandmother's house to be prayed over. I remember a lady who visited my grandmother. She was about middle age, and was dressed in dark clothing. I really couldn't understand too much of what she was saying, since they were they in another room, and she was crying so hard. I peeked through the crack of the bedroom door, and watched as my grandmother laid her hands on the woman's head. Grandma closed her eyes and started to pray very softly. I noticed how the woman relaxed, and actually started to look peaceful. When the woman was leaving she started kissing my grandmother's hands as she thanked her over and over. My grandma told her in Italian to keep praying and believe that God is healing her.

My grandmother was well known for her gift. In fact, even people in the medical profession believed in her faith. Doctor Leopardi would always send patients to her when they couldn't be helped by conventional means. Once he heard of a baby way out in the Philadelphia area, who was very ill. He referred the family to my grandmother. Grandma asked them to send her a shirt. Not a clean one, but one that the baby had worn. After she prayed over it, and anointed it with oil, she returned it, instructing them to put it on the baby and pray, believing that God would heal him. Lo and behold, the baby was brought back to health! The family sent my grandmother a large check, thanking her for healing their beloved child. However, Grandma send the check back. She *never, ever* accepted any payment for her prayers from anyone. She told the family, "I only prayed for your baby; *God* is the one who healed him! You give Him the honor and glory!"

I meet people to this very day, who come up to me and tell stories about the healings that have occurred through my grandmother's prayers! I tell them what I know Grandma would say, "You too, can pray for the sick, always believing that all things are possible with God!"

Mary Jane and I lived the closest to our grandmother, so we saw more of her than most of her grandchildren. Since she came from Italy she spoke very few words of broken English. (I really used to think that when people became old, they started to speak with an accent). Our grandparents on my mother's side also spoke Italian, so when I was younger I was able to understand quite a bit of this beautiful language. I was even speak enough to be able to communicate.

To this day, I regret that I never learned or remembered more of the language of my ancestors. Although I still find myself speaking in Italian once in a while. Every now and then, while entertaining at a birthday party, I hear people speaking in Italian, and my heart jumps. I find myself rushing over, telling them my, "My name is Jo Jo!!" and "How do you feel?" in the Italian language. They get all excited and they think I'm very "WONDERFUL!" But then, for some strange reason I am compelled to speak more to them, so I blurt out the few statements I can remember. Although they have little or no bearing on the birthday celebration, and I'm probably speaking in very bad Italian: "Did you say your prayers?" "Do you want to eat?" "Give me a kiss," " Come on, to go to bed!" "You're getting fat," "What time does the bus come?" "Be patient and wait a minute," and of course I always have to count to ten for them! And then they probably think I very...WEIRD!

Visiting my grandmother was always a pleasure! How I loved to climb the apple tree in the back yard. There were many other trees: juicy pears, peaches, plums and cherries that could be picked right off the branches to be eaten anytime. My Aunt Mary— who is Aunt Annie's twin sister—Uncle Jake and my cousin Rossie would come to visit Grandma. Rossi, and I would play for hours in the back yard and in the apple tree making up all sorts of exciting adventures. Way in the back of the property was an old coal breaker, and we would go exploring, finding pieces of coal and several times we even found a stone arrowhead from a real Indian arrow.

My grandmother also did some comical things. Since she couldn't read English, she once made delicious potato pancakes. The only problem was she thought she was making them with flour, but she used Plaster of Paris instead! And once she stated that the oil had an awful smell after she poured it into the frying pan. Thank God, she decided not to cook supper in it, since it turned out to be Lestoil!

We would love to hear about our heritage. When my Grandmother lived in Italy she was very wealthy, in fact, she was a Countessia! Her maiden name was Constantine—we are directly related to the Emperor!

My grandmother even had a handmaid, who used to draw her bath and comb her hair! She had the finest clothes, and could have lived out the rest of her life in luxury. However, as fate would have it, her life took a turn and changed forever.

Grandmother came to America to visit a cousin who had moved to this great land of freedom and opportunity. It took several months to travel to America by ship. During the long voyage my grandmother met many people. One young man was smitten by her beauty and charm. They developed a friendship, and before long, he fell deeply in love with Josephine Constantine! But there was a problem—although my grandmother felt a fondness for this gentleman, she was not in love with him. He begged her to marry him, telling her that he couldn't live without her. He did all that he could to win her heart, but to no avail.

They finally arrived in America and parted, each going their own way. She left him with a broken heart. That man was, Marconi, inventor of the wireless telegraph!

So my grandmother came to this new and very different land. She was visiting with a relative; they owned a boarding house in the area of Carbondale, Pennsylvania. In those days, paved highways and interstates were not even heard of. All the roads were rough, narrow passageways and it would take sometimes a day or two just to get to another town with a horse and buggy. So Carbondale at that time might as well have been in another state from Old Forge. In fact, that town was probably not even established yet. Years later, they moved to Old Forge, and she set up housekeeping.

I find this fact ironic, since here it is over a hundred years later. I grew up in Old Forge…I now reside in Carbondale! My mind ponders over such things, was this just a coincidence…or was it fate?

Years before I moved there, I was residing in an area called Lake Ariel. One day I received a phone call form a nun, Sister Eleanor Kalafut from St Rose of Lima Church in Carbondale. She had heard about my expertise in composing poetry and putting together a Christian program. We made an appointment to talk about the great plans she had a special person, Msgr.Thomas Horan. He was about to celebrate his fiftieth anniversary as a priest. I felt so honored she chose me to be a part of his celebration.

Following the directions to Carbondale, I started to feel a sense of peace as I neared the small city. As I drove into the area my heart was filled with joy. The old, beautiful buildings reminded me of a train layout underneath a Christmas tree. I fell in love with St. Rose's church; it was absolutely breathtaking and one of the most beautiful churches I have ever seen.

Sister Eleanor was the principle at Sacred Heart School which belonged to the church. What a great lady she was, and she had even greater plans to make Msgr. Horan's big day a fine success. So we plotted and planned to make his celebration a day no one would ever forget.

Sister wanted it to be a surprise for everybody, so no one knew I was coming, with the exception of the caretaker. She gave me all the information and I composed a three page poem all about his life. We took pictures of his cow in a field. Planned everything with zest...why, it was just like a Broadway stage production...songs, music, the works!

Now, Sister was so nervous, being the perfectionist that she is; she called me every day with such messages: "I want this celebration to be perfect! I don't want any mistakes! Make sure you have the music just right! Have everything in order; it must be just wonderful!" My son, Dominic, was my assistant "Jasper" at the time, and we practiced and practiced! By the time the big day arrived, I could have done the show in my sleep!

Our game plan was: Sister Eleanor would say, "Hark! I think I hear someone!" Then the production would begin...Jasper would enter with the music from Godspell—"Prepare ye the way of the Lord"—while he was pushing a large broom. As he would reach Msgr Horan, Jasper would then turn around, reveling a bold sign on his back: "Happy 50th Anniversary." Just about that time, the music would become faster and more lively. I would make my entrance carrying a huge bouquet of gold helium balloons, moving to the fast, joyful beat of the music. "Prepare ye the way of the Lord; everybody now, prepare ye the way of the Lord!" Jasper would throw confetti. I would dance around while handing Msgr. Horan the balloons, one at a time, and entice the crowd to clap to the tune of the energetic music. Wow! What an entrance; just like a New York theater!

Well, Sister said her part, Jasper did his part, and I performed my part—almost! As the music became louder, the tempo faster and more exciting, I made my grand entrance, then to my horror, I heard the music become slower, and SLOWER: *"Prreeepaaarree yeee thhe waaay offf thhe Loord, evverrbooddy noow, prreeepaarree yeaa thhhe waaay offf thhe Loord!* Oh my God! The batteries in my sound system were dying! I glanced over at poor, shocked, Sister Eleanor, and if looks could kill, I wouldn't be alive to write this book.

My mind raced remembering there was a Woolworth store in town, I grabbed Jasper, shouting, "Come on! Let's go!" and ran out of the church hall.

Flying down a one way street— the WRONG way—I sped up to Main Street, then made a right on Salem Avenue and pulled into a parking lot. As I started to run across the street I called out to Jasper to pull the old batteries out of my tape recorder. A man started to yell at me, "Hey you, Clown, you can't park here; this is for the taxi! I yelled back that I would only be a minute, as I ran across the road, almost getting hit by a garbage truck, and stopping traffic. The man was yelling something about calling the cops. By the time I reached the door, my adrenaline was sky high, and my heart was beating so fast I thought it would burst through my costume. All I could think of was Sister Eleanor; I was a clown on a mission: find batteries, and get back to the church ASAP! I threw open the doors, and ran into the store, screaming so loud to the lady at the checkout one would think I was POSSESSED! "BATTERIES! BATTERIES!, quick, where are your batteries?" Of course, she looked at me like I was a mad woman! I yelled at her again, "I SAID, where are your BATTERIES... I mean NOW!" in a much too sinister voice. She didn't speak, but pointed to the wall on the right, and I ran to my destination, loudly praying: "OH GOD PLEASE, PLEASE, LET THERE BE D CELLS!" As I scanned the racks, I yelled, "YES! THANK YOU JESUS!" I grabbed the Coppertops and spun around; everyone, both customers and employees, were literally stopped dead in their tracks, just looking at me! In my crazed state of mind, I yelled, "What are you all staring at? Why don't you take a picture; it will last longer!" Then, to add insult to injury, I pushed past everyone in line saying, "PLEASE...PLEASE, let me get ahead of you, it's an EMERGENCY, a matter of life and death!"

Finally, I was at the counter and I said anxiously to the cashier, "QUICK! HURRY! How much do I owe you?"

I was ripping the batteries from their package, when all of a sudden she began laughing, and said, "Oh my God... I get it; we're on Candid Camera! I can't believe it; where's the hidden camera? Where is Alan Funt?"

I stated, "NO, you are NOT on Candid Camera, *this is NO JOKE! Now please do your job, and tell me how much I you NOW!"*

As her smile left and tears glistened in her eyes it suddenly hit me, I was picking on this poor, innocent lady; what kind of a "Christian Clown" was I, anyway! I felt so bad, so I reached over for her hand and softly said, "Oh, I'm sorry, please don't mind me; I'm having one of THOSE days! Placing the money on the counter, not even waiting for the change, I blew kisses to all the people I cut in front of, smiling and saying in my worst, Elvis impression, "Thank you, Thank you, Thank you very much!" I burst through the doors and ran across the street. The man at the taxi station was arguing with my son about my van, so I gave him a big hug and said , "God will surely bless you for this!"

As I sped back to the church, I noticed all the people in Woolworth's were looking out the windows. I prayed that I wouldn't have a heart attack!

There, outside was Sister Eleanor, she pointed to me and said, "THANK GOD! I thought you RAN away, I have the caretaker looking all over for you! What happened; where did you go? You're the MAIN entertainment!"

Breathlessly, I said, "Sister, you have no idea!"

As they say, the show must go on! Jasper and I made our grand re-entrance and it was a smashing success...much to the relief of Sister Eleanor!

Now, in this boarding house where my grandmother was staying, lived a man named Salvatore. He too migrated from Italy and he came to America to start a new life. This gentleman was hardworking and of modest means, and like his future sons would become, he too was a coal miner.

Salvatore, a handsome man himself, was also struck by my grandmother's gentleness and beauty. And like Marconi, he fell deeply in love with her. At first she was reluctant and thought of him as just a friend; but Salvatore wouldn't give up. He followed her, played the accordion, sang love songs and wrote poetry to her, he did everything he could to win her over, wanting her to become his wife.

Now my grandmother was used to a certain lifestyle. Back home in Italy, she had a title and wealth. Living in America and marrying this coal miner, she would have to give all that up. She would have to learn to do things for herself that she had never had to do. Simple things like cooking, doing laundry, and even styling her own hair. This was really a big decision, one that would change her whole life.

Lucky for me, love won out! Soon, Josephine Constantine became Josephine Scorzafava.

Unfortunately, I never had the chance to know my grandfather; he left this world soon after I was born. I was told he was much like my father, a coal miner, a kind, goodhearted man who loved his friends and family. Like anyone else, he had his good and bad sides, and like my father, he also enjoyed having a few glasses of wine.

My mother would tell me this heartwarming story: On the day of my Christening, my mother, father and grandparents had to take the trolley to the city of Scranton, then another to the town of Dunmore. I was to be baptized in St. Anthony's Church on Smith Street. This was my mother's church, and she and my father were also married there four years before. Dunmore is where my mother grew up and where her family still lived.

Once they arrived at their destination, they had to walk up this steep road, appropriately named Hill Street. They were going to my Aunt Rosie and Uncle Johnny's house, who are my godparents. My grandfather, was carrying me and all the while he was short of breath. Both my mother and father wanted to take me from him, but he held me close to his heart and said, "Don't take her away from me, this is the last time I will ever hold her in my arms!" My grandfather died shortly after that day.

One of the things that always laid heavy on my grandmother's heart was that she never had the chance to go home to Italy again. Grandma always talked about it, but was never able to return. Therefore, she never had the chance to say a real goodbye!

So my grandmother left behind a life of leisure, wealth and security and moved forward to a life of growth, hardship and blind faith. My Grandma Scorzafava contributed many things to this world, most importantly, she gave life to nine babies, including my father... and in turn, he gave life to me!

Chapter 8

Aunt Annie & Family

All of Grandma Scorzafava's children had grown up to marry and leave the nest. All except one of her twin daughters... Ann.

I simply cannot remember when Aunt Annie wasn't a part of our life. No matter what occasion, celebration... or problem that arose, you would find her there. I am closer to her than I was to any of her brothers and sisters. Not that I loved them any less; I loved them all very much. It is just that we lived nearby, and we are able to see her more often. In fact, her sister Paulene (Parmie), had taken me out to her home in Long Island, New York several times. Aunt Parmie, her husband, Uncle Sonny, and cousins, Roche and MaryAnn, lived in a beautiful house in Jericho. When I became a little older, my mother would put me on a Greyhound bus. My Uncle Sonny was a successful fashion designer in Manhattan and he would meet me at the Port Authority in New York City. I remember that once he wanted to go for a ride in Harlem, where he grew up. As we rode through the streets, he gave me a tour, pointing out his old house and other places that held meaning for him. At first he was so excited to be in his old neighborhood, then as we passed by burnt cars, graffiti, run down buildings with their windows boarded over, my uncle's mood began to change. His enthusiasm turned to great sadness. He then passed the church where as a child he attended Mass and was an altar boy. It had a high, chain link fence all around it. There was a padlock on the gate and a sign proclaiming which hours the church would be opened.

He stopped the car and I thought he was about to cry. "I can't believe it!" he said, "When I was a boy, you could go into that church twenty-four hours a day, it was never locked! Harlem was such a beautiful, well kept neighborhood, I can't believe it, I just can't believe it... how could they let Harlem get so trashed and run down like this!"

My heart went out to him and I shall never forget that day. Uncle Sonny was a big, handsome, strapping man; he was always the life of the party and was very comical. He wasn't afraid to laugh and sing and just have a good time, and let people know that he loved them. So to see this side of him truly tore at my heart.

My Aunt Parmie was so beautiful and glamorous to me. She always treated me so special, and made me feel grown up. I enjoyed visiting her and playing with my younger cousins, Mary Ann and Roche. I especially loved seeing all the places I never saw before, like the Empire State Building How I loved to brag to my friends that I had a "rich" aunt, who lived in a "very expensive house" with a swimming pool and all! I also have several second cousins; I am especially fond of my cousin Allen.

The Communion Dress

Aunt Parmie came to the rescue one summer day. My sister was getting prepared for her First Holy Communion. We didn't have enough money to buy her a new dress. So my mother looked in the back of the closet for my communion dress. It was so beautiful, all satin and lace, and layers of ruffles to make a little girl look like a princess. "It's a little yellow, and since you are chubbier than Mary Jane, it needs to be taken in, otherwise, it's good condition," my mother said to me as she carried it downstairs. She put it in a paper bag, and stated that we would take it to my grandmother. "Your grandma will know what to do to get the yellow out, and Mary Jane, you try it on and Grandma will take it in for you—then you'll look beautiful!" my mother said. She put the bag on the kitchen table, and that is the last time anyone saw it ever again.

That afternoon, as we prepared to leave to go to my grandmother's house, we couldn't find the bag with the communion dress! We looked upstairs, downstairs and everywhere in between. I must have looked under the table a zillion times. It was so weird, she left it on the table, and no one took it, no one came to visit… so how could it have just disappeared into thin air?

My mother was retracing her steps; I heard her talking to herself as she walked out of the kitchen, into the hallway, "I took it out of the closet; Mary Jane tried it on, too big, brought it downstairs, now let me think… Nicky told me he was going to Salerino's to tend bar for a while on his way out… I told him to take out the trash… humm." We couldn't hear the sound of her voice anymore, only her footsteps as she climbed the stairs… then all of a sudden she let out a scream, "OH NO! OH MY GOD! YOUR FATHER THREW THE DRESS OUT IN THE GARBAGE!"

My mother made me run across the street to Salerino's. I ran into the bar, almost out of breath, exclaiming, "Daddy, Daddy… I hate to tell you, but Mommy said you're in BIG trouble!" I expected him to get all upset when I blurted out what he did to the communion dress, but he and all his friends just burst out laughing! His buddies were teasing him about being in "the doghouse." Boy, was I relieved! I ran back home, all excited. "Mommy, I got good news! Daddy didn't throw out the communion dress; he put it in the dog house!"

Immediately, I ran out to the back yard calling out to Daisy Mae, "Here girl… come here… come see me!" Patting my legs, as I coaxed her out of her house. She wagged her tail excitedly, and started to lick my face. I then got down on all fours, and stuck my head into the opening of the dog coup. I then heard my Mother's voice… "Joann! Get out of there right now! There's something wrong with that kid!" I heard her say to my father, who had come home from across the street.

Soon, one of his buddies came to our house, and we all jumped in this stinky truck and off he drove to the dump.

Wow! What a great place the dump was! I'd never seen anything like it before. It had mountains of garbage, all kinds of broken furniture and other neat stuff. It sure didn't smell too nice, but what the heck… you might find treasures here!

We searched the dump, climbing over piles of everything. More often than not, I would yell, "Hey… look at this; can I take it home?" My mother would burst my bubble, and yell back to me to stop fooling around and drop that filthy thing, and to look for the bag with the communion dress.

Later that evening, we sat in galvanized tubs of water, to wash all the "dump stuff" off our bodies. Believe it or not, after all that we still never found the bag with the communion dress. I found quite a bit of other great stuff that I was sure if I washed it good, and fixed it a bit, it would be just as good as new. But no, my mother ruined everything and wouldn't let me take any of it home.

Aunt Parmie was visiting from New York, and when she heard of our dilemma; she gave my mother money to buy Mary Jane a new dress. The following day, we walked up to Main Street and purchased Mary Jane a new communion dress from Gladstein's Department Store. She did look beautiful, but I know she would have looked even more beautiful in MY communion dress with all the lace, satin and layers of ruffles. But of course, being the kind, thoughtful big sister that I was, I never let her know.

Joann's 1st Holy Communion day, pictured with Mary Jane, in Grandma Scorzafava's yard, on Moosic Road, in Old Forge. Notice how Mary Jane always hung on to her big sister. This is the infamous Communion dress that sparked a trip to the dump.

A memory I know I can never, ever, EVER forget was on one of my bus rides home from Aunt Parmie's house. I was around eleven years old. Uncle Sonny put me on the Greyhound, kissing me goodbye. He told the bus driver, "You take good care of my niece and make sure she doesn't get off until Scranton." I was sitting there alone, until the next stop, when a very heavy African American man sat next to me. He was very nice and told me he had a daughter about the same age. We were riding along, when all of a sudden, I felt very ill and nauseated. I wanted to go to the restroom, but the man had fallen asleep and since he was so heavy, I couldn't get around, over or under him. Then, I began to get these awful pains in my stomach; I didn't know what to do. So I pretended to cough and sneeze as loud as I could. The rest of the people heard me, but the man next to me just kept on sleeping. Finally, I stood on the seat and told the lady in the back that I felt sick, she went up to the bus driver, and the next thing you know, he pulls the bus over. The bus driver came to me asking, "Are you ok?" as he touched my forehead.

"I just want to get to the bathroom!" I answered. By this time, the man next to me was awake, and while I went to the back of the bus, there was a big discussion about what they should do in this situation. A woman gave me some cold soda, and in a little while, I felt a little better, so they continued the trip. I was never so embarrassed in my whole life... that is until I got to the bus station!

I never wanted anybody to hear what happened. I can't believe I made such a commotion, that they even stopped the bus. I sat there for the rest of the trip, not letting anyone know that I was still not feeling well and had an awful headache.

When we arrived in Scranton, my mother was waiting for me. I thought to myself, I will act normal and never let her know what happened, otherwise she will yell at me and say something like, "Can't you do anything right!" or "Do you always have to make a big deal out of everything!"

I waved to her and Mary Jane through the window of the bus. Carrying my suitcase, I descended the steps, smiling and waving as if nothing had happened, then I got dizzy and almost fainted right on the spot! The bus driver and most of the passengers crowded around and told my mother what had happened. I could hear the bus driver saying to my mother, "I think you better take her to the doctor; maybe there is something really wrong with her!"

My mother looked worried and whispered to me, "You didn't let anyone *bother* you, did you?"

I said, "Ma, how could anyone bother me on a bus full of people!"

I had to go to the restroom and she followed me right into the stall to "check things out." After a moment, my mother look relieved, and then got the biggest laughing fit and started singing, right out loud, while clapping her hands, "JA got her period... JA got her period!" Mary Jane happily joined right in and started clapping too, although she didn't have a clue as to what was going on! That wasn't bad enough—when we went back out to the terminal, she told the bus driver and anyone else who would listen, including the heavy, black man who sat next to me on the bus, "Oh she's not sick! She got her period... for the very first time!"

At that moment I was positive that I would never, ever speak to my mother again! I just wanted to crawl into a hole and die, so I would never have to face anyone ever again! Dear God... I couldn't believe it I finally got the "curse!"

Another relative that I would see often was my Uncle Tommy. He lived in the next town of Duryea with his wife, Aunt Marie, and cousins, Johnny, Frankie and Paula. Uncle Tommy and my father would go hunting, fishing, picking mushrooms, and of course have a few drinks together. I would see my Aunt Marie and cousin Paula for holidays at my grandmother's house. Later on, I saw them more often when they moved into the apartment attached to her house.

Uncle Tommy looked a little like my father, and he was a comfort to me when my father died. I would visit my Aunt Annie, and he would always be there, mowing the grass and fixing things. Since he reminded me so much of my daddy, sometimes I would pretend that he was my father, and he was still alive!

When Uncle Tommy died, my Aunt Marie moved to the housing development on Dunn Avenue. There she didn't have to mow grass or take care of furnaces, so it made life much easier for her. We wanted my Aunt Annie to do the same, since she would have to do everything herself, however, understandably, she didn't want to leave her home.

I remember my cousin Paula gave such a beautiful tribute to her father at his funeral Mass. As she stood at the pulpit in St. Mary's Church, I remember her statement: "My father was not a rich man, in the sense that he had money, but he was very rich in other ways!" I felt her pain, for I knew the sorrow of burying your daddy. As I sat there listening to her, I suddenly realized that the things she was saying, I could say about my own father! Uncle Tommy had been my "substitute daddy" for many years. Suddenly I felt such an overwhelming sense of heartache, and I realized it was like burying my daddy all over again.

My Aunt Mary, her husband, Uncle Jake, and her son, Rossi would come to visit my grandmother. They once lived in Binghamton, New York, but moved to California, to work with her sister Rose. My Aunt Rose owned a nursing home. When I was really young, I couldn't understand why my Aunt Mary looked and sounded just like my Aunt Annie! At one point I actually thought I had two Aunt Annies! Of course it was because they were twins.

Aunt Mary was such a gentle, loving soul, and very close to the Lord. She also loved to tell us funny, true stories. One of my favorites was what I like to call "The Egg Story." One day, she decided to have an egg salad sandwich for lunch. So she put an egg on to boil, when she was called to the apartment downstairs, where her niece lived. She only meant to stay a few minutes, but they got to talking, and she forgot all about the egg. When she finally did remember, quite a bit of time had passed. So she ran upstairs and found the pan; all the water had boiled out of it. The pan was actually red hot, but the egg was... gone! So she figured that Uncle Jake must have taken it out when he came home, but forgot to turn the stove off.

Later that evening they were all eating supper, and she leaned back in the chair to relax a moment. She just happened to look up, and there was the egg! The force of the heat just propelled it right up, and it actually stuck to the ceiling!

The only one of my father's siblings I hardly knew was my Aunt Rose. She moved to California when I was very young. She and her husband, Uncle Louis, had one daughter named Lucille.

It's amazing, although we rarely saw each other, Aunt Annie would keep us so informed about one another that it felt as if they were always around.

My father had two more brothers... Sam and Ralph, they both lived in Buffalo, New York. I did see them a bit more often when my grandmother was alive. I remember them always smiling and happy.

I really used to be so proud; I thought that one of them was the real "Uncle Sam!" In front of the post office stood a poster with a man in a big hat and matching red, white and blue jacket. His finger seemed to be pointing right at me. Underneath his picture was written the famous slogan, "Uncle Sam wants... YOU!" I used to think that the picture really didn't look too much like him. It was probably because after he took the picture, he shaved off that awful gray beard!

I especially recall my Uncle Ralph. He would get on his knee, open his arms wide and say, "There's my favorite niece!" Off I would go, running into his embrace!

We would also see my Aunt Angeline from time to time. She lived in Binghamton, New York, with my Uncle Joe, and cousins, Nicholas, Sammy and Joan. A few times we traveled to her house, but most of the time she would come to the old homestead.

My mother always thought she was a little strange, and even seemed a little afraid of her, but not me...I loved her! She spoke with an Italian accent, and I loved to listen to her stories! People said she had physic abilities, and... so do I! Well, I think I do... maybe!

We would laugh and share stories of strange things that we saw, or that happened to us. One day she looked me right in the eye and said, "Joanna, you *know*! You have the *gift*!" Wow! Was I excited! She said not to be afraid of it, because it comes from God's own Holy Spirit. Now, some people don't believe in this sort of stuff, but I sure did! The way I saw it, if God gave His Holy Apostles powers, and we are His followers, then why can't these blessings happen to us also!

Many times I would pray for people to be healed, or ask Him to help them with a problem, or for good fortune to come their way, and God would allow it to happen! And many times unusual things would happen to me that were sort of like a "miracle!"

Well that was then, and this is now. Why, I was just a naive child in those days. Now that I am older and much wiser, I realize that all that talk, and all those stories we shared together, was just a bunch of silly ideas between an aunt and her niece to entertain each other... right? Strange and unusual things like that don't really happen to me now! Err, um... or do they?!

JOANN M. JORDAN

Pictured is one of Joann's many alter egos..."Cassandra."

Cassandra

I received a phone call from Harry Myers, one of my talent agents, in the fall of 1989. He usually called me to entertain at large corporate affairs and resorts. This time he said, "I need a magician, a fortune teller, and a clown—however, I don't want you to be the clown."

Confused, I stated, "What do you mean, you don't want me to be the clown! I can get Darius the Magician, since he works for me. I can provide you with extra clowns, since Rainbow, Bashful and Patches are my sidekicks, but just *where* do you think I'm going to get a fortune teller? And again, *why* don't you want me to be the *clown*?"

Harry started to chuckle over my indignation and said, "Calm down, Jo Jo, we all know you're the best clown in the land! To answer your other question, I'm speaking to the fortune teller!"

Still bewildered I said, "Harry, am I missing something here?"

Harry then stated, "Come on, you of all people, with your acting ability, can pull this off! Besides, I've known you a long time, and many things have occurred that you were strangely aware of. I do believe that you *are* a little psychic... aren't you?"

I really couldn't tell if his last statement was metaphor or not, but I thought about it for a moment and said, "Oh what the heck... a job is a job!" After all, it was only for fun. I wasn't *really* going to tell anybody's future, and I surely wouldn't do this again, so it is not like I'll get kicked out of the Catholic Church for joining the occult or something.

So there I was, dressed in this beautiful gypsy getup, reading the tarot cards and... "Cassandra was born!

At first, I would study the cards and say whatever the picture on it looked like: "I see you have a bad pain in your back.".... "The cards show that you are going on a trip."... "I see you will receive much money!"... "There is someone in your family who is ill," etc.

However, the people would always gasp and say things like, "Wow! The cards are really right!" After a while, I really got involved and told people some very intimate details about their lives. By the end of that job, I found myself actually crying over these people's heartaches and pain. Strangely, somehow I really reached these people.

I was listening to my messages a few days later and I hear Harry's voice, "Hey, Cassandra... What did you do, get a private eye to check these people out so you would know all about them? You got rave reviews! I already have several other jobs for Cassandra lined up!"

For many years after that day, every time Harry would get me a job, the same thing always happened—I would read the cards and would get a feeling deep inside, and somehow, I would sense all about them! The people were amazed! Harry was amazed! Most of all... I was amazed! Sometimes I was even frightened! I think I said more prayers to St. Michael the Archangel for protection while reading the cards, than I ever did in my whole life!

How could this happen; it was a job... "For entertainment purposes only." Then I remembered an aunt looking directly into a little girl's eyes and stating, "You *know*! You have the... *gift*!"

Was it a gift or just a coincidence? Whatever it was, the people I was entertaining loved it and responded with such enthusiasm. When they would see me at the resorts again, I would always hear, "Everything you said last year was absolutely true!" I made it a point from there on, if people actually believed in this stuff, I would use it help people. When troubles or trials came up, I would tell them to pray and put it in God's hands. Sometimes, I gave them my favorite prayers to say and I put them on my own prayer list, asking God to help them If I actually knew a doctor, lawyer, or... Indian Chief who could help a certain person, I would refer them. When good things came up, I would remind then that this was a blessing and to thank God for all they were about to receive! There were times when someone was tense and stressed out; I told them about relaxation techniques that I had learned to relieve my own stress.

I vowed to myself, and to God, that I would not lead others to depend on me to help them. I also made a promise that I would only do this when hired as an entertainer, and I would always make a point to mention that it was for "entertainment purposes" only! It was very tempting to know that I could have quit clowning, put a sign up on my door and I would probably retire a millionaire! However, I wanted people to trust and believe in the only person who could truly help and bless them, their Creator!

Once, I saw a medal of the Blessed Mother around a woman's neck. The cards were showing problems and she confirmed them. I shared with her that I noticed she had a devotion to Our Blessed Lady and gave her a special card with a Novena to Mary for her to follow. Well, this other woman that I had previously read the cards for, was eavesdropping and said, "Hey, how come you didn't give *me* that prayer to read? I'm having almost the same problem!"

I looked up at her and said softly, "Well, sweetheart, I see you are wearing the Star of David and I respect the Jewish faith. So I didn't share this with you because Mary is the Mother of my Lord and Savior... Jesus. Besides, I honestly don't have another prayer card.

She promptly turned and quickly walked away. A minute later she came back with a pencil and note pad, saying to the woman whose cards I was reading, "Do you mind if I write down that prayer to Jesus' Mother? I can use all the help I can get!"

The lady sitting across from me handed her the Novena and stated, "Sure it will help you, after all, Jesus and Mary were Jewish too!"

If walls could talk, that big red house on Moosic Road could sure tell a lot of wonderful stories! I remember it was always busy and full of family and friends. My grandmother even had pet cats and birds. It was always full of life, and aromas of delicious food cooking for some celebration.

Now, it is a bit quiet, and my Aunt Annie lives there by herself. Several times the question has come up, maybe she should move to an apartment for senior citizens, but her answer is always the same: "Where will the family come to, if there is no homestead?"

Aunt Annie is like a second mother to all of her nieces and nephews. Once she told me, "Well, I guess I never married and had children because God knew I would be needed to take care all of you!"

She worked in Brooks Manufacturing, a pants factory near the middle of town. Often she would stop to visit on her way home from work. Sometimes, she would be carrying in a bag of groceries. My mother would brew tea, and Aunt Annie would pull out a package of Stella Dora sponge cookies; they were my favorite! (I still love the soft, anise flavored goodies!)

Aunt Annie took care of her mother all her life. Because of her love and sacrifice, my grandmother was able to live out her life in her own home, the home where she had cherished memories of her husband and children until she died, at nearly one hundred years of age!

Aunt Annie really loved her garden. We would find rocks and she would paint them white, making borders around flowers and trees. I loved when we would go into the woods. She would pull up anything she thought was beautiful, be it a wildflower or weed, then transplant it in her yard. I know I got my green thumb from her and my father. In the woods we would also look for items to eat. She would not only pick the usual mushrooms, but dandelion greens, grape leaves and milkweeds. Back home, she would boil them, then fry them in olive oil & garlic. Sometimes she'd make soup by adding a little meat and potatoes. Everything always tasted so good!

Aunt Annie could make delicious meals out of almost anything. Mary Jane and I still laugh about the time we went to visit her with several of our friends. She was about to cook supper. Sticking her head in the refrigerator, she mumbled to herself, "Gee, I only have one egg." She took the egg out and asked us to stay for dinner. "I'm going to make you a nice omelet."

We all looked at each other, knowing what the other was thinking: "She's going to make us a nice omelet out of what? She only has one egg!" There we sat, watching her, both amazed and amused! She beat the egg with a little milk, then went back and forth into the refrigerator pulling out all kinds of things. She poured the egg into the frying pan and began to add a little of this and a little of that. Then before we knew it, we were all eating the most wonderful tasting omelet! We were all handed a fresh piece of Italian bread and butter and she poured us a cup of tea. And when we had eaten all that we could, she even had leftovers! "See!" Aunt Annie said, "God provided, just like He did when He multiplied the fish and bread!"

Although she is well into her eighties, she doesn't know that she is not too young anymore. Many times she would say, "I hope I will be able to still take care of my house… when I get old!"

I was visiting my sister in her lovely Victorian home in Scranton. Mary Jane was not feeling too well, so to pass the time we looked at home videos and old pictures. Naturally, we started to reminisce about old times. We laughed and even cried a little, sharing stories about our childhood. My sister and I also spoke about how our lives made many twists and turns along the way, both good and bad. We sure had made plenty of mistakes, but somehow, no matter what, we always made it through! Then we starting talking about Aunt Annie, and we both agreed that she always took the time for us, and was always there when we needed her. Not only when we were children, but even now. As we looked at the video of Mary Jane's grandson, George's, Christening, we noticed that in the corner of the church sat Aunt Annie! And we both realized that in every home video and every old picture, there was our Aunt Annie, sitting right there in the corner, smiling at us like everyone's Guardian Angel!

Chapter 9

The Change of Life

When I was about in fourth grade our landlady began to have much work done on the old house. Painters came to scrap the weatherbeaten outside walls and brighten the long neglected structure with fresh coats of white paint. They tore down the rotted front porch and hauled away the rusty supporting beams.

I recall how shocking it was when I came home from school to find that they had torn out the front doors of the old butcher shop... the doors that no one was allowed to ever open, even with the forbidden key, replacing it with just a plain solid wooden door. They even removed the large glass windows that I'd spent so many hours sitting in front of, awaiting the arrival of my father from work in the coal mines.

My mother would say to my father, "She is going to ask us to move! What do you think, she's doing all this work for us?"

When the rent was due they asked the landlady if they were going to be evicted. She said, "Oh no... you can live here just as long as you want. We're just fixing it up a little." However, my mother sensed it wasn't true; she kept nagging my father to look for a new place. My daddy was such a trusting person and he would tell her that the landlady, even as nasty as she sometimes was, wouldn't lie. And she certainly wouldn't force us out with no warning, especially with two kids. So the work went on for months and the landlady would come for the rent.

As Mary Jane and I approached our house, coming from school one day, I could hear people yelling. My mother was crying and she was arguing with the landlady. "You old witch! I just knew this would happen! You kept us on a string so we could pay you rent to fix your damn house... then you throw us out into the streets like bums!" She then yelled at my father, "I told you this would happen, but oh no, Mr. Goody Two Shoes, you believe anything anybody says! Your problem is you don't care about your family! You care more about those damn friends of yours and getting drunk, than looking for a place for your family to live!" My poor father, the look on his face was heart wrenching! He tried to tell my mother that it wasn't true, that his family meant everything to him, but there was no sense talking to her, when she got in one of her moods.

Then my mother turned and screamed at the landlady, "You old, bitch, bastard, you... Get the hell out of my house! The rent is paid until the end of the month, so until then this is still MY house! So get out... or I'll throw you out!"

The landlady backed away and as she quickly fled out the door. Once outside, she yelled that my mother was crazy and threatened to call the cops if we were not gone by the first of next month; she also began screaming a few choice words of her own!

Mary Jane and I stood there numb. My mind was trying to absorb all that had just gone on. I had such mixed emotions, feeling both sorry and angry with my mother for being so mean to my daddy. I felt heartbroken for my father; he looked so sad and defeated. At the same time I wanted to say, "Why didn't you listen to Mommy; she tried to tell you!" but I didn't. How could I be upset with someone who had such a trusting nature, and my remark would only add to the pain and frustration he was feeling already. So I tried to be witty and say something to help the situation. My mind raced, but for the first time in God only knows how long, I was speechless! I knew I *had* to say something, so before I knew it, without warning... out it came! "Wow! Ma, it was great seeing you finally telling off that old witch of a bitch, bastard for a change!"

All I got for my efforts in trying to make a bad situation better was a swift a slap across the mouth and my mother shaking her hand at me yelling, "You little brat, where did you hear such filthy things? You NEVER hear me or your father curse! Don't you EVER let me hear such dirty words come out of that mouth of yours ever again or I'll wash it out with soap!"

The Search

Everyone's heart was broken. As I walked around the yard, I couldn't even imagine never seeing my daddy's garden again. Over in the corner was Daisy Mae's old homemade doghouse. Although she had died, Daddy told us she went to live on a farm so she could be free and happy with all the other farm animals. I would never let him tear it down just in case she missed us as much as we missed her, and wanted to come home again. Tears streamed down my cheeks as I was thinking, "What if she did come home and we didn't live here anymore... how would she find us?"

I probably would never see my friends again, especially Shirley next door. She lived out of town, but stayed with her grandmother and Aunt Clemey in the summer. When she comes back again... I won't be here!

It's funny, you don't realize how important things are to you until you lose them. I just couldn't imagine not living there for the rest of my life.

My mother, Mary Jane and I would walk around the town looking for a house to rent. It was difficult; either the rent was too high, or they were awful and run down. My mother would say, "We might be poor, but we are clean and have self respect! I'd rather live in a tent then that filthy old place!" We would look for a place while praying, "Good St. Anthony, please come around; we need a place to live and none can be found!"

Finally, my father came home from making his rounds all excited. He heard of an apartment down on Oak Street; people had just moved out a few nights before. The landlord hadn't even put a "For Rent" sign on it yet! Not only that, since it was a friend of my father's, he would give us a break on the rent! Off we all went, walking down the other side of town to Oak Street, to see... the apartment.

At first sight, it looked overbearing and decrepit. It was a huge, gray building on the corner of Oak and Church, and was as close to the curb as it could get. We stood across the street, in front of Dolinish's Drug store, just staring at it. The place sure could have used a painting. It was a little shabby looking with the exception of new, shiny brass letters stating the address... 413. It had a sagging front porch without any railings around it. There was no front yard, just a couple of bushes in front of the porch... and then the sidewalk. Around the side there was just a dirt pathway between the building and road leading to the back of the house. I watched the expression on my mother's face; she looked like she was about to... cry, scream, laugh or something! My father was saying that it wasn't too bad inside, but my mother said absolutely nothing! I waited for her reaction, when she surprised me by saying "Well, what are we standing here for! Let's go take a look; the inside can't be as bad as the outside."

"Ya have ta get to the apartment from around the back," my father stated as we all marched across the street. When we got to the back, I was happy to see that it did have a big back yard with two peach trees. My father said that he could still plant a little garden in the corner of the yard. "There's four apartments; the one we're gonna look at is upstairs." Daddy said. "See, here is the coal shed. It's not too far from the steps." I got a funny feeling in the pit of my stomach thinking that he would have to carry coal up all those steps. He was already showing signs of black lung and having a hard time breathing. How would he be able to carry up heavy pails of coal if we moved to this place?

A man called out from the apartment for us to come on up; he was the landlord. As we climbed the stairs, a little boy poked his head out of the other apartment. I heard a lady say, "Get in here and mind your own business!" The door slammed shut before we got to the top. It seemed so strange to have other people living in the same house with you... that didn't even belong to your family!

We walked inside. To our relief, it was a bit better and cleaner than the outside. The first room we entered was the parlor. It was a nice size room, but painted a dull dark green. To the left was a big kitchen and full bathroom with a bathtub. My mother seemed impressed. There was still no hot water, but she said that at least she only had to fill it with heavy pots of boiling water and then simply pull out the plug to empty it! On the other side of the kitchen was a pantry which had several shelves and cupboards. There was even a back door with a porch. I was so thrilled to have a porch! Then the landlord said, "The porch is real old; I need to fix it one of these days. So please keep it locked and don't let the kids out on it!" I couldn't believe it! Not again; what is this with the porches already?

My mother turned to me, shaking her hand in front of her and said, "Joann! Did you hear that? Don't you ever go out on that porch, or you'll fall through and kill yourself! Then you'll be in big trouble!"

"Ma!" I said, "How come you're always hollering at me; you never say anything to Mary Jane! It's always me!"

Well, if looks could kill... I'd be dead! "Because you're the oldest, honey, and your little sister does everything you do," she said a little to sweetly, with a smile. I know it was because the landlord was listening, but her eyes warned, "If you ever talk to me like that again, especially in front of people, you'll get it... and get it good!"

Back through the parlor, on the right of the apartment was a bedroom, and through that room was another bedroom. "I don't like the fact that the kids would have to walk through our bedroom to get to theirs," Mom told my father.

The landlord spoke up, "Why don't you just make the front room your bedroom?" But my mother explained that the first room was larger, and she could arrange her bedroom furniture better.

My father then opened his mouth and said, "I don't know what all the fuss is about, most of the time they sleep with you anyway!"

I could see my Mother was trying to keep her cool in front of the landlord, and stated, "Oh ya, well there's no room in here for *your* bed, and the kids are too old sleep in bed with us. So as you can see, they need their own room!" Embarrassed, I asked if Mary Jane and I could go downstairs and look at the yard.

We sat on the back porch, wondering if this was to be our new home. It was so different than having a whole house all for yourself. Looking around the neighborhood, everything seemed so strange and different too! I was used to a big yard that was all mine. Also a big field to play in with my friends, past the yard. This yard was not even as big as our old yard, and we had to share it with three other families. Gazing in back of the yard, I saw an alley, and a large cinder block garage. A far cry from a field to play baseball! I tried not to, but the tears came streaming down my face. I started to quietly sob, and Mary Jane started to cry too. I put my arm around her, thinking that the poor little thing must be feeling the same loss and fear of an unknown future as I was.

Hugging her, I said that everything will be alright, and she looked up at me with those big, wet, blue eyes of hers, that always melted my heart and whispered, "JA... what are we crying about?"

The Big Move

For the next several days it seemed like all we did was cry and wrap things up in newspapers! My father made several trips back and forth from the Beer Gardens, bringing us cardboard boxes to fill with our belongings for the move. Mary Jane would ask me to read what was written on the boxes. I couldn't understand all the words, so I would make up things like, "This is a good box to put your clothes when you move." Or, "Please put heavy cups and dishes in this box." Some of the words I actually could read, and that was enough to understand that most of them had once contained bottles of wine, whisky and other spirits. I do remember that one of my father's friends said, "How do ya like that?" pointing to the writing on one box, "The Stegmaier Brewery, made in Wilkes Barre, Pennsylvania. Why that's just down the line a piece!"

There was so much to do, in so little time. The apartment would not be large enough to take everything we had in the house, so some things we gave away. I remember that my father's bed with the fancy iron foot and headboard was given to my Uncle Tommy. My father gave some of his other possessions to friends. My mother said that she couldn't believe all the stuff you can collect over the years. She even threw away a box of items including some chipped bowls and an iron that was broken, saying, "I don't know why in the world I kept this junk!" Not me… I kept all my personal belongings, broken or not. It was sad enough that I was leaving my home, I wasn't about to leave my memories in the garbage. It was so hard putting your whole life into those little cardboard boxes.

All too soon the day arrived for the men to put our furniture in the truck. I just couldn't believe we were going away from our home! My heart felt like a stone as I walked around the house, trying to memorize every nook and cranny. I did the same outside, taking in the yard and around the neighborhood. What was even harder was saying goodbye to a few of my friends and neighbors. Although we were only moving across town, it seemed like we were moving to another land.

My mother made us sweep and clean up the place. I asked her why, if we were moving. She told us that you should have pride in yourself. If you left it messy, people would talk about you. The landlady showed up right about then, and it was the first time I felt anything positive about moving. "At least we won't have to look at, or listen to *you* any more!" I whispered under my breath.

Since they were riding in the truck, my father and his friends arrived at the new apartment first. So by the time my mother, Mary Jane and I finished cleaning our old house and then walked to the new place, the men were just about finished moving everything in.

We climbed the stairs and walked into total chaos. They had just plopped the furniture and boxes down… anywhere and everywhere! "What a mess, Ma! It will take us the rest of our lives to straighten this all out! Why did we have to move here… I hate it!" I cried.

To everyone's complete surprise, my mother, of all people, was very calm about the whole thing. She said, "Joann, you run up to Sambo's for bread, bologna and cheese to make sandwiches. (Sambo's was called "The biggest...little store" although it was tiny, you could find almost anything there! I loved the way it always smelled like bananas.) At least get the beds up and made so we can sleep tonight."

Everyone was in shock over her calm reaction. She looked at us… looking at her, and started to laugh! Then she said in a very peaceful and determined voice, "When life hands you lemons… make lemonade!" And what was even more surprising was, first that she didn't yell at me for my outcry. Second, when I asked her what it meant, instead of getting annoyed at me, as usual, for asking questions, she sat down on one of the boxes and explained, "Life gets hard sometimes. Things change, and there will always be things that will happen to make you sad, or be hard for you. So you have to think about what is happening, and try to do the best you can to make it better; then you ask God to help you, and things will get better!"

I could hardly believe my ears! My mother was far from philosophical, and I don't think I ever heard her say anything so deep or positive in her whole life.

How many times did I hear myself say those exact same words to my children and family? Up to this very day, I try to live by, and truly believe in those words!

Chapter 10

Mama's Family

Both of my mother's parents were also born in Italy, and came to America seeking a new and better life. My grandmother had such a beautiful name, Dominica Maria. In America she was called Mary. She came from Italy with her father and several sisters and a brother. Her mother had died in the "old country." They settled in a house on Smith Street in Dunmore, Pennsylvania—a town on the outskirts of Scranton.

My grandmother and her sister were very close; where one went, so did the other. When they each married, they bought a house at 620 Cooney Street. It was a large, two story building. They also made rooms in the attic to make it three floors. My grandmother lived on the second floor of the house, and her sister on the first. (It always amazed me that the number of both my mother's and father's parents' address was 620!)

My grandfather's name was Joseph. So Mary and Joseph had several children: Vincent (Jimmy), Ralph (Popeye), Nancy, Antoinette, Rose, Andrew, and the little baby girl... my mother, Carmella. Grandfather worked at the reservoir, but there came a time when there was no work, so they moved to the neighboring state of Connecticut. The two sisters missed each other and after a while they moved back into the homestead on Cooney Street. My grandfather still worked in Connecticut but would commute back and forth. One Easter Sunday morning, when he was about to return to his family, he was killed by a hit and run taxi driver. My mother was only three years old.

Mary was sitting outside, under the grapevine, when a friend came to her and said, "Come in the house, I want to tell you something important."

My grandmother stated that she didn't want to, it was such a beautiful day and she was waiting for her husband to come home. The friend insisted that she come into the house, away from the children, but my grandmother said, "No, you can tell me here; I told you Joseph is coming home today, and I want to wait outside for him."

Finally, the friend said, "No, Mary, he is not coming home, he died today." My grandmother was devastated; everyone in neighborhood could hear her cries as her heart was breaking.

Grandma's sister also died, leaving behind her husband, Salvatore, and several children—Rose, Antoinette, Andrew (Terry), Sam, Carmella (Millie) and Josephine.

After a few years, my grandmother married Salvatore, making everybody one big family. So my mother's first cousins were now her stepsisters and brothers.

Grandma moved downstairs. My Aunt Nancy, who was now married, moved to the second floor. Of course, I never knew my true Grandfather Joseph, but I hear he was a good, hardworking person, who loved his family.

The only grandfather I ever knew was Salvatore. We always called him by his last name… "Grandpa Bio." I loved him and he was good to me and to everyone else. There was never a time when I didn't think of him as my real grandfather. He used to make grape wine in the cellar. My cousins and I would go under the house to see Grandpa working at his wine press. What I recall most is, no matter how hot it was outside, once we entered the cellar, it would always be cool, giving us relief from the hot sun. There was always a strange mixture of aromas from the dampness, grapes and pipe tobacco, which somehow was pleasing to the senses. Grandma would always have strings of hot red peppers hanging to dry from the rafters.

My grandparents had a large garden, and quite a long grape arbor which grew down the middle of the yard. There were several benches inside the grape tunnel for us to sit on. In the yard were several sheds, bread ovens and coops for the chickens they raised.

I used to follow my grandfather around the yard asking him such important questions as, "Grandpa, how come chickens don't wear pants?"

I wish I had more time to share with my grandmother; she died when I was still in grade school. What I do have are warm and fulfilling memories! We would pick fresh vegetables from the garden, then sit under the grape arbor and shell the fresh peas, and I would help her make homemade chicken soup.

One thing I remember about my grandmother was her large, soft breasts! I was almost four years old, and there was such excitement! In a few short hours my mother would to give birth to my baby sister. I had no way of knowing that she was crying out in pain due to the upcoming blessed event. In those days, children were not told of such things. So when they had to take her to the hospital, I started screaming and crying, "Where were they taking her? I don't want her to go away!" Why, I thought I was never going to see my mommy ever again!

My grandmother tried to comfort me, telling me in broken English to be a good girl, and my mother would bring me home a big surprise. I didn't care; I didn't want a surprise! My mommy was crying and sick; I wanted her back! I was truly confused and terrified.

Grandma washed my face and carried me out to her green wooden rocking chair that was on the front porch. As she rocked, she sang to me in Italian; I finally settled down and relaxed. Grandma was a large woman and so soft and cushy. She and my Aunt Nancy had been baking in the outside ovens that very morning. The wonderful aroma of the fresh baked bread still lingered on her clothing. As she gently rocked me back and forth, I snuggled down, taking comfort in her soft, warm body. As I closed my eyes, I felt so peaceful and safe, drifting off to sleep with the gentle motion of the rocking. How comforting it was hearing her sweet voice singing softly, my face buried in her large breasts, smelling the aroma of the fresh baked bread. (To this very day, whenever I smell that special aroma of fresh bread baking I think of my Grandmother's breasts!)

My Aunt Nancy, her husband, Ralph (Butch), and my two cousins, Catherine and Ralph Jr. (Butchie), lived upstairs from my grandparents. Above them in the attic apartment was the home of my Aunt Antoinette, her husband David, and their four daughters—Ada, Mary, Donna and Nancy Ann.

I do not recall too much about my Aunt Antoinette, since she died of cancer when I was quite young. However, I do remember my Uncle Davey, who raised three of his daughters. The youngest, Nancy Ann, went to live with my Aunt Rosie.

What adventures we had, and what trouble my older cousin Donna and I got into! We would lock the door, and put on her sister Ada's dresses, high heels and make up, pretending to be movie stars. And there was the time she talked me into taking the bulletins from all the pews before Mass at St. Anthony's Church. The best was when she had me tie a rope to the kitchen stove, then around her waist, while she tried to climb out the attic window. I tried to hold her, but the rope slipped through my fingers, and she fell on top of the upstairs porch roof, which was at least thirty-five feet above the ground! My Uncle Butch had to rescue her. Naturally, I was the one who got in the most trouble.

My Aunt Nancy would always invite us up for Thanksgiving and Christmas dinner. Sometimes, we would take the bus, but most of the time Uncle Butch would come and pick us up with his blue Ford. It was very exciting to ride in a car, since we never owned one.

Uncle Butch had a brother who owned a dairy farm in the town of Moscow, about ten miles away. We would love to take a ride with him to the country and get milk fresh from the cows. Since I didn't know too much about cows, I really thought that white milk came from the black and white cows, and the chocolate milk came from the brown cows.

I must have owed him hundreds of dollars; every time the man with the merry go round ride or the ice cream truck would come around, I begged him, "Oh please, please, Uncle Butch, can you lend me a dime? I'll pay you back… honest I will!"

My two cousins were older than me, so they left home when I was little. Catherine became a nurse, and married her husband, Al. They lived in New Jersey, where they had three children— Michael, Alex & Cathy Ann.

Her brother, Butchie, went to the seminary, and became a priest in the diocese of Scranton. He died of a heart attack when he was in his late fifties.

My mother's brothers—Vince, (Jimmy), Ralph (Popeye), and Andy— were always in our life from time to time. Uncle Popeye was my sister Mary Jane's godfather. He also walked her down the aisle when she got married.

Uncle Jimmy would always come around and help us with things, especially anything electrical, since he was an electrician. We became really close as he got older. He became ill and I helped him as best I could. In fact, I was at his bedside when he passed away. He was in a semi coma. While holding his hand, and sitting next to him in the hospital bed, I kept telling him not to be afraid, Jesus loved him, and was waiting for him.

The youngest, Uncle Andy, was close to my mother. He was only about three years older than she. With the exception of my mother and her sister Rose, all of her siblings are diseased.

My mother would tell stories of all the mischief she and her brother Andy would get into. They would always stick up for one another, because if they didn't they would have both been in trouble quite a bit of the time. One day they skipped school and went gallivanting through all the stores in Scranton. They thought they really got away with it, when in the Scranton Dry Goods Store… up they were rising on the escalators… and down came the principal of the school on the other side!

I used to really *use* that story to get myself out of trouble with my mother, over my own capers!

Joann and her godmother, Rose Scripp. This same Christening dress was also worn by Joann's daughter Mary Ann, and her granddaughter, Sarah.

Joann and her grandparents. From Left to Right: Salvatore & Josephine Scorzafava. Three-week-old Joann and Dominica & Sam Bio. Photo taken at 620 Cooney Street Dunmore, Pennsylvania.

The Godparents

Some of my happiest memories growing up were at my Aunt Rosie's house. She and her husband, my Uncle Johnny, are my godparents. I would love to spend my summer vacations at their house, on Moritz Street, in Dunmore, a town on the outskirts of Scranton. My mother would often take us on the bus to visit her favorite sister, Rose.

How I love my Aunt Rosie—she is my second mother! I recall only happiness being around her loving, fun personality! She gave me the attention which I always craved, along with discipline, which I always needed. Her faith in God made my faith stronger, and most important, she gave me love! She would have big cookouts in the woods next to her house. We didn't need a fancy barbecue grill, Aunt Rosie would arrange rocks in a circle and light a fire, cooking the best franks and burgers around.

There was never a time when you went to her house that she wasn't cooking, making pizza, or baking something.

One of my favorite things was to go deep into the woods, across the railroad tracks and pick huckleberries. We would come back hours later, with pails of the blue, juicy berries, which Aunt Rosie would make into pies and other delicious pastries.

Now, our favorite huckleberry patch is part of Interstate 81. Once a peaceful place, where a family picked berries, laughed and enjoyed each others' company, it is a noisy, busy concrete highway, filled with thousands of vehicles speeding off to... wherever. Although I, myself, am one of those busy persons, I still feel a little sadness in my heart, for a part of my childhood that can never happen again, each time I fly by the Drinker Street exit in my "Jo Jo mobile!"

My Aunt Rosie is the cleanest, neatest person in the entire world. She was always cleaning, scrubbing, and polishing, yet her house was comfortable and homey. Why can't I be like her! I am such a slob! Not dirty—deep down my house is clean... just messy and disorganized! How many times have I heard myself cry out loud in anguish, while tearing the house apart looking for something, "God WHY, WHY didn't you make me neat and organized like Aunt Rosie!"

Uncle Johnny used to be a coal miner, like my father. He was heartbroken when the mines closed. Unlike many people, he really loved working there. As he grew older, I would ask him questions about the mines, and his eyes would light up. He loved to tell tales about what went on and what he did there.

After the closing of the mines, it was hard to make a decent living in the area, so he had to find work in New Jersey. He would usually only come home on weekends, so I didn't see him as much as I did Aunt Rosie, but I was always so happy when he came home. He is a quiet man, and really didn't say too much, unless you sparked up a conversation with him, but I always felt he was glad to be my godfather, and I felt loved around him. He must have loved me—after all, he didn't even get angry with me when I went up into the attic and put my foot through the floor. He had just finished putting up fresh sheet rock... how was I to know that I was only supposed to walk on the boards? I was up there looking for the blackboard they were giving me, and I stepped in between the boards, and the next thing I knew, my chubby little leg was dangling down from his bedroom ceiling, and I was screaming and hanging on for dear life! I thought I was going to get killed, either by falling down into the bedroom, or by my Aunt Rosie and Uncle Johnny! I'm still here, so neither happened. However, that wasn't the first mishap, and it surly wasn't the last. I was always getting myself into one kind of trouble or another.

They had two daughters—Ann Marie, and Mary. Ann Marie entered the convent to become a nun when I was little, so I really didn't see too much of her while growing up, but Mary is another story. She was always my idol, like a big sister in my eyes. I always thought she was so beautiful and smart, and wanted to be just like her when I grew up. And I am sure she loved me too. Well, I think she did, even when she got in trouble because of me sometimes. Well, I didn't mean to step on the nail that was in the board, while she and her friends were making a playhouse, and I didn't mean for her to get punished just because she was older and should have been watching out for me. And I didn't mean all those other things I did... and I didn't want her to get the blame! Honest, I didn't. After all, I was younger, and just got into things, but I never meant any harm.

Mary worked at the GLOBE STORE, which was one of Scranton's finest department stores at the time. She would dress so beautifully and fashionably. In fact, she almost started a new fad, when one day, being in a hurry, she found herself wearing two different shoes going to work!

I used to love to tell all my friends that she was my cousin. She lived at home for quite a while, until she moved to New York; there is where she met Henry, her husband.

My cousin Ann Marie had left the convent due to health reasons, and in time, met and married John. I love sharing with John about such important matters as Tai Chi. Ann Marie is so clever; she makes beautiful wreaths and centerpieces. They have a fantastic garden, filled with roses and other fragrant flowers. People have been known to stop their cars and get out to admire and take pictures of it. We see each other more often now than we did when we were younger, and you can bet we would always have a good laugh as she would tell all about my antics as a child. She loves to tease me about being a spoiled brat! To tell the truth, I really don't remember being bold, or spoiled! In fact, I thought I was always quite nice... honest!

As my Aunt Rosie and Uncle Johnny started getting up there in age, they also began having health problems. Mary and Ann Marie would spend weeks with their parents, to take care of them. Finally, Mary and her husband Henry moved back home to live with my godparents. Everyone loves Henry. He is a jack of all trades, and very talented, doing all sorts of odds and ends around the place. Most importantly, he treats my Aunt and Uncle as if they were his own parents. Mary and I are not just cousins, we are close friends. We can talk about anything, and everything, and I value her opinion. Because of Mary and Henry, my godparents can live out their lives in peace, and in their own home.

Chapter 11

Growing Up in the Real World

The Poster

After we moved to Oak Street, my life just never seemed the same. I do not know if it was because I missed my old house... the house where there were so many fond memories of my friends, my dog Daisy Mae and especially my black daddy walking down from Main Street, returning home from the coal mines. Or perhaps I was just growing up, and no longer seeing the world through rose colored glasses. I suspect it was a little of both.

I tried to make new friends, which was difficult at first, especially since the only other children in the apartment house were two little boys. Not that I didn't have male friends in my old neighborhood. Nicky Calvetti, and Patty Sebetta were two of my friends, but there was a whole group of kids, boys and girls, that played together—we were like a family!

All too soon I was realizing that life was not always fair, and my home life started to become a little more unsettled, and far less comforting than it used to be. As I grew older, I began to resent the fact that my father drank, and that my mother was always yelling at me just because I was the oldest and "should know better." The worst part was that my parents were now fighting all the time. In the morning, I didn't wake to them laughing about what they had done and said to each other, when they'd argued the night before.

When I was little, how I loved to go with my father to the bars as he made his rounds. I thought he was the smartest, greatest man alive! But now, his drinking was an *embarrassment* to me. The kids at school would make fun of him and call him an "old drunk!" Sometimes I would get so angry; I remember once yelling back at one of my classmates, "Oh yea, if *your* father didn't own a bar and give booze out, people wouldn't get drunk!" But most of the time I just put my head down and pretended not to hear their remarks, acting as if what they said didn't hurt. I would also become so angry at my father because of his drinking problem. Although he was not a falling down, slobbering drunk—in fact, he was neat, always wearing his clean, white dress shirt and fedora hat—I still felt humiliated. Sometimes, I would see him coming down the street from one of the bars, and if there were other kids around, I'd turn up another road pretending I didn't even see him... even if he waved and called out to me.

As of this very day, I am still ashamed and upset with myself over this! As a child I did not realize that he couldn't just stop drinking; Alcoholism is a illness and he needed help.

I really never said anything to my father about his drinking and I didn't love him any less—in fact, I felt sorry for him. I think I even loved him more because of the guilt I felt over being ashamed of him. I would give anything to see him now, walking towards me with that beautiful smile, waving and calling out my name once again—drunk or sober!

My mother started to slowly change too. Something was missing from her usually proud, humorous and spunky spirit. When I was younger, she was organized, and preached the morals of having a clean house. And no matter how little we had, she would always conjure up something for a meal. Now, there were some days we would come home from school to find the house messy... ashtrays filled with cigarette butts, and half empty coffee cups scattered about. There were even days that she would be laying in bed when we got home. Mommy would yell out from the bedroom, telling me to make us a peanut butter sandwich, or a package of Lipton soup mix. Sometimes she would let the coal stove go out, and it would be freezing in the house. This would lead to a blaming war: Daddy would scream at her that she was too lazy to go downstairs and get coal, so she let the fire go out... she would yell at him that he was too busy drinking with his bum friends to come home and take care of it, so it was his fault!

She even started to let her personal appearance go. My mother was a very attractive woman, with chestnut brown hair and green eyes. Normally she would always look beautiful. But now, sometimes she would be sitting at the kitchen table, smoking her Newports, and she had not even combed her hair yet. I also noticed that sometimes she would wear the same dress, not even changing into her nightgown to sleep, for days.

Once in a while, we would come home to hear her singing. The house would be neat as a pin, and a delicious aroma would greet us, as supper cooked on the stove. She and my father would be joking around just like old times. When we came in he'd say, "Hey, there's my girls!" I remember one day as we ascended the stairs, we delighted in the rich, sweet fragrance of something good baking. Mary Jane and I were sure it came from one of the neighbors' apartments. However, to our great surprise, my mother was in one of her good moods, and had made us a chocolate cake. We would never know what we would find as we'd climb up the rickety steps of that old apartment house. My heart would always pound as I reached for the handle to open the door. This always made me feel confused, insecure and even frightened.

I know poor little Mary Jane felt the same way. She would often cling to me, and have a look of fear in her eyes as we approached the apartment door.

Of course, I was too young to realize that my Mother was beginning to suffer from depression, and severe hypertension, obstructing her arterial flow. This condition was contributing to her strange actions. Unfortunately, this caused her to have a stroke when she was only forty-one years old. *If someone had only known and got her some help, she may not have had the stroke.* My daddy was also depressed, and troubled by my mother's mood swings and shifts in behavior. With no steady job, his own health problems, and especially his unsettled home life, made him take even more solace in alcohol.

We didn't have much money, and I also resented that fact. We never did anything, or went anywhere. I couldn't buy nice things to keep up with the other girls at school. How I hated the second hand clothes given to us by other people. "Thank God you have a roof over your head! After all, money doesn't grows on trees!" my mother would always say. And I heard my daddy say at least a million times, "Be happy with what ya got. When I was yer age, I was pickin' slate in the breaker!"

I recall once when were walking down Main Street, a girl pointed at me, and said so loud that the whole town could hear, "Hey Ma, look—she's wearing that old dress that you were going to throw out. Aren't you glad we gave it to the *poor* people instead?" I know she must have meant well, but at the time I was mortified!

I was lucky enough to have two *good* dresses that my mother purchased for the holidays, at Gladstiens Department Store, where they allowed her to make payments. My father would jokingly call them, "Yer Sunday go to meetin' clothes!" But I even hated them, especially, when after Mass one day, some of the "upper class" girls were giggling about me. I heard one whisper, "God... she lives in that old thing. Doesn't she have any other clothes!" It was a blessing that we had to wear uniforms to school; at least we were all *equal* in that respect.

I know now, that my parents did the best they could, with what little they had. I especially realize this after raising my own children. And in spite of all their arguments, and hardships... they loved us, and tried to be good parents.

Mary Jane and I attended St. Mary's School. Most of my classmates were better off financially than we were. To top it all off, I was not only considered poor and stupid... I was overweight! My Mother made a lot of pasta, rice and other starchy foods. She prepared meals like melting lard in a black iron skillet, then mixing in flour and milk, to make a thick white gravy, then poured it in a bowl, over hard chunks of buttered Italian bread... to fill us up. Believe it, or not... not only did this dish have about a zillion calories, it tasted delicious! So I was also the brunt of many jokes and name calling, like, "Joann Scorza...pig!" or I would hear, "Moo moo," as I passed by. Once, my teacher caught some of the boys passing around a piece of paper, but not before I got to see it. Someone drew a picture of an elephant with red, curly hair. Underneath, was written: "What's real ugly, fat and sits in the back of the second row?" As each boy received it, they would write a derogatory comment underneath, referring to me.

I realize now that I ate just a little too much for the same reason my father drank. It was my source of comfort; it helped ease my pain. (Until this very day, whenever I am stressed out, troubled or in any kind of pain, I have to fight the incredible urge not to eat everything in the whole house!) Certainly, I must have eaten a lot more than Mary Jane, because she too had a weight problem—she was skinny! She also had eczema, a skin condition that made her break out in rashes and sores. Naturally, others made fun of her too. I spent many a recess defending her.

How I hated school! The other kids made jokes about my weight and my family. I was rarely invited to join in the schoolyard games. The only time they would let me play jump rope, was to use me to do the turning; they never let me actually do the jumping! How I longed to skip rope as we chanted, "A... my name is Anna, and my husband's name is Al... we come from Allentown, and we sell...Apples!" But no... I was told I was *too fat...* what did I want to do, "put a dent in the pavement?"

Another thing, I was also afraid to answer any questions that the teachers may have asked in class. My worry was that if I answered incorrectly, I would REALLY get made fun of. The sad part was most of the time I knew the answers. However, being intimidated, and not answering, only succeeded in making me look dumb! It seemed like the harder I tried to be accepted as one of the others, the more I got shot down.

There is a memory instilled in my mind, that even now it is painful. The memory still makes me feel embarrassed every time I think of it! The last Friday of the month, was "poster day." Sister would select a few children to work on a certain theme for their poster. After their presentation, the class would vote on the best one, and the winner would receive a blue ribbon. The best part was that the winning poster would be put up in the main hall, for all the school to see!

It took several months for my turn to come, since the name Scorzafava was near the end of the alphabet. I was so nervous, knowing that all too soon, my turn would come. Finally, Sister Immaculatta called my name, and she gave me my topic: "The White House." Wow! I couldn't believe it! Just the day before, my father had brought home a copy of *Life Magazine* from the bar, and it was all about First Lady Jackie Kennedy, and she was re-doing… The White House! How lucky could I get? The article contained several pages with colored pictures!

I was filled with hope that this would be my turning point. Loaded with ammunition and confidence, I would finally prove myself! I may not have been rich, and I might have been overweight, but I certainly was not *dumb*. I was determined to make this project perfect… the best thing I ever did in all my ten years of life!

Excitedly, I shared my ideas with my mother, and she gave me fifty cents to purchase not one, but two poster boards, from Cherry's Book Shop. Each and every night I worked diligently… cutting, pasting, drawing, and memorizing my presentation. My poster was beautiful! On the front of the first poster, I glued a large picture of the outside of the White House, then I drew red and blue borders all around the white poster board measuring exactly two inches apart. I measured it correctly with my father's yard stick, making sure it was one inch wide, all the way around the edges. On top it simply stated, "The White House," in the same colors as the borders. In the lower right hand corner, in small letters I proudly wrote, "By Joann Marie Scorzafava." The two posters were held together with shiny gold ribbon that my mother, fortunately, had tucked away with the Christmas decorations. The first poster may have had only one picture, but then it opened like a book. I practiced dramatically, as I explained my project.

What a masterpiece! At first, everyone saw only the top poster, with just one picture on it. I shared the story of how President John F. Kennedy's wife,

Jackie, remolded the famous structure. Then I unfolded the top page, revealing all the wonderful before and after photos of the rooms.

I spoke eloquently and with confidence about the history of the White House as I carefully explained each photo. I even shared the fact that some people believe that it is *haunted* by President Abraham Lincoln, and that Jackie herself, had been known to see the ghostly figure!

For the first time since I started school, I felt pride. At last, I would finally be accepted! All my days of hard work would finally pay off; my classmates would no longer think that I was *stupid*. They would finally see me as a person of worth, and not just some dumb, overweight kid to make fun of…someone who had no feelings.

The others took their turns showing their posters, and I must admit they too were nice—however, nothing could compare with mine! I was so excited; I couldn't wait to be voted… BEST! I imagined my poster with my blue ribbon hanging from it. I could picture it on the main wall of the hallway, for the whole school to see. Finally, I would be admired and shown respect!

My heart was beating so fast as we cast our secret votes. Everyone had to write the name of the person that they felt was the best on a piece of paper. Sister Immaculatta would then count them, to determine the winner. I was practicing my acceptance speech that the winners had to give, in my mind, when Sister got up from behind her desk. She spoke clearly, with anger in her voice. "Children! What have you learned about fairness! I cannot believe you did this! All the posters were wonderful, and all four worked hard on them, but we ALL know, that there was one project that was far above the rest! Joann Scorzafava only received TWO votes! The whole class knows that she should have won… shame on you!" She then put the blue ribbon on my poster saying, "Congratulations, Joann! You are today's winner!" Glaring at my classmates she instructed, "Now class, let me hear your applause!" My peers halfheartedly started to clap… but it didn't mean anything. I was crushed! I felt my eyes welling up, and I excused myself and ran to the bathroom. As the tears streamed down my face, I locked myself in one of the stalls. I felt like such a fool! And I don't think I was so hurt, and so disappointed, since the day I realized that my black daddy was no longer going to come home from the coal mines.

Since it was the last period of the day, the bell soon rang, but I was still too embarrassed and devastated to come out of the restroom. Finally, Sister Immaculatta came in and spoke to me. Knocking on the stall door she whispered, "Are you alright?"

Still crying, I sobbed through the gray, metal door, "Oh, Sister, how could they be so mean? I worked so hard on my poster, and I PRAYED really hard to win! I really thought for sure I would be the winner, and be accepted! How could I be so stupid! They are right—I *am* stupid, to think that ANYTHING I would do would make them like me!"

Sister told me to come out of the stall. I obeyed, and she handed me a piece of toilet paper so I could blow my nose. Then she had me wash my face and look into the mirror. She spoke quietly, saying, "See that young girl... she is accepted! God accepts her, and she was made in His Image, so she is wonderful! You must learn not to be so sensitive, because life is not always fair. You and I both know you did a great job, and so do the other children. No, it was not a nice, or fair thing they have done to you. Just because they didn't vote for you does not mean that you are not a *winner*! Please remember this all your life... always, *always* do the very best that you can do, no matter what. Trust me, as long as you do your very best you will always be a... *WINNER!*" Then Sister tried to make a little joke about the situation by saying, "Well, you have a few friends, at least *two* people voted for you!" I pretended to laugh, but deep inside, I was too hurt and ashamed to tell her that actually, I had only one vote... I voted for myself!

Later on, I learned that the other person who voted for me was a girl named Lorraine De Angelis, and till this very day she holds a special place in my heart!

At every Celebration, Jo Jo the Clown invites the children to get into a circle, and says, "Now, children, we are going to do this silly song and dance, but I am going to make a game out of it. So whoever sings the song the loudest, and makes the actions the best... will win a prize!" The music starts, and they all begin dancing around to the "Hokey Pokey."

"You put your right hand in, you put your right hand out, you give your hand a shake, shake, shake and turn yourself about." Everyone sings, dances and laughs. When the song is finished, Jo Jo says to them, "Now I will pick out the winner!" She goes around the circle, batting her long eyelashes at each child, then says excitedly, as she points to a child, "You're the winner..." then to another, "... No, you're the winner..." then to another, " No, no you're the winner!" Acting confused, and putting her hands to her head she states, "What to do, oh, what to do... I can't pick out a winner! Wait, I know! I am going to give you ALL a prize!" As she pulls out balloons to shape into a puppy dogs, cats and other assorted prizes she softly says, as she looks into each of their little eyes, "You

know, all of you are wonderful and very special, each in your own way... God didn't make anyone in the whole, wide world exactly like you, and all of you did your very best, and remember all of your lives, as long as you always do your very best... you will ALWAYS be a winner!" As Jo Jo looks at the children sitting at her feet, they are looking up at her smiling with joy, and most importantly... PRIDE in themselves.

A Child's Betrayal

Child psychiatrists in this day and age know that children can truly suffer from depression and other physiological disorders. However, in my day, no one ever even heard of such problems with children. You were just labeled: "shy, a trouble maker, lazy, retarded" or some other such thing. Daily life was becoming a real challenge for me. I hated to go to school, knowing I would be tormented. After the incident with my poster, "Teacher's pet" and "Cheater" (I was accused of not making my poster at all... I was too stupid to make it! I must have had my mother make it for me) were added to the list of names they called me. I pretended to be sick often, so I could stay home, but I don't know if that was any better. My parents were always yelling. I lived in fear that they might even hurt each other, *really* bad.

My father was also suffering more severely from his black lung disease. If I wasn't mad at him for drinking, I was crying and worried about him because he was gasping for air, and coughing up blood. I would have him sit down, and put cold, wet wash cloths on his head after one of his coughing spells. "Daddy," I would say, "maybe you shouldn't make your rounds today, because it will make you feel worse. Why don't you just stay home today and rest?" I meant it for that reason, but I also hoped that he wouldn't go out, so he wouldn't come home drunk, and all the fighting would begin.

Also, my mother was also becoming worse with her problem. I recall her coming to walk us home from school one day, and she had a "babushka" on her head. She was also wearing a heavy winter coat, and she was in open sandals. I was totally embarrassed. Not only were her feet obviously very dirty, there was no need of a coat or hat of any kind, since it was a very warm day. Our house was also a mess, Filled with clothes, dirty dishes, and soiled ashtrays all over. Soon, I tried to became a housekeeper, cook and child care giver. I was too young for all this responsibility, and believe me, very soon I really started resenting it! I would become angry at my mother, saying some unkind things like, "Ma, I am only a kid! Why should I have to do all the stuff around here? Get out of bed, and stop being so lazy!" Or, "If you didn't smoke all those cigarettes, you'd be able to get more food!" And my most popular insult, "What kind of a wife and mother are you? no wonder Daddy drinks!" Later, I would always be so very sorry and ashamed for my outbursts, but no matter how many times I said that I didn't mean it, and I was sorry, the words were already spoken and the hurt I caused by my big mouth was done! This would make me feel so guilty and terrible, only adding to all my other heavy burdens that lay on my heart and soul.

Poor little Mary Jane, who adored her "Big Sissy," even she would get on my nerves, and none of it was even her fault! I would tell her to stop hanging on me. And to leave me alone. Why did I have to take care of her, and get her up, fed and dressed for school? This would make me late, and I would get in trouble. Why did she always have to hang around me, and do everything I did? Not that I was able to do that much anyway. This too, added to my guilt, because I loved her, and realized that she had no one in the house to really take care of her, except me.

Then, one awful day, I was also presented with another horrendous problem, which still haunts me. We had no school buses, so everyone had to walk to school. There was an old, dilapidated house on Sussex Street. The kids would take a short cut to school, walking through the back yard of the property on which the house was situated. There was an old man who sometimes would sit on the back porch, smoking a pipe. He never said anything to the kids that passed through; in fact, he would even wave at us.

One day, Mary Jane and I were walking behind the other kids, (in fact, I always lagged behind, knowing no one would want to walk with me anyway) and the old man got up and called me over, "Hey, Red. Come over here a minute!"

For a second I was stunned, thinking I was in trouble for something. So I slowly walked over and stated, "I didn't do anything wrong!"

He smiled at us through broken, yellow teeth and said, "No, no you didn't do anything wrong. I just wanted to talk to ya." I became a little nervous, asking what about. "Oh, I always see that ya always walk behind the other kids. What's the matter, ya ain't got no friends?"

He seemed harmless enough, so I relaxed and said, "No they just walk faster than me."

The old man, clearly not believing my excuse, stated, "Well, don't you worry, old Jack (not real name) here will be yer friend. Come and talk to me anytime."

After that when I saw him outside, I would stop and talk for a few minutes. It really seemed good to have someone talk to, even if he was old. Soon, I actually looked forward to seeing him on the porch. Slowly, I began trusting and confiding in him. I started telling him how the other kids made fun of me and my sister. Mary Jane was usually with me, hanging on to my uniform. He would sympathize with me, even telling me sad stories about himself when he was growing up. We never went into the house. The closest I came was to stand on the porch once or twice, and I only visited a few minutes. However, I started to think of Jack, as a grandfather. I was glad to have someone to share my feelings with; he seemed to really understand.

It was a damp and rainy day a few months later. Mary Jane had stayed home from school. I had a particularly stressful day in class and was feeling very down. As I was walking through Jack's yard, he called me over for one of our usual talks. He said, "Let's go in the house, out of the chilly rain."

My parents had warned me never to go into anyone's house alone, but by this time I felt knew and trusted Jack. Thinking about it for a moment, I agreed. I climbed the old creaky steps and entered the house as he held the door open for me. His kitchen was old, but surprisingly neat and tidy. I could smell chicken soup simmering on the stove. "You look so sad," he said, "Tell old Jack what's troublin' ya." Well, I immediately burst into tears, telling him all about that day's episode. "There, there," he said, as he came and put his arms around me. It felt good, feeling warm arms around me, even if he did smell like tobacco, so I put my arms around him too, and cried against his chest. He kept patting me on the back, saying soothing things like, "Cry it all out; it's ok. It will make ya feel better."

After a while, I did feel better. My tears, and his tenderness gave me some relief from my pain. Jack then pulled up the rocking chair and sitting down, he gently pulled me on his lap. "I don't know why everybody is so mean to a sweet little thing like you," he stated, as he started to rock us. Jack gave me a kiss on the cheek and said, "How about givin' yer old pal a kiss." Thinking nothing of it, I gave him a kiss back. His unshaven face prickled, and his breath didn't smell too good, but I didn't care; he was my friend, and being Italian, we always kissed our friends. Jack went on saying all the sympathetic things I longed to hear. "Put yer head against me, and relax for a while," he said soothingly.

Leaning against him felt so good. He started playing with my hair saying, "Yer hair smells like flowers." I was so glad my mother had a good day a few days before. She washed my hair and had rinsed it with Lily of the Valley cologne. It made me happy that I pleased him, because I didn't seem to do anything right for a long time. It felt so comforting that I could have nodded off. I remember thinking this is how it would have been if my *real* grandfathers hadn't died. Jack started to rub my arm softly and said something about my skin being so soft and white.

I was just thinking all I ever wanted was to be loved and accepted; why can't everyone be like Jack, when he said and did something that shocked me beyond belief! "Ya know yer titties felt real good against me!" and he actually grabbed me (I was very developed for my age), shoving one hand down the blouse with such force, the button popped off and went flying to the floor! With the other hand he groped my crotch area, as he stood us up and pushed me against the wall. He was kissing me on the lips and tried to put his tongue in my mouth. I kept moving my head away and spitting because it was making me sick. As Jack pressed himself against me, I could feel something hard from his body. I squirmed away, yelling, "Stop it! What are you doing! You were hurting me!"

His eyes looked glassy, and his breathing became heavier, while I became more terrified. "Come here," he said. "I won't hurt ya! Ya know I love ya! I just wanna make ya feel better! Old Jack is yer friend!" As he came closer, he unzipped his pants and pulled this *thing* out saying, "I won't hurt ya; I just want ya to touch it, that's all. Just hold it like a good girl!" I had no idea why he was doing this, or what he even got out of it, but instinctively, I knew it was wrong! He came after me and grabbed my hand, pushing it on himself. With his other hand he quickly slid under my uniform, and into my underpants.

I yelled, "Get away from me! You're hurting me!" Then, with all my strength I picked up my knee and pushed him as hard as I could, catching him off guard. He stumbled and fell against the corner of the table. He just laid there... I could see blood trickling down his forehead. My first reaction was, "Oh, my God, I killed him!" I would go to Hell! Then, after a few seconds, thankfully, I heard him moan, and then he blinked open his eyes. My whole body was shaking so bad, that teeth were actually chattering! I slowly moved a little closer, then unbelievably, I found myself saying, "I didn't hurt you, did I?"

He took the opportunity to grab my ankle and hissed, "Just where do you think yer going? I ain't done with ya yet!" I got my other foot and started kicking him as hard as I could; this caused me to actually fall on top of him. He let go of my leg for a second, and I pulled away from him, crawling towards the door. In the midst of all this trauma, I remember seeing and grabbing my little white button. He screamed out at me, "You little bastard, don't ya tell anybody! They will blame you; it was all yer fault! I'll put ya in jail for hittin' my head!" Standing up, I ran out the door. He followed and yelled, "If you ever tell anybody, you little fat, little bitch, I'll *kill* you and yer sister! I *know* where you live! If you tell, I'll get you!" Running out of the yard crying hysterically, my heart was racing so fast, I thought I would have a heart attack!

That was the worst thing that had ever happened to me in my whole life. Should I tell my mother, my teacher, or the cops? I didn't know what to do. As I ran home, I was glad it was raining, because I was so frightened I wet my pants! When I got there, my mother started to yell at me, "Where the hell were you? How come you got home so late?"

Not knowing what to say or do, I finally blurted out that Sister asked me to stay after school to clean the blackboard and erasers.

I spent most of the night crying, worrying and praying. What if he died after I left? What if I really murdered him? Should I tell anyone? Maybe he was right, maybe it *was* my fault? Did I commit a sin? Will I get pregnant? I really didn't know much about sex, or even what it really was. Of course since there was no actual sex act, and I was too young, I couldn't get pregnant... but how would I know? We were never taught anything about sex in school, and were told very little about it by our families. I was told never let anyone touch you *there,* in certain places on your body. It was a big sin, and you could get a baby in your stomach. (For the next several months, I would check my stomach each morning. I'd look in the mirror to see if it was getting any bigger, then I'd check my uniform to see if it was any tighter. I was so scared; what if there was a baby in there! Would they kick me out of school? Would my parents beat me and throw me out of the house? Most of all, I worried how and when would the baby come out of my stomach?)

My mind and thoughts were going crazy. One minute I'd think, "In the morning I will tell my mother." The next minute I'd think, "No! she'd hit me and say Jack was right; it was all my fault!" After all, I did go into his house, and I did hug and kiss him, didn't I? Or maybe he would kill me and my sister to get even, if I told. I noticed he had a gun on the wall, he could shoot us! I even wondered if I had committed a mortal sin, and maybe I should go to confession. But I thought better of it, being too embarrassed to let the priest know. Then I'd think, "What if he bled to death after I left, and the cops would find out it was me, and I would be arrested!"

The more I thought about the awful, creepy feeling of him touching my body, the sicker I got. Finally, I had to throw up. I felt so *dirty and ashamed*, and wanted to take a bath. How I hated my body, especially my breasts! It was one thing to have the kids make fun of them, but for someone to touch them like that! Why didn't I have little ones, or better yet, *none* like the rest of the girls in my class? Maybe he wouldn't have done this if they were *normal*!

I think what hurt the most was that he betrayed my trust. I actually don't know how old he really was. I suspect that he was younger than I thought at the time, but I thought of him like a grandfather, and he knew that… I told him so! My own grandfathers were dead, so it was so nice to have one, even if he was only a substitute. How could I ever trust anyone ever again?

For the next several days I stayed home from school. My mother thought I was sick with the flu, but I was sick in my heart and soul, and the shock of what had happened actually made me physically ill. When I finally did go back to school, I made sure I didn't take the short cut. However, I did sneak a peek, through the hedges just to make sure I hadn't killed him. There he was rocking away on the back porch, smoking his pipe, just as if nothing ever happened! The only evidence was a Band-Aid across his forehead. I was so mad at him for doing such a terrible thing to me! I was also angry that I'd lost his friendship; he was the only real friend I had! All I could think of was some friend, he never even me asked me my name; he just always called me "Red." I vowed then—because maybe it was my fault, maybe I deserved it, maybe he'll kill us… maybe, maybe, maybe… for all the wrong reasons—that I would never, ever tell anyone. This terrible secret weighed heavy on my soul, and has caused me grief, pain and guilt most of my life. I have kept my vow, and never did share this experience with anyone… until now.

I have decided to tell this story, and share my awful secret. I know now, that unfortunately, there are other little girls, and boys, who are also being molested. They too, might be feeling as I did, too frightened to tell anyone. Their little hearts and minds troubled and guilt ridden. There are many signs: If a usually happy, outgoing child suddenly becomes quiet and fearful. When you get close to them, or try to hug them and they pull away, especially if they always hugged you before. If a usually good child suddenly becomes angry, and gets into trouble quite often. Some children may start to wet the bed, begin crying all the time, or get promiscuous, even at a young age. Also, if a child claims he or she is sick a little too often, or becomes upset if they have to go with a certain person, or to a certain place, that they never feared before. All these changes may be signs that they are being molested. Of course, all or some of these reasons do not always mean that this is true, either. However, if you know a child, or if your own child is showing these symptoms, I hope and pray that you feel this innocent, little life is worth enough to at least check it out. And if anyone, child or adult, reading this is being harmed in any way, please... please, don't be afraid; God is with you! TELL SOMEONE!

My Calling

Naturally, I always went to school the long way, after my harrowing experience. I avoided looking at or talking to almost everyone. This was a far cry from that joyful little girl with the outgoing personality, who sang and danced in the beer gardens just a few short years before. What ever happened to my life? I would think about my past, as if I lived a hundred years ago. We had our problems, but were a warm, happy family. I felt content then, living in a small, sheltered world which consisted of going to church, making the bar rounds with my daddy, playing in the front cellar with Mary Jane or the back field with my friends. How I missed my father's beautiful grapevine and garden. I also missed my almost daily visits to our grandma's house. Now, we lived way across town, and it was too far for me to walk alone. We didn't have too much then either, but things were different. Our home was clean and cozy. They may not have been real fancy, but we always had meals. There might have been fights between my parents, but there was love and laughter too. Most importantly, then I felt safe. Now, I felt frightened, unprotected and... empty.

Since that day I walked around in some sort of fog, building an invisible wall around myself. When the kids made their rude remarks, I pretended that their words hit this wall and I couldn't hear them. Quietly, I did my school work and ate my lunch, not even bothering to look around or say anything. I'd return home and do whatever my mother asked of me, usually no questions asked. I spoke only when spoken to, with as few words as possible. When I did talk, my remarks were more often than not sarcastic. Then I'd go into my room, close the door and listen to country and western music on the radio. Listening to all those losing, leaving, divorcing and dying songs, seemed to somehow help me cope. No one ever asked me if something was wrong, and I was glad, because I sure didn't want to talk about what happened. Once I overheard my mother talking to Helen, the neighbor who lived in the next apartment, and she said, "I don't know what's the matter with that girl; she must be going through one of those stages or something!" I judged any hug, or show of affection from a relative... even my own father! When he kissed me, or touched me affectionately, I thought it was in a *bad* way. I started to pull away, not wanting him near me. I began avoiding all physical contact from everyone, especially men, with the exception, of course, of my little sister Mary Jane. I knew she wouldn't hurt a fly, and besides she gave me no choice, she was always hanging on to me. When I relate back, I think she realized something was wrong, because of the sympathetic, unusual way she would look at me. She would softly rub my arm, and say, "JA, I love you; don't cry today... ok?"

I truly do not know what would have happened to me, if I did not believe in God. They say He works in mysterious ways, and I am sure He did on that day in 1961. That was the day that I believe literally changed my entire life and future!

It was near the end of the school year, and we only had a few weeks left before summer vacation. My schoolmates and I were all outside, since it was almost time for school to let out for the day. The other kids were playing, but I was standing by myself, near the schoolyard wall. Some of the nuns were walking up Grace Street from the convent. They were carrying what looked like clothing. Sister Rose called out to me, "Joann, come and help me with Father's vestments." I hurried down to meet her, thinking it was an honor! At least the nuns liked me. She told me to hold out my arms, and she laid some of the vestments across them. "Hold them just like that; I don't want them to get wrinkled," she said. They were shiny, ivory colored and made of silky material, so as I walked, they started to slide from my arms. I tried not to let them fall on the ground, but as they kept sliding I had to grab them, not only making wrinkles, but some of the material became soiled as it slid down to the ground. I accidentally stepped on it, causing the whole pile to fall at our feet! My heart seemed to stop, as I looked at Sister Rose. Her whole face turned as red as a beet! Before I could even try to apologize, or explain, she started to scream, "You little idiot! Do you know how long I worked on these vestments? It took me two days to wash and press them! Why don't you watch what you're doing!" I tried to say I was sorry, but she cut me off, "Sorry? Sorry? Is that all you have to say for yourself? You never listen to anything, or are you really that dumb?" Naturally, I started to cry and was totally frightened and embarrassed, especially after realizing that the whole playground had become quiet. Everyone had stopped playing and talking, to listen to her yelling at me. Then she said something in a deep threatening voice, that till this very day, I cannot believe a nun would say to any child, no matter what they did, "Save your crying for Hell, because that is just where you are going, straight to... HELL! You deserve it for ruining the priest's vestments! These are what he wears to say the Holy Mass, and YOU will be punished!"

The other kids had a field day! I just wanted to die... just wanted to die! This was the last straw; I didn't want to live anymore. Yet, if I died I was going straight to Hell. I didn't know what to do, what to say or where to go. I felt like a trapped animal. It seemed like forever until the bell finally rang. Mary Jane was not in school that day, so I didn't have to wait for her. I ran across the street as fast as I could, into the large field that led to the path we took to go home. There was a large, flat rock off the path that Mary Jane and I liked to sit on for a while on our way home from school. (Years later, Insalacco's grocery store was built on that spot.)

I clearly remember the day... The weatherman would call it "partly sunny." You know, one of those days that the sun comes out, then goes back in under a cloud, and in a little while it comes back out again. Breathless, I finally reached the rock, and fell down upon it crying harder than I ever had before. "Dear God!" I sobbed, "I am so sorry for everything I did wrong! I didn't mean it—honest!" A million things came into my mind... all those maybes again! Maybe if were really good, my daddy wouldn't drink. Maybe if I didn't say those mean things to my mother, she would be well by now. Maybe if I didn't hug Jack, he wouldn't have done what he did. Maybe, maybe, maybe... all the maybes, guilt, sorrow and pain, everything I ever felt deep down inside of me, welled up and came to the surface. I honestly and truly couldn't take it anymore. I really, *really* wanted die. "Please, please let me die! I am stupid, ugly and no good, no good at all! Everyone would be better off, the whole world will be better off without me! God, please forgive me! I know you love me, so please don't send me to Hell for messing up the priest's vestments; I didn't mean it! Please let me go to Heaven with you and be at peace!" I closed my eyes, took a deep breath, held it and waited... to die.

The sun had been under a cloud and I felt its heat as it came back out again. Only this time it was different! I felt the heat, and it was so bright... I couldn't open my eyes. And as hard as I tried, I couldn't hold my breath anymore. Then, all of a sudden, a miraculous thing occurred! I felt as if I were lifting off the rock, and actually floating! Maybe I was on my way to Heaven! This warm, beautiful feeling came over me, that was so fantastic, all the books, in all the world could never express. And as I experienced this "ecstasy"... God spoke to me! No, I did not actually hear His voice, but He spoke to me alright, I heard Him *LOUD and CLEAR,* in my heart! He said,

"You get off of that rock and get on with your life! I have wonderful plans in store for you! It is *NOT* your time to come home to me! I want you to use the many gifts and talents that I have given you to make the world a better place to live in! If you love and obey me, you will bring great joy, happiness and peace to others, through fun and laughter—they are *healing medicines*! I love you, Joann! You are my beloved child; now go forth with the blessings I bestow upon you... and bring about my Kingdom!"

I honestly do not know how long I *floated* there, feeling a peace that passed understanding. My joy was incredible. I also realized the light, which was so bright that I couldn't open my eyes, was not the sun in the sky—I believe it was the Son of God! I also believe that I was truly in the presence of the Father, Son and Holy Spirit all in one God!

After a while, I felt the firmness of the ground beneath me, and I was finally able to open my eyes. I sat up and was in awe! I thought, "What in the world happened? Did it *really* happen? Was I imagining it? Was I dreaming? I must have been dreaming; *why* would God speak to me? Did I finally go... NUTS? I'll tell you, at that moment I didn't care what it was. I felt so *LIGHT* and *WONDERFUL*! It felt like all the pain and sorrow that was trapped deep inside of me came right through my body and drifted away.

All of a sudden, the whole world seemed different, and worth... *LIVING!*

As a guest speaker, I have related this story many times before. After hearing mine, other people have also shared their experiences with me, and they too believe God spoke to them. There are people who have faith in God, and they absolutely believe it happened. Other people chose to think that I AM nuts. But it doesn't matter to me, because I KNOW my Lord spoke to my heart, and I absolutely KNOW that He has called me to use "Jo Jo the Clown" as His instrument to bring about His Kingdom, and that is all that matters. I have no need to prove anything to anyone. I also believe that God speaks to all of us; we only have to listen, to hear Him! I read a card once that summed it all up: "For those who believe, no explanation is needed, for those who do not, no explanation is possible."

I arose from the ground and was so happy that I skipped and sang all the way home. As I approached my house, for the first time since I moved there, I was glad to be home. I came around the house to the back, and my father was digging in his little garden. Watching him, I realized all the pain and sorrow he must be feeling. I also comprehended the things that caused him to drink—the war, the mines closing, his health, his wife's depression and yes, even his little girl growing up and pushing him away! As he knelt, I watched how tenderly he placed the tomato plants in the soil. I felt a rush of love! I ran up to him and said, "Daddy, I missed you today!" I hugged and kissed him so hard we both fell in the fresh dug earth. We both started laughing so hard, as our shoes and clothes got covered in dirt.

"Hey what's come over my little girl?" he said, his blue yes glistening.

"Nothing, Daddy! I just want you to know I love you, that's all!"

But he sure knew something was different about me. I could see he needed me to be his little girl. I promised myself that I would never, ever be ashamed of, or avoid him again.

My mother leaned out the window to hang some clothes, and I yelled, "Hi, Ma... I love you!"

She looked down and said, "What in the hell is going on down there; have you lost your minds?" But I detected a giggle in her voice. I also saw her in a different way, a woman who was struggling to keep a family together, and fighting her own pain. She was married to an alcoholic, which had its many problems, and from that moment on I realized that she was ill, and she *needed* me to help her.

I ran upstairs to see Mary Jane, no longer looking at her as a pest, or someone I had to look after, but as a little child who loved her "Big Sissy," and I loved her too! She *needed* me watch out for her. I hugged and kissed her, whispering in her ear, "Mary Jane, I love you so much! I don't ever want you to be afraid. I will always, always look after you and take care of you forever!"

She whispered back, "JA, you mean you are not going to cry anymore... ok?

"Well, Mary Jane" I said, "I promise you I will not cry all the time, anymore... ok?" This seemed to please her. Why didn't I see all this before? Here I was feeling neglected, unloved and sorry for myself, and I was *needed* all along!

The big test was when I went to school the next day. But I should have known that God is good! Yes, I saw this situation differently also. I realized that the kids who made fun of me had problems too. There must be pain in their own lives, to want to cause others sorrow.

My eyes were finally open. I was always wallowing in my own self pity, and always feeling so sorry for myself, that I never realized that there were other kids that were being made fun of, too. There was the boy who was tall and skinny, that they called "String Bean." Also the girl whose teeth stuck out so much they called her "Bucky Beaver." Another girl had real thick eye glasses, they nicknamed her "Four Eyes." I realized that if you were different in any way, shape or form, you were made fun of. No, life sure isn't fair, but I decided it could still be… good!

Before the first period was over, I got called down to the office. I had been called down to the principal's office before, however, this time I wasn't worried or frightened. There sat Sister Rose; she looked a little embarrassed, as she said how sorry she was for yelling at me. "Sister," I said, "I know you didn't mean to yell at me, just like I didn't mean to drop the vestment. Let's just forgive each other, ok?" All of a sudden, to everyone's surprise, I jumped up and hugged her! In fact, I felt so happy… I wanted to hug everyone in the whole, wide world!

As the days passed, I started to talk with all the other "less than perfect kids." So we all got together, and before school was out for the summer, we all became friends. Another marvelous thing that happened—as time passed, I didn't care if others made fun of me. I am not saying it still didn't hurt, it did, but it wasn't the most important thing to me anymore. I realized, and also recognized one of the many gifts that God had bestowed upon me. He had given me a sense of humor. I never knew I could be silly. Sure life isn't always fair, but it could still be fun! In fact, when the other kids were about to joke about me, I joined right in and made a joke about myself first! Soon, instead of laughing at me, they were laughing with me. I guess you could say I became the class clown.

Of course life is not perfect, and I still had my share of sorrow and troubles. In fact, a few times I thought God had gone out to lunch. Sometimes I still got sad, upset and I even cried, but now my problems had a light at the end of the tunnel, and I knew God had to come back from His lunch break sometime. I was able to get through my troubles, without *despair*, because I knew He was taking care of me. I even pulled my mother's old cliché out of the cobwebs, "When life hands you lemons… make lemonade," and started practicing that rule again. I began looking for signs from God, so I could do whatever it was that He was calling me to do.

It took a long time, and I know it will never be forgotten, but I was actually even able to forgive old Jack, for what he had done to me. I know now, that he had a problem; he was a sick man, and needed help. I only wish that I had the strength at the time to tell someone so he could have received the help he needed. I also hope and pray that no other little child was hurt by him because of my silence.

Every day I try to find humor in even the most trying situations. And even if at the time, I am troubled. I seems that no matter how serious a situation may be, afterwards, when I think back about it, or relate it to someone, we could always find something in that situation... to laugh about!

New Friends

Well, I thought, if I could make friends at school, I could make friends around my neighborhood. I also decided that they didn't even have to be my age. My mother had already gotten aquatinted with a lady named Madeline Pugliano. She owned a little grocery store, located on Oak Street, just one block from our house. The store was small, however, you could get milk, bread, newspapers and other small essentials, and especially, Newport cigarettes.

This storekeeper was a single, older woman, who also had a weight problem. She was quiet, and some of the kids even thought she was a little mean. However, I made it my business to find the "real Madeline." As I shopped in her little store, I would compliment her beautiful, dark brown hair, or other incidental things, that may make her feel good. Soon, my mother would make a habit of visiting her, and they would drink coffee and smoke cigarettes together.

Madeline was also self conscious about her weight, but before she could say something to cut her self down again, I would relate a funny story about my own weight, and we'd have a good laugh! Then I'd say something like, "Hey, heavy people are sure lucky, there is more of us to love!"

The age difference didn't matter to me, she was my friend. Later on, she had to have her legs amputated. I would visit and run errands for her . I started to befriend several older people, like Jenny Morino, who lived across the street.

Not only did I enjoy doing little errands for them, but complimenting them and listening to their stories. Old people have a wealth of knowledge and wisdom. It is sad that many times they are thought of as a burden, so they are neglected, ignored, or perhaps, thought too old enjoy life. I found that by listening, and sharing with them, they blossom.

By joining an organization called Serving Seniors—formally Interfaith Friends—I have had the wonderful opportunity of volunteering and entertaining in each and every nursing facility in the Northeast. I had just finished my show at the Lackawanna Long Term Center. How exhilarated I felt as we all laughed and sang our way down memory lane! My dear friend, the activities director, Tony La Mania, hugged me and said, "God Bless you, Jo Jo! The residents really love when you come here! You really make a difference in their lives!"

I said something that was very true, "Tony, all the volunteers and entertainers are wonderful, and so are you; we all make a difference!"

He agreed with me, and then said, "You're right, Jo Jo, we all do. But you know, I noticed that when you visit something happens. Several residents have come up tome and asked if I thought you would like their dress, tie, or maybe a piece of jewelry. They want to get all dolled up for you! So today I really watched you, and now I know why; you really pay personal attention to them. Not only do you tell them how wonderful and special they all are, you went up and hugged each person and gave a compliment to every one. You mentioned how nice they looked, or how pretty that color looked on them. I loved it when you told ninety-year-old Vito that he looked sexy today! Why, he just grinned from ear to ear!"

To be honest, until that day I never realized that I did that. I just wanted these dear, sweet people to know they were loved, and noticed. But I used Tony's kind words as a learning experience. Every time I meet up with anyone, young or old, I always look for something that I really find pleasing, and give them a big compliment! Not only does it make that person feel good, it makes that little girl who still lives deep inside me, the little girl who would long for a compliment from anyone, feel much better too!

Soon, I found friends in the neighborhood. Right across the street lived a girl I never even noticed before. Her name was Elsa Revello, and we became close friends. Down Church Street, I met a real interesting family; they had a whole house full of kids! I can't remember how many, but there must have been at least ten. I became fast friends with Barbara, Helen and Andrea Dudack, and Annette La Tempa. We could have fun doing practically nothing. I also became friends with a whole family, the Garvins. They also lived on Oak Street. My favorite was the youngest daughter—although she was about ten years older than me, she had the heart of a little girl, and always would. Christine had Down's syndrome. She was full of nothing but pure love. There were many other people, young and old alike, that became my friends over the years.

What always amazed me was they were always there, right in front of my eyes. But before, I was all caught up in my own sadness, troubles and self pity to even see them.

Chapter 12

The Teenage Years

Although I had a much more positive outlook on life, things at home had not become too much better. At a young age I thought that there were many things I was responsible for, like my father's drinking problem, and my parents almost constant arguments. I tried to be a peacemaker and smooth things over when they fought; sometimes it worked, most of the time it didn't. The arguments weren't always my father's fault. Yes, he was the one with the drinking problem, however, there were times he came home in a good mood, singing and acting silly. My mother was the one who would start nagging him; sometimes, it seemed as if she wanted to fight. More than once, my father went to bed to sleep it off, and she would nag and badger him. Finally, he'd have enough and get up, then he'd go back to the bars again.

I took care of Mary Jane on my mother's off days, which were becoming more frequent. My experience taught me how to cook, clean, sew, and do just about any household chore, almost as well as an adult. By watching and helping my father, on his good days I learned how to paint, use tools and become an all around handyman. Not only did I look and act years beyond my true age, some days I felt *really old*!

I loved both of my parents, and it hurt me to see them so unhappy, and always hurting each other. Their constant bickering also made me angry, and it hurt Mary Jane too. Some days, I really didn't think I could take it, but of course, I always made it through. I couldn't wait to grow up, and marry Mr. Wonderful. How I looked forward to getting on with my *new* and *perfect* life!

When I was about thirteen years old, my friends and I started doing what most of the young people did. We did small jobs to earn a little money. I babysat, did housework and even worked at Renna's Dairy, which was located way down on West Oak Street. I used to help make and sell ice cream. When payday came, I would not only to buy food, I also bought little things to spruce up the house a bit. Of course, I also started fixing myself up a bit, too. My friends and I would go to Gmitter's Five & Dime to buy the usual teenage essentials: lipstick, toilet water, and earrings. We'd all go to Reba's Pizza Place on North Main Street, or Marianelli's Bowling Alley or Shaefer'sDrug Store for a Cherry Coke, which were located on South Main Street. But it really wasn't so much to eat or bowl; they were usual hangouts for the teens in the neighborhood. We'd whisper about the cute boys, and who we would like to *go steady* with.

I was outgoing, yet shy (if that is possible) at the same time. Although when I was little, people were always saying how cute I was. And when I was three years old, I was the winner of The Children's International Beauty Contest, sponsored by the Scranton Dry Goods Department Store. Friends would say things to my father like, "When she grows up, she is going to be a real heartbreaker!" or "Isn't she gorgeous, with those big green eyes and red hair!" My parents, especially my father, always told me I was beautiful, but of course, that was only natural. Parents always think their children are beautiful, no matter what they look like. All this didn't matter; I always had a hang up about my looks. Although I had nice features—a small nose, large eyes, straight white teeth and a clear complexion—I always felt *UGLY*, and of course *FAT*!

Painfully, I recall one humiliating incident that contributed to my low self esteem: We lived only a few blocks away from the border line of the next town of Taylor. This town was in the east direction, and you would need to pass through it if you were going to Scranton. In Taylor was another popular hang out for the kids, Thomas's Movie Theater. One day a few of the popular girls came up to me at school and said that this boy in our class, "was dying to get together with me, at the movies!" They told me that he thought I was really cute. Of course I didn't believe it at first. Even my friends Barbara and Ann Jo thought it was a joke. Especially since this *certain* boy was really popular, and extremely handsome. He was also on the football teem, and could go out with anyone he wanted to. So why in the world would he want to date me? For weeks the other girls kept insisting that he had a *crush* on me, but he was afraid to talk to me, which was really hard to believe!

Well, when he started to wink at me in the hall and wave to me, I began to wonder. Then one day he slipped a note to me :

"Dear Joann, I would like to know if you are not busy on Saturday, would you meet me at the movies? I think you are real nice, and I love your long red hair. I also think you are very smart; I liked the poem you composed for English class! Will you meet me. I really want to get to know you better. To be honest I'm really sick of all those snobby cheerleaders who think they are all it!"

Discussing the matter with friends, the big question was: "Do you think I should go?" So after reading his note about a zillion times, we decided the answer was…yes! I saw him after school and told him I would meet him.

For the next few days I practiced fixing my hair in a dozen o different styles. I went to "Sally's" (our name for the Salvation Army Thrift Store) and bought a brand "new" outfit. I fixed it all over, hoping I didn't look fat. Carefully I applied my make up and looked in the mirror, holding in my stomach. My friends stated that I looked stunning, and much older than my age. To tell the truth, looking at my reflection, I had to admit I didn't look too bad at all.

Saturday finally came, and my friends and I walked up to Thomas's Theater. We were all so excited since this was my first date. He was waiting for me! I was so nervous as he took my arm and boldly walked me right up the center isle. Barbara and Ann Jo naturally sat somewhere else. Of course it was in a good spot where they could see everything that went on between me and my date! As he and I sat down, he mentioned that I looked very lovely. After a few minutes he even put his arm around me! My heart was pounding! The movie started. *House on Haunted Hill* flashed on the screen. After the movie was playing for about ten minutes, he leaned over and *kissed* me quickly, but right on the… *lips*! He said (*rather loudly, for being in the movies*), "You are so beautiful, and I want you to be my girl!" As you can well imagine, I could have fallen over! I was stunned, and at a loss for words! After a few moments of listening to Vincent Price talking about the spooky house in the movie, my date leaned over and stated, "What is your answer?"

I was taken aback, but of course I said, "Yes!"

He then stated, "I can't hear you, what is your answer?"

I said again, "Yes! I will be your girl!" I thought I heard some boys in back of us giggle.

All of a sudden he gave me another quick kiss on the lips and said, "I'll be right back; I'm going for popcorn." Then he got up and left. I sat there so happy and excited! I couldn't believe it actually happened and I couldn't wait to tell my friends that he wanted me to be his girl! Wow! Now I will be popular in school, and hang out with the *in* crowd!

About five minutes passed by and I started to get that funny feeling in my stomach. I hated when I got that feeling, because it always meant that something was wrong. More and more time just ticked away. About a half hour went by and I knew he was not coming back. I got up and slowly walked up the aisle. I felt the tears welling up (how I hated those damn tears) and I needed some air. My friends suddenly joined me, saying, "Where did he go! What happened?" But as we walked home, I couldn't say a word.

The weekend was terrible; I felt like such a fool. I didn't matter what my friends said or did to comfort me, I couldn't have felt any worse. What an idiot I was! I thought nothing could make me feel worse, that is until I got to school on Monday. I was turning the combination on my locker, and *he* passed me by, with one of the most popular cheerleaders on his arm. That was only the beginning. His buddies and a bunch of other kids joined them, and were actually handing him money! "You won the bet! Man, I thought I'd piss my pants when I saw you kiss that ugly, fat slob!"

His girlfriend said, "God, I hope you washed your mouth with Listerine; I don't want to catch some disease!" They all just stood there, actually blocking my path so I couldn't leave. All of them were laughing and saying degrading, humiliating things, about the *big bet* he'd won, as if I weren't even there. The words crushed, humiliated and heartbroken, could never even begin to describe what I was feeling. Somehow I found the strength deep down inside of me to close my locker and push past them, but not without first turning around and stating, with all the dignity and sarcasm I could muster up, "I hope your mouthwash was really strong, because, hey… you never know!"

(It seemed like I had several bad experiences concerning that movie theater. Once a man yelled to me and my friends from the bushes. He had his pants down and was waving his "private part" at us, saying obscene things. Another time, Mary Jane and I were walking home from the movies and this older teenage guy was walking towards us, and all of a sudden he grabbed my breasts and said, "Beep…Beep!" I was carrying this huge purse full of junk, and I started to hit him with it, yelling that he was a pig. Everything was flying all over… my makeup, change, papers, pens etc.! The man was so shocked that he started yelling, "Help! Help! Somebody, she's trying to kill me!" Mary Jane had not seen what he did, so she had no idea why her sister suddenly flipped out and was hitting this stranger with her purse. She was frantically picking up all my "wares" that were falling and rolling down the sidewalk, when the man started running down the street, exclaiming loudly, "You're crazy!")

As teenagers we did everything we could to make ourselves look better. And although I still had a weight problem, I did slim down a bit and was told I had an *hourglass* figure. But it didn't matter to me, I always found fault with myself, no matter what I did.

I laugh at all the beauty rigmaroles and diets my friends and I tried, to achieve the ultimate look. We gave each other Toni Perms, and lightened our hair with hydrogen peroxide, darkened it with henna, got bee hives, page boys, rooster combs, pony tails and flips. We scrubbed our zits with coffee grinds and oatmeal, and tanned ourselves, covered in lard and iodine. I applied make up around my eyes so thick, that I could pass for Cat Woman! And the Hazel Bishop lipsticks! The big rage was either white or blood red; both colors made us look like the brides of Dracula!

We would buy second hand clothes from The Salvation Army (still my favorite store) and The Goodwill. I'd cut the sleeves, change buttons, lower the necklines, sew on lace, until it looked like a completely different garment!

Then we would follow the Vinegar Diet, the Grapefruit Diet, the Carrot and Celery Diet, the Crackers and Water Diet, the Banana Diet—even the very dangerous Liquid Protein Diet. We even did the Stick Your Finger Down Your Throat and Make Yourself Throw it All Up Diet!

I still have so much trouble controlling my weight, all I need do is look at a picture of a slab of chocolate cake, or a piece of lemon meringue pie, and I gain weight! And I am always on one diet or another. I tried such drastic measures as prescription diet pills, shots of embalming fluid and even fasting. I drank only water with lemon for almost three weeks. However, as I've gotten older and wiser, at least now, the diets are healthy and good for my body like: Tops, Weight Watchers, Atkins, Stillmans, and of course, Richard Simmon's, Deal a Meal!

Along with my usual dancing around at birthday parties, I also exercise with Richard and Denise Austin, and do yoga and Tae-bo on a daily basis but, even so, I have lost and regained the same twenty pounds, for the past thirty years! To be even more specific, I probably have lost and gained at least a thousand pounds in my lifetime!

My journey to lose fat has inspired me so much that, as a young girl, I received The Golden Poet Award for composing the following humorous poem:

The Battle of the Bulge

I don't think that life is fair... skinny people can eat a big éclair,
also cookies, candies, cakes and pops... while I look on, and lick my

chops!
All of my life I've been so "Pleasingly Plump", and it causes me top get "Down in the Dump"... because no matter how hard I try... I still end up with a
lumpy thigh!
In my life, I've tried most every diet... "Weight Watchers", "Stillmans"... you just name it... I tried it!
I do exercises on the floor each day, eat "Saccharine", use Diet Pills, and even... Pray, but when I get on the scales to see, why is there always more of me?
Oh how I long to go into a clothing store, and buy size eight, ten or even four... or go to the beach in a little bikini, right out in the open where could see me!
I'm so sick of lettuce and cottage cheese, carrots, celery and things that look
like... trees!
I want chewy caramels, fudge and chips, plates of macaroni, pizza and sour cream dips...
but alas, I know I must decline to a milkshake, or even a glass of wine, because if I look this way now, if I eat all those things, I'd be as fat as a ... cow!
No, I don't think that life is fair... skinny people could eat a big éclair, and all those wonderful things I've mentioned before... and when I taste them,
I gain weight galore!
Now, there are a lot of people who believe what I've said... and they all know
that it's not just inside my head...
They all believe what I say is true... because they are all fighting the "Battle of the Bulge" too!"

Besides exercising, we took long walks to burn calories. One of our walks took us to the next town of Moosic. There, was another favorite teenage hangout, called Kay's Drive-in. We would get dressed up and go there for their famous burgers, to dance and most important, with high hopes of meeting that special someone. That is where we met Mario Leo, John Cimini and Dominic Pio. They were teenagers fresh from Italy. This made them very attractive to me, considering my Italian heritage. I loved their rich accents and it was fun trying to remember Italian and speak to each other in the language I loved so much. Well, I told Mom all about them, especially after Mario asked me out. I realize I was a bit young, but as I said, I was much older in looks and spirit. Looking back, I think my mother was trying to live the life she always wanted, through me. She was always a romantic, trying to fix everybody up with someone or other. So she talked my cousin, Mary into going on a triple date with me.

We all met, and dated (behind my father's back), although it didn't last long, especially when after the first dance he wanted to have sex! In order to preserve my virginity (we were forever warned, we were not supposed to "do it" until you got married), I lied, saying, "We can't, because I have a awful disease and you will catch if we *do it*!" I know it was drastic thing to say, but my God, we were only kids and he insisted we go outside and have sex right then and there! I had to do or say something to discourage him. It discouraged him all right, he got so scared I never heard from him again!

Chapter 13

Johnny on the Merry Go Round and the Actress

We also had another favorite place to walk to, Rocky Glen Amusement Park. Since the way to the park was past my grandmother's house, we usually stopped by to visit her (still picking her the same Blue Bells).

Rocky Glen was full of fun and excitement! I was really drawn to all the activities, rides, music and fanfare. I would think how great it would be to go into show business. But it also held another and bigger interest for me—a ride operator named John. He would come around to collect our tickets, and I would get all *happy*. Of course, he was so cute and full of charm that all my friends were infatuated with him. I am sure we all had our fantasies of becoming his steady girlfriend!

Now, the first time I met him, my friend Barbara and I were trying to get into some club at school, so were being initiated. They made us do all sorts of dumb things to prove we were worthy. Just the week before, we had to go everywhere wearing two different shoes! This week was the final test, because it was almost the end of the school year, and it was also the most challenging. It was Nationality Week! Whatever your family's background was—Polish, Italian, Irish, German etc—you had to talk with that accent, using as many words as you knew in that language, and pretend that you just came from that country. We had to do this with no matter who we met. They told us that they had spies out and we would always have someone watching us at all times. One slip up and we were out! So when John came and stood next to me as soon as the ride started and asked me my name, I was flabbergasted! Not knowing what to do, I looked at Barbara, but she shrugged her shoulders. I had no choice but to say, "How do you do; my name is Joann," in my best Italian accent.

He proclaimed, "Hey, you got a real cute accent, where ya from?"

I then said, "I comma from Italy, but I'm living with my aunt and uncle in

Old Forge." I looked over at Barbara again and thought she would fall off her horse!

When we got off the ride we both laughed so hard, it hurt my side! "God, Jo," she said, "I can't believe you did it! You sounded so good, just like a real person from Italy!" I told her it really wasn't hard, since some of my family came from there and they all speak Italian, or have accents. So the next time I saw him, which was the very next day, I spoke to him again with my accent. It was so much fun! I can't believe the story I composed: My parents sent me and my younger sister to America with the money my father saved for many years, doing carpentry work. He wanted his children to have a better life in the "new country." I told him how my little sister, Maria Jana, became very ill on the ship coming over here, and a kind hearted doctor nursed her back to health, asking no fee, since his own dear child had died just the year before. John believed every word I said!

Barbara would laugh and say, "If you and little Maria Jana here, came from Italy, and I told him I came from Poland, speaking with my Polish accent, doesn't he wonder how the two of us became such good friends? Well, naturally we had to concoct the story of how we met!

Each day we'd walk to Rocky Glen, giggling along the way. I loved the intrigue of it all. It was so exciting pretending I was someone else, and I couldn't believe how easy it was for me. I joked to my friends, with my very dramatic accent, probably sounding more like Dracula than an Italian... "I am a great actress! When I grow up I will be discovered and be in movies and show business! I will become famous and everyone will know my name! Please, please get away, no autographs for little people like you!" We all laughed so hard, I had to wipe away the tears.

I was finally sharing my story with my mother, and as we laughed, Mary Jane brought me to my senses, "JA, How *are* you going to tell him you are joking; won't he be mad at you?" I never thought of that. At first, I figured that after I finally got into the club, my friends and I would explain the situation to him.(After all this, we never did make it into the stupid club.) But now several months had passed and I had gotten so caught up in it all! I enjoyed making up stories, pretending I was someone else, but it just went a little too far. Would he be mad? Or would he think I was making a fool out of him?

Talk about a great actress; I not only had him fooled, I had his family fooled too! I wanted to tell John the truth. I knew it would be difficult and I would have a lot of explaining to do, but the very next time I went to Rocky Glen, he greeted me all smiles and said, "I have a surprise for you! My brother Steve's wife, Ann

Marie, has parents that came from Italy, and I told them about you!" Guiding me by the arm to these people who were waving at me, he joyfully proclaimed, "And here they are! They are dying to meet you!"

Let me tell you, I got myself in many a predicament in my young life, but this was the pits! I felt my face get hot and I knew without looking that it was bright red. I honestly started to feel faint. They come rushing up to me rattling in Italian, hugging and kissing me, as if I were one of their very own! My mind was racing, as I said, *"Como sta?"* (How are you?) and wondering what to do next. I stated my name is Joann, and a few other things I could remember in Italian. Then it came to me, *Yes! I have it!* I called John over and whispered, "John, I know they are Italian, but they must have come from a different part of Italy; they speak with a different dialect than I do! Tell them that I find it hard to understand them!"

As John walked over to explain the situation, my friends Barbara & Ann Jo, were catching it all in. Ann Jo whispered, "Where in the world did you come up with *that* one?"

I told her, "I don't know; I think I remember learning something about it in school. If there were two people from the same country, and one came from the north and one from the south, they may have difficulty communicating. You know, like the people from Louisiana have a tawny accent and use different kinds of expressions, so sometimes we can hardly understand them."

We watched them talking, and then John came over to us. I realized I was actually holding my breath! "Did you explain it to them?" I said. He smiled and nodded. They all bought it... lock, stock and barrel! Believe it, or not we all had a great time. They tried telling me things, and since I did know some Italian, we were able to piece together some sentences and have an *almost* conversation!

It is hard to believe, but this "Italian scenario" between John, his family and me, actually went on for over a year!

In my carrer, I have not only acted in several plays and commercials, I've been called by Ed Curry Theatrical, and many other agencies to play such characters as Mae West, Rita Heyworth, A Russian Immigrant, a Geisha Girl, and even a German Prostitute, among others! I am told I am a great actress. However, the only real acting lessons I ever had in my whole life, was when I was fourteen years old, at Rocky Glen Park!

I started to go to the park, even when my friends couldn't. I was really falling for him. He liked me too, and he was so kind to me. I would receive handfuls of tickets that he was supposed to tear up, so I could have a ball on all the rides... free! When it was time for his break, he would buy lunch to share. John would always make me laugh with his comical stories. The more I got to know him, the more I found we had in common. We both loved country and western music, five hundred rummy, scary movies, French fries sprinkled with vinegar and of course the excitement of the park. Most important, he liked my heart and soul, he also thought I was "very pretty!" When I mentioned my weight to him once, he said, "You are NOT fat, and don't ever let me hear you say that again! You might have a little bit of extra meat on you, but I like that in a woman; with a little padding, there is more of you to hug!" and then he gave me a hug for the first time! If someone told me that now, I would take his remark to be crude. But back then I thought his words were music to my young ears! (I not only lied about who I was, I had also lied about my age—he thought I was nineteen, when I was only fourteen. Of course HE lied too, saying he was twenty-one, when he was really twenty-nine!)

The funny thing, John and I never really dated, and we were never really alone with each other. I would go to the park as often as I could, just to be near him. I could sense he really liked me just the way I was.

I told my mother all about John, and she loved hearing every detail. As I said, she was an incurable romantic. We would whisper when my father was home because he would *kill me* if he knew. My mother, on the other hand, actually encouraged me. In fact, she and Mary Jane even spent money to take a cab to Rocky Glen just to meet him! To top it all off, she went right along with my story, telling him I came from Italy, and she was my aunt! There were even one rare occasion when he actually come to my house, when we knew the *coast was clear*, and my father (err, I mean my uncle) was away at camp!

We didn't have a telephone until about a year or so later. John said that if I got one he would help me pay the bill. It was so exciting to wait for his calls, and he called me quite often, always wondering what I was doing and where I was. He was jealous! I loved it! I never had anyone, other than my family, show me such attention or affection. As I said, we were really never alone, in fact he had never even kissed me, well, not a *real* kiss. I do remember the first time I received a real kiss! I stayed a little too late at the park to walk home by myself. John called my mother, telling her I would be late and not to worry; he would get me home safe. Since he didn't own a car, he said he would walk me home. We left the park (with Mary Jane tagging along) and were walking down the road. He stopped and said, "Don't the lights from the rides look beautiful in the dark?" I agreed that they sure did. The night was warm and magical; we could still hear the calliope music playing faintly from a distance. He then said, "Look at all the stars!" As I raised my face to look up, he took my chin in his hand and just very lightly, very tenderly kissed my lips! "I've been wanting to do that for a long time." He said. Wow! I could have melted into the ground!

Then he kissed me a little harder. All of a sudden, my mind raced back to the horrible situation with Old Jack. I remembered how Old Jack started kissing me and tried to stick his tongue in my mouth, how he groped at me. I pushed myself away from John and said in a panic, "Please, stop! Don't do that!" I really thought he would be mad, but to my surprise, he stated that he was sorry. We started walking again, but didn't speak or hold hands like we did before.

After a while, he reached for my hand and said, "Someone really hurt you, didn't they?" I just nodded, afraid to say anything or I would burst out in tears. "Do you want to tell me about it?" I was almost tempted to divulge my secret, however, I was afraid he would blame me, or worse…hate me!

"No," I whispered. "Not now; maybe someday," I said we continued walking and he stopped again, saying very strongly, "Look at me; I am not the person who hurt you! I swear, as God is my witness, I would never, ever hurt you! No matter what!" After a short pause, he stated, "Joann, I think I am falling in love with you!" Then he bent down and barely touching my lips with his, ever so gently. "Baby, I know I love you!" he said. Tenderly, slowly he planted tiny kisses all over my face, before reaching my lips again, finally, giving me a long, moist, romantic kiss! Something stirred inside of me! I never felt like that before, when the kiss was over, I reached up for him pulling his lips upon mine again, kissing and hugging him with such feeling, and then said, "I love you too!" Mary Jane didn't say a word, she just watched it all, smiling.

I never really kissed a boy before that night. Even when I went out on my other so called dates, they were just getting together at hangouts with the rest of our friends, and we just had fun and never really did anything intimate.

As we walked home, he shared personal things with me, that he said he was afraid to tell me before—like he was divorced and had two children. I was shocked and a little upset, because becoming involved with a married man was a big taboo in the Catholic Church. But I really couldn't say anything, since I too was keeping my big secrets from him. And to be honest, at that moment, I was so happy… I didn't care what the church said!

Finally, I had the nerve to tell him secrets—after all, didn't he just tell me he was divorced? "John,",I said, "I, too, have been lying to you ever since we met. I don't know how to say this. Please don't think I was making a fool out of you, I just didn't know how to tell you!"

He said, "Please don't tell me you're married, or have someone else!"

I burst out laughing and crying at the same time, and blurted out the whole "Italian" story as fast as I could. Mary Jane tried to help me out by interjecting a few times. I held my breath, and waited for his reaction.

"Get the hell out of here!" He laughed, "You gotta be kidding! I can't believe it! You mean to tell me that everything you ever told me was made up?"

I said, "No, not everything; one thing I told you is the absolute truth... I love you!"

When we got home that night, I couldn't wait to tell my mother what happened! She was all excited as I explained everything. "I am so relieved; I finally told him the truth about everything! Now I don't have to worry about it any longer!"

I was so up and happy, until she dropped the bombshell, "What did he say when you told him how old you really are?" Oh, no, I had not even thought of that! It didn't even cross my mind, when I was telling him about all the other stuff. I should have just told him then. I told her I forgot to tell him. She said the sooner the better, before you get yourself in a mess again, but I never had the nerve to tell him, after that.

My personal life was looking up. However, my home life was becoming worse. Not only with my parents' relationship, but with the *house* itself. It wasn't the first time that I had passed through my parents' bedroom to go to the bathroom in the middle of the night, to find a rat in their bed! This night I saw a rat that was almost a huge as a cat, standing on my father's leg! I screamed... it ran and my mother and father jumped so high, I thought they would go through the roof! "My God, what in the hell is the matter with you!" my mother yelled. This was her usual saying when she thought I'd done something wrong. My father was also angry and questioning my sanity. Why was his fourteen-year-old standing by his bed, screaming her head off in the middle of the night?

Well, let me tell you, I was angry myself! I yelled back at the two of them, "What's the matter with ME? What's the matter with YOU, and this damn house! I've told you and told you before about the rats, but oh, no one ever listens to me! They could have bitten you, me or Mary Jane!" I was so upset, I didn't care what they did to me at that point. I was screaming hysterically. "I'm sick and tired of doing everything around here! I'm sick and tired of getting yelled at like I was a two year old! I'm sick and tired of your fights!" Then I pointed to my father, and said to his face what I never said to him before, "And I'm sick and tired of *you* embarrassing me, coming home d*runk* all the time! I hate this fucking house, and I hate both of you!" Then I ran out the door in my nightgown, and with no shoes on my feet.

I sat on the bottom of the steps, shaking in the chilly night air. I couldn't believe I screamed so loud; I probably woke the whole neighborhood! I couldn't believe I spoke to my parents like that and said such terrible things, and mostly, I couldn't believe I actually said a curse word! I heard the door opening, and my sister's voice called down to me, "JA, where are you?"

I looked up and said, "Mary Jane, I'm ok; just go back to bed."

Of course she didn't. Down the steps she came, with my jacket, and placed it over my shoulders. "Daddy sent me down here; he said for you to come upstairs; he's not mad at you."

I looked at her and said, "I don't care! I'm mad at them! Things are going to change around here, and I mean it!"

Mary Jane sat next to me put her head on my shoulder and started rubbing my arm, something she hadn't done in a long while, then she started to giggle. "JA, I almost died when you said the 'F' word! I thought they were going to kill you!"

I too started to laugh, "I know! I can't believe I said that! What about me telling Daddy I'm sick of him drinking?"

She said, "And that you hated both of them!"

There was a pause, and we both stopped our chuckling. I then stated, "Boy, I've said some terrible things when I got mad, but *that* was the worst!" Getting up, I told Mary Jane it was time to go in. Walking up the steps, my heart was heavy, I knew I must face the music. I deserved any punishment they gave me. Opening the door, I saw my mother in the kitchen, smoking a cigarette, I could smell the aroma of the coffee she set on the stove to perk. My father was sitting in the green living room chair, smoking one of his Camels. I entered and said, "Ma... Dad, I don't know what got into me, and why I said those awful things to you. I'm so sorry. I don't hate you; I love you both very much. please don't be mad!"

My mother stared straight ahead, and kept right on smoking. She didn't say a word. My father got up from the chair and simply stated, "I'm sorry too... that I'm such an embarrassment to you." Then he walked into the bathroom. I went into the kitchen and pulled out cups from the cupboard, then poured us some coffee. I sat down, my father came out of the bathroom and sat down across from me. However, no one said another word. I noticed that the coffee cups had several chips on them. Finally, to break the silence I said, "When I get paid from the dairy on Friday, I'll take a bus to John's Bargain Store and buy us some new cups."

Mary Jane joined us, and we all sat there drinking our coffee, in the quiet hours of the morning. I could see that each of them wanted to say something, but what could they say? What could they do... I was too old to spank! Their oldest daughter was ashamed and disgusted with them? Were they also thinking that the child they created was a loudmouth witch? Or worse yet, did I make them feel like they were not only failures as parents, did I make them feel like they were failures as *human beings*? All I knew was, I sure felt like a flop of a *daughter,* at that moment! Then the thought occurred to me, what if my mother tells my father about John? All of a sudden, I'm sure it was the stress of it all, I jumped up and started singing! "I *love you truly... truly dear*!" Dancing around the kitchen, I kept on singing and going from one to the other giving them a hug and saying, "I see your face cracking!" About that time, I'm sure that they were thinking the child they created was not only a bitch, but insane! Pretty soon we all started laughing; why, you would think we were having a party. I didn't make any further apologies, and they never said a word about the incident. We just drank our coffee, sang and laughed! My God, maybe we were all lunatics!

No one ever mentioned that night good, or bad again. The next day my father came home really early (and not too drunk) carrying two rat traps which he set in the corners of the bedroom and parlor. My mother also straightened up the house and made supper.

Without... Daddy

Things were a bit better at home for a while, but slowly they returned to "normal." I tried very hard not to say anything offensive to my parents, or anyone else, for that matter. Praying to God, I'd ask him to make me calm and not lose my temper. Most of the time my prayers were answered. As usual, I tried to be happy and make things better for everyone.

The traps my father set did catch two fat rats, however, I made up my mind we were no longer going to living there. I would walk the streets with Mary Jane and my friends, searching for "For Rent" signs. Acting as sophisticated as I could, I'd ask to see the apartment. After looking around, I'd ask the price of the rent.

John and I were getting very close. If I wasn't at the park with him, we were talking on the phone. I wanted him to meet my father, but I knew he would forbid such a thing. To my father I was still a child; as he would not too politely put it, I was still "shitting yellow." One day, after a particularly bad fight between my mother and father, I came up with this very great and *selfish* idea! "Ma!" I said, "I looked at an apartment over on Hickory Street; the landlord and his wife are really nice. You should see how clean and bright it is, and we can afford the rent! How about we go look at it and if you like it, we can move there, without... Daddy!"

She looked at me and said, "What do you mean, *without* Daddy? Where is he supposed to live?"

I said anxiously, "Ma, not for good. He can go stay with Aunt Annie and Grandma for a while, and we can visit him there. Then I could tell him about John. I know he will get mad, but after a while he will get used to the idea. Then, when he realizes how much he misses us, he will *stop* drinking, and he can come live with us again." This was partly the truth, I did want him to realize how much he missed his family, and hopefully, not drink so much. To be truthful, the main reason was I wanted a place where John could come and visit me. I also wanted some peace and quiet for a while. I had no idea that this would never come true!

My mother liked the place; but wasn't too sure about moving in without my father. I finally cried, "Ma, I can't stand it anymore! If you don't do this, I will run away! I swear you will never see me again!" Mary Jane was mad at me for talking my mother into moving without her Daddy.

The events that followed will forever cause me anguish. We did it without my poor father even knowing. First we moved boxes in my wagon when he was not home. Then one day, we had a friend of John's from the park come with a truck to get some of the furniture. In the middle of the move, my father showed up. "What's going on! What are you doing!" he said. My mother told him we were moving, however, it still didn't sink in. He said, "Why didn't you say so? I could have got my brother with his pickup truck to move us!"

My mother said, "I didn't tell you, Nick, because you are *not* coming with us."

I shall never forget the bewildered look of disbelief and hurt in his face! I said, "Daddy, we are just going to be by ourselves for a little while; you can stay with Grandma to think things out. After a while, then you can come and stay with us again."

I don't think he heard a word I said! He shook his head, and with tears streaming down his face, he said, "I can't believe you did this, Molly; you're *killing* me!" Then slowly, he walked away.

Mary Jane was so upset, and so was my mother. "Maybe we should call him back," she said.

I stood there, confused and in turmoil. My mind was racing, "Why *did* we want to move without him?" I went over all the reasons and they really seemed trivial, until I got to the one where John could come and visit me. "Ma,." I said, "it will only be for a few weeks, then we will work things out. You know Daddy, he'll have a few drinks with his friends, and he'll be alright. And he won't be alone; he will stay with Grandma and Aunt Annie." My words sounded so good, but why was my heart heavy? In the end we continued to move in without our father.

We had to walk around the back to get to our apartment. Actually, it was one big house and they sectioned a part of it to rent out. When you entered, you came into a pantry. There was a sink on one side, and large cupboards from floor to ceiling on the other. An archway led into a kitchen. It was large and the walls were covered with cheery wall paper. The bathroom was also located on the left. It had a bathtub, with running hot water! There was another door in the kitchen, but it was locked from the other side. Beyond that door was the landlord's apartment. From there you had to walk upstairs where there were three rooms, a parlor and two bedrooms. All the rooms were freshly painted.

I still couldn't get my father out of my mind and spent a sleepless night.

John came over the very next day, and I told him what happened with my father. He could tell it was really bothering me, so he said, "Well, it looks like I will have to meet him, and *ask for your hand* sooner than we planned!" I really didn't know if he was just joking to cheer me up or not, but it sure sounded good to me!

For the next several days we were busy unpacking and getting settled. I called my Aunt Annie's house, but my father wasn't there. As the days passed, I found that it was so nice not worrying if there would be an argument between my parents. John would come over and we'd play cards, or watch the television he brought over. I really loved the peace and quiet. Although I missed my father and felt guilty about hurting him, things were much nicer... for me, anyway.

My mother also seemed in a much better frame of mind.

I called my grandmother's house again, and he wasn't there. Mary Jane didn't say too much, but I think she was still mad at me. John was always nice to her when he came over, making her laugh. Soon, they became friends. We were all starting to be really happy.

One day, my father showed up at our door, and he and my mother talked for a while. I even heard them laughing about something. Maybe everything would work out after all! But before I had a chance to come downstairs and talk to him, he left. I anxiously asked my mother several questions all at once, "What did he say? Did you tell him how happy we are? Is he going to come back? He could come live here, if he stops drinking! Is he alright?" My mother really didn't say too much, and kind of left me hanging.

It was so good to see her taking care of herself and the house again. I would say to myself that I was right, living without my father for a while is really doing her and everyone else good! I called my Aunt Annie's but my father wasn't there again, so I finally decided to go visit my grandmother and Aunt Annie to wait for him to come back. When I got there, my cousin, Lucille, was in from California. She was about two years older than me. Her father had recently passed away, and she came to visit for a few days. The minute she saw me she started to cry and scold me, "How could you do something like that to your poor father! You don't see him cry for his family! He sits here, so sad! You just *broke* his heart! You never saw your father die like I did! I would give anything to have my father back! How can you all be so cruel! You are mean and rotten!" She then rushed into the bedroom. I was stunned; did I really hurt him that bad? Was I fooling myself, thinking he was drinking with his friends and was happy, that the booze kept him from feeling pain?

My dear grandmother came in from the back yard. She couldn't really understand English, but she knew that there was something going on between me and my cousin, and she knew it had to do with my father. Instead of becoming angry with me for hurting her son, she said in very broken English, "I know, it is hard living with a man who drinks. (My Grandfather had also been a drinker). "But you know, God helps you to forgive so families can live together in peace." She put her arms around me and gave me a hug. I always found it so comical when we would hug. She was so short, I felt like I was hugging a child! I missed my grandma. I missed her faith, wisdom and especially her love.

We made tea, and before the hour was up, my father came in. I was so happy to see him. I ran up to him hugging him so tightly, "Daddy, I missed you;

every time I called you weren't here." I could tell he missed me, too. He sat down at the table with us, talking to my grandmother in Italian. I could understand a little, and he was telling her that he and my mother had a talk. She told him that he couldn't come back yet, that we were really happy. There was peace in the house, so until he got help to stop drinking, he had to stay away; it was up to him. Then he told me they were going out to Salerno's to eat on Saturday. "You and Ma are going out on a ... date!" I laughed. "Wow, this is great!" I stayed for a while, and we talked longer than we had in years. He did want to stop drinking, but it was so hard to do. He missed us so much, and felt lost without us. I suggested that he could get come help form the Veteran's Hospital. He said he would look into it. My cousin joined us, apologizing for her outburst. Life was looking up!

My parents did go out to eat a few times, and my mother seemed happy about the situation. She would actually get all dressed up for her *dates*. He was also giving her money to help pay the rent and buy food.

John and I were really getting closer too. Although, I would never let him *go all the way,* we were into some petting. We loved each other so much! Finally, I thought, life is wonderful! I felt guilty keeping this relationship from my father, so we decided it was time to tell him. It was time for them to finally meet. This time I knew he wasn't joking when he said he was going to ask for his daughter's hand.

The Mass Card

The phone was ringing; I looked at the clock, and it was almost two a.m. At first I was annoyed. Who in the world was calling at this time in the morning? Then I realized that something must be wrong! My mother was talking on the phone, "What hospital is he in? Ok ,we'll be there just as soon as the buses start running." She looked at me and said, "Your father is in the hospital. He is bleeding in his stomach, and his asthma is really bad; he can't breathe without oxygen."

My heart fell to my stomach! "Why did this have to happen, especially now that everything is going so good! God, God I prayed, Why did you let this happen?"

We met my Aunt Annie in the waiting room of the intensive care unit, at the Scranton State Hospital. She was crying. "It looks bad; he needs a serious operation. He is bleeding and has already lost a lot of blood. I had the priest come and give him the Last Rites. You can go in to see him, but only one at a time. They gave him medication for the pain, so he is kind of sleepy."

I almost fainted when I saw him. Tubes were going in and out of him every which way! They had several IV solutions going into one arm, and in the other, he was being given blood. He was wearing an oxygen mask to help him breathe. I sat down beside him, and held his hand; it felt so cold.

"Daddy, it's me, Joann. I am here, Daddy... can you feel my hand?"

He opened his eyes and tried to smile, but it was hard with the tube going down his nose into his stomach. He was trying to say something, so I moved real close to him, and he said, "Shut the window... those dogs barking."

I said, "Daddy, there are no dogs outside." He seemed agitated and again mumbled something about the dogs, then feel into a sleep. It tore at my heart! I started crying, so sorry for hurting him, so ashamed I lied to him, and that I was seeing John behind his back. I just wanted him to get better and then we would straighten everything all out. I felt so small and helpless. I wanted to do something to help him, but there was nothing I could do, but pray.

Finally they took him to the operating room. We were sent to the waiting area, and Aunt Annie asked the nurse how long the surgery would take. She said at least two hours. While my mother stayed at the hospital, Aunt Annie, Mary Jane and I walked a few blocks to St. Peter's Cathedral to pray. We sat in the darkened church, but I was feeling so frightened, I couldn't even think of a prayer. All I could think of that it was my fault that he wasn't with his family. I couldn't get him out of my mind, with all those tubes! I whispered to my aunt, that I couldn't even pray. She said just be still in the Lord, He knows your prayers, without you even saying them. After a while, she said, "Let's go to the rectory to get a Mass card." We spoke to the receptionist, explaining that my father was in surgery right at that moment, and we wanted a Mass for the Sick. We went back to the hospital, bringing my mother coffee form the cafeteria, and waited. Finally, after what seemed like forever, the doctor came out to tell us the operation was over. He was doing as well as could be expected. They repaired a bleeding ulcer and did some other work. The doctor then exclaimed, "I never saw anything like this! Did he drink a lot of baking soda?" We told him that he was always taking baking soda for heartburn.

"Well,",the doctor said, "I had such a time cutting through his abdomen; all that baking soda hardened and was like cement!" We were told that it was just a matter of time, and the next twenty-four hours were critical.

I sat by his side the next afternoon, and just talked to him, not really expecting him to talk back. I just wanted him to know he was not alone. I watched him breathing and it sounded better; he even had some color in his previously almost white skin. They even took out one of the tubes. I was elated when he finally opened his blue eyes. He finally spoke, his voice weak, and to my surprise he said, "Joann, I know you have a boyfriend. I just wanted to meet him and tell him to take good care of you."

I said, "Daddy, I'm so sorry I hurt you, and lied to you." But I don't know if he ever heard me; he was already back in a deep sleep.

By the next day he looked and felt even better. I just knew he would get well soon. I just sat next to him, holding his hand, vowing to myself that I would never lie to anyone again. I thought he was sleeping, because his eyes were closed, when he whispered, "Well, I guess I will have to meet your boyfriend in Heaven." I became upset, and told him not to talk like that! He would get better and come home soon. He did get better; by the following day, they had him sitting up, and were giving him sips of water. He was starting to really look good.

The following day we went back to school, so I didn't go to the hospital with my mother. Mary Jane and I were sitting in front of the television doing our homework, when she came home. "How is Daddy doing?" I asked, without even looking up from my school book. She didn't answer. "Ma, how is Daddy feeling today!" I said, even more persistently. "He's doing real good, right?" I got that funny feeling in my stomach, and my throat tightened up so I could barely speak. Tears started rolling down my face, and I choked out, "He will be able to come home soon, right?"

My mother never answer me. However, without her saying a word I already knew the answer—my daddy was dead.

I was full of sorrow, and haunted by guilt. How did this happen; he was only fifty years old! He was fine when I left him and *was* getting better! My mother explained that when they opened him, they found along with everything else, he had sclerosis of the liver. He really didn't have too long to live, but they had given him at least six months to a year. However, he took a turn for the worse, and only lasted a few days after his operation.

The next few days were just a blur. It was a horrible experience picking out a coffin. All I could hear were my cousin's angry words to me: "You didn't have to see your father die! I'd give anything to have my father back!" She was so right... I'd give anything!

As we entered the funeral home, my legs became weak; they felt like rubber. I was holding on to Mary Jane, as she cried softly. The poor little thing, I remember how she was shaking. It seemed like we walked a mile, before we got to Daddy. How handsome he looked in his gray suit. I was struck by the peacefulness on his face. I stood there looking at him, but I still couldn't believe it; I must be dreaming! I know for me, the worst part was seeing my grandmother. As small as she was, she literally tried to take him out of the casket, into her arms, crying out in Italian that she was supposed to die before her children!

Sitting in the back of the Palermo's Funeral Home, I cried to Aunt Annie, "I feel so guilty! Maybe if I didn't make my mother leave him, he'd still be alive! I loved him and didn't want anything to happen to him. It was so mean, what we did to him! It's all my fault! I think he died of a broken heart!"

Aunt Annie sat quietly for a moment, then she opened her purse, pulling out a card. She said, "I was going to show you this later on, but I think this is the best time. I believe God knows the very day when we will die and go to Heaven. Do you remember the day of your father's operation, when we went to church to pray?" I nodded, and she continued, "Do you also remember that we went to the rectory and I told the secretary about your daddy's surgery, and asked for a Mass for the *Sick* card?" Again, I nodded in agreement. She then took the card out of the envelope, and while handing it to me she said, "I looked at this card yesterday... read what it says."

I slowly opened the card and read: "A mass for the Repose of the Soul of Dominick Scorzafava, will be said," etc... not even finishing to read the remainder of it, I laid the card in my lap and said, "Oh my God, this is a Mass for the *Dead*!"

Aunt Annie said, "See, it wasn't your fault; God called him. It was his time to go home."

We finally arrived at The Cathedral Cemetery, on Oram Street in Scranton. We were sitting at his grave site, and my mother whispered, "We got a spot under a tree; he always loved to sit under a tree." The priest finished his prayers, someone from the VFW folded the American flag that covered his coffin, and presented it to my mother. Shots were fired, giving him a twenty-one-gun salute, and his good friend did his best, as he tried to play "Taps" through his tears.

That was it; everything was done. It was time to go home, forever in this life... *without Daddy.* Just before we left, I whispered, "Daddy, we will see you again someday, and when we reach Heaven, I want you to greet us with your arms open wide and say those wonderful words... "There's my girls. Daddy is here!"

In my life I have learned many lessons, this experience taught me the greatest lesson of all! Truthfulness, honesty, integrity, faith and loyalty should remain in our lives each and everyday. If you have these things, you have... love and peace!

I have suffered greatly over my Father's loss, not only over the fact he was taken from us at such a young age, but what truly stabs at my heart, is the fact that through my dishonesty and selfishness, his last weeks on this earth were filled with heartache and remorse. He also never got his last wish... to meet the man, he felt was taking away his little girl!

Chapter 14

Here Comes the Bride...Almost

After my father died, I quit school. Although I wasn't even quite fifteen yet, I was discharged because I was needed to help support the family, and given working papers. My mother and I, both got jobs at the Taylor Hospital. Since it was only a few blocks away from where we lived we were able to walk back and forth to work. I loved my job, although it had no title. I guess you could call me a nurse's aid, kitchen worker, housekeeper, errand girl! Anything that needed to be done I did it, with the exception of laundry; that is where my mother worked.

The hospital was very small and could only accommodate about fifty patients. I would get them up, washed and fed. I was instructed on how to take temperatures and blood pressures. When they were short of help, I even gave out medications. Then I would make the beds and clean the wards. Afterwards, I would take the dirty sheets and towels down to the laundry room, where I could see my mother.

I loved helping the people, especially the elderly and children. When my chores were done I would try to make time to talk with some of the patients. They would tell me all about their families, and their illnesses or accidents. What I really loved the best was taking a peek at the newborns.

One day, I was looking through the glass at the newest baby; he'd been born just the day before. All of a sudden one of the nurses tapped on the window and motioned me to come in. "Here, put this mask and gown on," she said as I entered the nursery. "Two of the nurses are out sick, and I need someone to help me feed the babies." Glowing with joy, I fed him his bottle. As I rocked him, I couldn't believe how tiny and warm he felt. I put him over my shoulder to burp him, his little face brushed against mine, and I remember how soft his face was. He smelled so clean, like baby powder. I couldn't wait to get married and have one of my very own!

John and I were deeply in love, but something was really troubling me. He was coming to see me on a daily basis now, and several times when he came to visit he would bring beer, or other alcoholic beverages with him. He didn't seem to get drunk, but I was surprised, since I had never seen him drink anything other than Coke or coffee before. I was also surprised at the amount he could ingest, and yet he never looked or acted drunk. (Later I learned that if you have a certain amount of liquor in your system, you are definitely intoxicated, whether or not you show it).

We were seriously talking marriage now, but there was a fly in the ointment. I still had never told him my real age! Finally, we set a date. We decided to get married in four months, on the 23rd of April, in Saints Peter and Paul Russian Orthodox Church. Since he was divorced we couldn't get married in the Catholic Church. That made me sad, however, I was so much in love and figured at least we would be married in some kind of church.

I bought a gown on sale at Sullum's Bridal Shop, and had my pre-bridal picture taken for the *Scranton Times* newspaper. It would be in the Society Page, along with all the other brides the day after the wedding. We booked Dante's to hold our reception. The wedding invitations were printed and mailed out, the flowers were ordered, we took our blood tests, our rings were purchased and engraved. We did the whole works. Everything was done except the marriage license. My mother said, "I guess you will have to tell him how old you really are. You'll need your birth certificate, and you won't be able to get a marriage license without my signing for it."

I have no clue how I thought I could get away with this one! How could I go get a marriage license without telling him my true age? Through my many experiences, I had learned to try to be truthful about everything... except this! Actually I was more mature than my mother, in many ways. Although she had many good days, sometimes she was very childlike and acted a little strange. I had to take control of many things around the house, contribute financially and even make major decisions. Not since I was a little child had she disciplined me. Oh, sometimes she would yell at me, or even give me a slap now and then, however, only if I were disturbing her personally: If I took one of the last few Newports, (I'm happy to say, although I smoked like a fiend, I quit smoking many, many years ago) made her get out of bed so I could change it, forgot to buy the tea bags etc., but as far as anything else, I could DO and GO anywhere I pleased, just as long as it didn't inconvenience her. This sure seemed great at the time, however, deep down I longed for discipline. It was difficult knowing if I was doing the right thing. Since I was so young, I made several bad choices, and made many mistakes, not only causing pain to myself, but to others. I also longed to be cared for, and not have to worry about everything.

This had taught me to not only show much love, affection and support to my own children, it also made me realize how important it was to discipline them. This was a winning combination! Each one of my children have grown up to become wonderful, honest, hard working people, who have a strong faith in God. They are also fantastic parents! What gives me so much peace, is that although they each have their own families, they are still close to one another. They also have much love and respect for me, and each other. They are such a blessing to me. Just to think of them, my heart fills with pride and bursts with joy!

When John came over that night, I was so nervous that my mother had to tell him. She said, "Joann is not as old as you think she is. I will have to sign for you to get the marriage license."

John looked at her with a puzzled expression. "What do you mean, you'll have to sign for her... is she underage? I know her almost three years, she told me she was nineteen then—how young is she anyway?"

I lowered my head and said, almost in a whisper, "I'm fifteen... I won't be sixteen until August."

Counting on his fingers, he said, "Holy shit! You mean to tell me she was only thirteen years old when I started going out with her! God, I could have been arrested!"

I quietly corrected him, "No, I met you when I was thirteen; we didn't go out for almost a year later."

I could see he was clearly and rightfully upset, as he said, "Thirteen, fourteen, what the hell is the difference? I don't know what to believe anymore! What other lies have you been telling me?"

By this time my heart was pounding, and I was crying, "Please don't be mad; we could still get married. My mother will just have to sign, that's all! We love each other, that's all that matters! What does age have to do with it?" I pleaded.

He put his hands up and said, "I gotta get out of here for a while." As he stormed down the steps, my mother followed him saying she wanted to talk to him.

I threw myself on my bed, my heart was breaking. I was crying hysterically, and talking to myself out loud, "That's what I get for lying!"

I should have learned my lesson, but no, I had to be so stupid! Why didn't you tell him the night he told you he was divorced, he would have been shocked, but he would be over it by now! God, I'm not a bad person, why did this happen?

My mother followed him outside, and Mary Jane and I tried to hear what they were talking about in the back yard. However, between both of our sobs, and being up on the second floor, we couldn't hear a word.

First my mother came in alone and a few minutes later, he followed. I sat on the couch, hoping to hear good news. They both came up the stairs and he announced, "Joann, I think we may have a real problem; guess what? I lied about my age to you, too. I told you I was twenty-one, and I was really twenty-nine. That makes me thirty-three in September. I'm just about seventeen years older than you!"

I jumped up, saying, "So *what*... I don't care! We are still the same people! My love for you didn't change! Did your feelings for me change?"

He shrugged his shoulders and said, "Well, I guess the wedding is on!"

All three of us went for the marriage license, and everything was ready for the big day. So if everything was so perfect, why did I have this sinking feeling in the pit of my stomach?

It was almost two weeks before the wedding. John and I went to Scranton to take care of a few minor details. He acted very happy, joking around as we talked about our wedding plans. When we finished our errands, we had lunch, and then he walked me to the bus stop. He kissed me very affectionately just before I boarded the bus to go back to Old Forge. That night he had to work at a local bar, where he was a bouncer, so he didn't come back with me. He stated that he was going to make arrangements with his boss for the *booze* at the wedding. As he waved goodbye, he shouted, "I'll call you tonight, baby. Love ya!"

Everything was wonderful, everything but the awful nagging feeling I had in my stomach. How I hated that uneasy feeling! I realized from childhood, when I got *that* certain feeling, something was very wrong!

I fell asleep with the phone in my lap... John never called. The next day I phoned his house, and his mother, Helen said, "Isn't he with you? He didn't come home last night." Now the dreadful feeling turned to panic! I called every friend and relative I could think of... still no John! In the evening I called the La Mar Tavern where he worked some nights. They said he wasn't there. Then I proceeded to call every bar in the phone book, with no results. My panic turned into fear. I even called the police station and hospitals. I couldn't eat or sleep and did nothing but cry, pray and make phone calls for the next few days.

The wedding was only a week away, and not only was my heart broken, I actually felt as if I was losing my mind! My mother was no help; she was in one of her weird moods. She would follow me around the house, clap her hands and actually sing, "Johnny left you and he won't come back to you no more!"

Poor Mary Jane, she was so worried about me and tried to comfort me. Once, she actually opened her mouth and yelled at my mother to "Shut up!"

I was beside myself. I had called his relatives so many times that they became annoyed with me. I decided that they must know something. How come they weren't in a panic thinking he was killed, kidnaped or in a ditch somewhere, like I was? Why weren't they worried that the wedding was right around the corner, and we had over one hundred guests coming? All the preparations were made, and we had everything but the groom!

Finally, his Aunt Dorothy, who was my maid of honor, (Mary Jane was too young to stand up for me, but in the future she got another chance…TWICE) called to tell me she wasn't going to be in the wedding, because she didn't think there would be a wedding. She had no other explanation when I questioned her. Now I was getting mad, so I decided to do a little detective work. Mary Jane and I took the bus to Scranton. I entered every tavern in town, looking and asking questions. I even went to his house, on Putnam Street, and hid in the back alley… trying to see him coming or going. Then, I actually went in the house, without even knocking. I demanded to know what was going on. With tears streaming down my face, I blubbered some powerful and unkind things like: "What kind of people are you anyway; you know where he is! God will punish you for not telling me what is going on! The wedding is only four days away! Should I call everything off, or is he coming back?"

His father, John Sr., finally said, without even looking at me, "No… he hit the road."

Then his mother added, "He took off with some *old* broad he met, named Anna Rose. I think she is older than me!"

I stood there rooted to the spot; I wanted to move, but couldn't. A gasp came from my body, and I realized I was holding my breath. Then I started to sob like an idiot. "Why didn't you tell me? I called you so many times; someone could have told me before! I have to cancel all the wedding plans; why didn't anybody tell me? How cruel can you people get!"

No one offered any comfort for what John had done to me. His sister Rose finally said rudely, "We didn't have to tell you anything!"

Helen got up and said, "Do you want a drink?"

I was finally able to move and as I walked toward the door I said, "A drink…

do I want a drink, is that all you have to say to me?" I looked at her for a moment, however, she didn't say anything else, so I just walked out the door.

Mary Jane and I cried as we walked all the way to Old Forge. I was in so much pain, and felt so humiliated; I didn't know what to do! How I longed for the love and stability of loving parents who would stick up for me and help me through this nightmare I was going through. I cried, "Daddy, I don't know what to do! Why did you have to die... I need you!" Then I said, "Ma, why do you have to be so crazy... I need you, too."

We stopped to rest on the bridge in Taylor. I exclaimed, "I feel so frightened and alone; I can't stand this pain."

Mary Jane said, "JA, you're not alone; you have *me*!" I took her hand, and we walked the rest of the way not speaking, but I felt comforted from the warmth of her hand.

What a task I had! Not only was I numb, and in agony, I had to call off everything. Hoping for some spiritual words of comfort, I called the church. Father Kudricoff was very angry. "I told you that you were too young, and this marriage would never work!" So much for words of comfort. Then I called the newspaper. As I hung up the phone, I had a fit of hysterical laughter. I was told that it was too late! The paper was already in print and it would be too expensive to reprint the page. The only thing they could do was put in a correction in the next issue. My God, I could see it now...our wedding photo with a big red X across it! Underneath it would say: "Sorry, this wedding photo we showed last week was a mistake. The groom ran away and they never got married!" I was still laughing like a *fiend* as I told my mother. Naturally she laughed too, thinking this dilemma was actually funny! "Why am I laughing?" I said to myself. "Oh God, I must be going mad!" After the last two episodes I figured I had to come up with some *better* explanation than... "The wedding is off because the Groom took off with an old lady!" I was so humiliated and embarrassed; how could I call everyone? I would be the laughing stock of the century!

As I dialed the catering hall I started crying again. I found myself saying, "I have to cancel the wedding because the groom... was in a terrible accident out of town, and was killed!"

I heard a gasp from the other end, then the voice said, "Oh, honey, how awful! You poor thing!" I couldn't believe my ears; someone felt sorry for me! So for the rest of the day I went down the list and called the florist, and all my guests...with the same story. It was so hard to tell the first lie, then it became easier as I went along. By the end of my calls, I almost believed it myself! Strange as it may seem, I felt better after the phone calls. Although it was a lie, and I know it was wrong to do so, I received such an outpouring of sympathy, it actually eased my suffering.

"Oh what a tangled web we weave when first we practice to deceive!" should have been tattooed on my head! I had an answer for everything. When I was asked when the funeral was, I told them that he would be cremated and buried in a family cemetery in another state. The lie got bigger and bigger! The larger it got, the more sympathy I received. Did I get sympathy… let me tell you, I didn't know which way was up! The neighbors came over with trays of cold cuts, and cakes. One of the girls from Nino's Sportswear, the pants factory where I worked, came to the house with a card that was signed by all my co-workers. It was filled with money they had collected for me. I received sympathy, and even Mass cards in the mail! I even got my non-refundable deposit check back from the catering hall. And of course the florist sent me flowers! "Oh, dear God, what a fine mess I got myself into this time!" I prayed.

Although I was heartbroken, it was becoming comical. "This is unbelievable!" I stated, "I feel just like I'm in a Lucille Ball television skit!" I didn't know how to stop everything. I even considered telling everyone the truth, and accepting the consequences, however, everyone was so wonderful and kind, I didn't want anyone to think I'd made a fool out of them, so I carried my feelings of guilt in silence.

The sorrow and pain in my heart seemed to become worse. The guilt about the lies I told everyone, and all the kindness they had shown me laid heavy on my heart. I became depressed, and had a hard time coping with everything. I didn't know if I was more angry with John, or with God! I was a good person. Ok, I had a few flaws, but I was kind and loving to others, a hard worker, looked after my mother and sister, went to church and always prayed. So *why* did God let this happen to me? I honestly don't know how I lived through the next three months.

Here Comes the Bride…Again

I was having this wonderful dream that John had come back to me. He was sitting on my bed, whispering my name, and telling me he loved me! I said out loud, "This dream is so real, it's like it is actually happening!"

Opening my eyes, I sat up, and there he was! He said, "Baby, you're not dreaming, I'm really here."

My heart leaped and I started crying, "Oh my God, is it really you?" All my anger melted as he hugged me and kissed my tears. I knew then, that no matter how much he had hurt me, and no matter what he had done to me, I would forgive him... no questions asked! This joy I was feeling, instantly replaced all the terrible agony I had endured over the past three months. A wise and *stable* person would have thrown him out, but not young and foolish me! I didn't care what he did; I couldn't bear to go back to that pain and sorrow.

We were both talking at the same time. He was telling me how much he loved and missed me, and how he was sorry for what he had done. I was kissing him, and telling him that I didn't care what he did! I didn't want to know *anything* about why he left! He was back and I loved him and that's all that counts. The pain was *gone*! The phone rang right about then, I wasn't going to answer it, but the only phone we owned had a long extension cord, and it was sitting on my bedroom floor. After it rang about twenty times, I finally answered it. My girlfriend Margie, from across the street, was yelling into the receiver, "Jo, is this you? Oh my God, Jo, you won't believe it; I saw a ghost, honest! I was walking home from babysitting at my sister Esther's house, and I heard someone calling out to me in the darkness, and when I turned around, it was John! His ghost was following me! I got so scared, I ran all the way home! My mother said I should tell you because he must be in purgatory and needs some prayers to get into heaven!"

By this time my mother and Mary Jane had joined us in the bedroom. All I could think of was, after all my lies, how am I going to tell Margie... John had *risen* from the dead? Oh no, how was I going to explain this to everybody else?

How I hate lies! If you tell one, then you have to tell another to cover up the first. I looked at John and said, "You sure put me in a predicament when you disappeared!" So I went on to explain my dilemma, and how it came about that he was supposed to be *dead*.

John shook his head and laughed, saying, "You sure are a great storyteller, however, I learned that from the first day I met you!"

John turned out to be just as good a storyteller as I was. He was the one who explained to everyone why I *thought* he was dead! He came up with some cockamamie explanation that involved an accident, his friend was the one really killed, burned beyond recognition, but he had John's wallet and there was a mistaken identity, he couldn't get in touch with me because was in a coma for months... and so forth. Wow! His story was even *crazier* than mine! I didn't say a word, and let him do all the explaining about his remarkable reappearance. I figured it's the *least* he could do for all the pain and suffering he caused me. The following week, I gave the girls from work back their money. It was still in the sympathy card; of course I never spent it.

I was sure learning my lesson about telling the truth! Lies got me into so many messes, and I promised myself after my father died that I would always strive to be truthful, but I certainly didn't keep my promise in this situation! However, after this escapade I vowed that no matter what happened, I would always tell the truth!

We had a small informal wedding, on August 23, 1965, the day after my sixteenth birthday. The Russian Orthodox priest would no longer marry us, so we got married by a Justice of the Peace in Dunmore.. (Months later, the priest did married us quietly in the church so we would no longer be living in "sin.") I actually had two small receptions; his sister Ann, who I still love dearly, threw us a party at her home and later that evening, we had one at Rocky Glen Park, with all the people he worked with.

Married life was wonderful, and all that I expected that first year. We lived with my mother for a while, then rented a small three-room apartment on Main Street in Old Forge. It was owned by the VFW, and since they knew and loved my father, the rent was very reasonable. I painted, wallpapered, and bought lovely plastic curtains from Woolworths. Soon, the apartment was warm and cozy. John and I played cards, went for walks and did everything together. I even went to work at the park and stayed overnight when he was night watchman. Finally, I was happy and had someone to love me.

However, my fairytale soon started to resemble a nightmare.

Every once in a while, instead of coming home from work, he would call me from a bar. He say that he was just having a few beers with the guys, and would be home in an hour or so. I would get that funny feeling in my stomach again. In the beginning he kept his word, but every so often he wouldn't come home until the wee hours of the morning. I would wait and wait, keeping his supper warm for him, until it was so late that I went to bed crying myself to sleep. The next day he would always be charming and loving, saying how sorry he was, and how he got caught up in a card game. He started to stay out more often, and I had the uneasy feeling that cards wasn't the only game he was playing!

Mary Ann

By January one of my biggest wishes came true; I was pregnant! Everyone was overjoyed, including John. He hoped it would be a little girl since he already had two sons from his first marriage. I couldn't wait to *show*, so the whole world would know I was with child. I made my own maternity clothes on an old Singer sewing machine, and started wearing them long before I needed to. We bought a secondhand crib that I sanded and painted, and fixed up the corner of the bedroom as a nursery. My mother bought me baby clothes and stuffed animals. Mary Jane was learning to crochet so she started to make the baby *something*. I was given beautiful a cradle, which I placed at the foot of the bed.

In those days, you were not able to find out the sex of the baby before birth, and even if you could, I didn't want to know. About a week before the birth, I saw my baby in a dream. The nurses handed me this pink bundle; inside was a beautiful baby girl. She had a full head of dark, silky hair adorned with a pink bow. St. Jude came into the room and told me you have to name her Mary, after the Blessed Mother.

I was way past my due date, so Dr. Kranick induced labor. I was in labor for almost three days, and on August 15, the Assumption of the Blessed Virgin Mary, my daughter was born. It was as if she waited so long so she could be born on the Blessed Mother's feast day. And just like in my dream, the nurse laid a pink bundle in my arms, she had a full head of dark, silky hair, with a pink bow! I looked at her beautiful, tiny face and whispered, "I will love you forever, and you will always *know* I love you!" I remember after the nurse left, I completely undressed her, inspecting every little detail. I was amazed at her tiny hands and feet, and the softness of her skin. I couldn't believe I created such a fantastic, beautiful little person! She was like a precious jewel! She started to cry, and I cried right along with her. I had cried most of my life over heartaches, however, this time they were tears of joy. As I held her to my breast and nursed her, I felt the presence of the Lord smiling upon us. Later they came to ask me what name was I going to give her, I instantly said, "Her name is Mary."

When John came to visit he was so thrilled that he got his little girl! He said, "If you want to name her Mary, why not name her Mary Ann. You know Joann… Mary Ann." So I added Ann, after myself and of course, St. Ann.

Chapter 15

The Honeymoon is Over

The birth of Mary Ann was like a miracle for everyone. John loved her and was a proud father. He started coming home right after work every night, and gave her lots of attention. I seemed to have a natural ability to take care of a baby, and enjoyed every second of motherhood. Even my mother was having many good days, and would come over every day to help me. We would cook for supper; she'd help me hang the diapers on the line (disposable ones were not even invented yet) and would have regular, *normal* conversations. I actually felt love and affection from a mother for the first time in years!

Mary Jane absolutely adored her new baby niece. The night Mary Ann was born, everyone was elated. My Uncle Jimmy had taken me to the hospital three days before, where I had a long, difficult labor. So when my child finally arrived, John, my mother, Uncle Jimmy and Mary Jane were celebrating. My mother even allowed thirteen-year-old Mary Jane to drink something stronger than Coke. Well, less than a glass later, she was looped! She kept crying out loud, "My baby, my baby! I love my baby!" And my quiet little sister made such a commotion that the neighbors came over thinking she was devastated because my baby and I died!

The day of Mary Ann's Baptism will never be forgotten, for several reasons. Was it because I dressed her in the very same dress that I wore at my Christening, the dress my godmother had bought for me? Perhaps it was because my Uncle Jimmy's girlfriend, Betty, got drunk and wet herself, in her newly dyed shoes, and made blue footprints all over my floors. Could it have been because the cake fell and landed all over the kitchen floor? Could it be because the toilet overflowed, soaking my living room rug? I bet I know what the main reason was… John and his brothers got drunk, and into a big fight! With all the yelling, screaming, throwing things and punching… the neighbors called the police. Not only was my house right on Main Street, now there were there several *flashing* police cars in front. So naturally, everyone from what seemed like the whole town, came running over to witness John and his brothers in a downright, on the ground brawl with the cops! Of course the police won the battle and carted them all to jail. Everyone left very quickly, my mother, promising to come back in the morning to help me clean. The house where I'd spent days cooking, cleaning and decorating was a total disaster. My husband was in jail, and I was alone and mortified. I felt like the laughing stock of the whole town.

Mary Ann... she slept peacefully through the whole thing. I said, "God, when you spoke to my heart, when I was younger, you said I would make people laugh! I surly hope this isn't it!"

Long after I cleaned up the mess, and took a long hot bath, I was still in shock at what had happened. As I rocked my baby in my arms, I was filled with fear. My mind raced, recalling the times my father came home drunk, and all the fights my parents had. Most of all I remembered how *terrified* Mary Jane and I would become. I also remembered the vow I made to myself: *"When I grow up I am going to marry a rich, handsome man who never gets drunk! We will never fight and my children will never cry over us and be afraid."* I looked down at my precious daughter sleeping, and softly cried, "Dear God, please don't let John and me end up like my parents! Please, please don't ever let my baby be afraid!" From then on, I promised myself I would do everything I could to make my marriage work, and keep my home peaceful and safe for my daughter.

Keeping my promise, I became Super... mom, housekeeper, cook, baker, and lover! I tried everything and anything I could to make him happy, and to want to stay away from the bars. Mary Ann was such a good baby. Our home was always spotless, I became a gourmet chef, cooking and baking fancy meals from recipe books, and I bought sexy outfits from Sally's—they looked pretty good, too. I was wearing only about a size twelve (which was tiny for me), letting my hair fall in loose curls down to my waist, just the way he liked it. I always acted alluring and ready for a *good time*... no matter how tired and exhausted I actually was. What more could he want? I don't know; don't ask me, because I didn't have a clue. It seemed the more I tried, the worse he became! At first, he would come home in the early hours of the morning; then there were times he would not even come home at all. I tried to be understanding and not ask any questions. I think I was actually afraid to know. How many nights I waited for him—dressed like a stripper, with a roast beef and an apple pie—I couldn't even count. When I finally had the nerve to ask him where he was, to my surprise, he slapped me across the face, accusing me of not trusting him! He always said he was sorry and didn't mean it, and would never hit me again... until the next time!

"Nurse, Nurse, Nurse and...Rock of Ages"

When Mary Ann was almost a year old, I received an anxious phone call in the early hours of the morning. Mary Jane was shouting at the other end of the receiver, "Something is wrong with Mommy! Come over right away! Bring a clean nightgown; she is throwing up all over!" she cried. I ran the few blocks to her house. Mary Jane was crying as I ran upstairs to my mother's room. My poor mother was lying naked on the floor and trying to reach for a glass of soda that was on the nightstand. I sat her up and tried to give her a drink, to my horror, her beautiful face was twisted to the side. Her mouth was all dried up and as she tried to drink, soda spilled it all over her. I called an ambulance, then washed her face and body down to her feet. Since my mother couldn't move her right arm and leg, Mary Jane helped me dress her in my soft flannel nightgown. I tried to comfort her, and my sister the best I could; however, I was terrified and shaking myself.

At the hospital they didn't know if she would live through the night. My sister and I sat in the waiting room of the Taylor Hospital, praying and talking. We agreed upon one thing, we wanted our mother to get well and started sharing stories about her. Mary Jane told me that the night before, Mommy was lying on the couch and she heard her yelling to someone. She said that my mother exclaimed that she felt like there was a weight on top of her back and she couldn't get up. Then she saw my father's hand and the plaid cuff of his shirt, he spoke to her saying, "Molly, I am so sorry I left you holding the bag!" This really gave both Mary Jane and me the creeps!

Then we started to talk about better things, and I said, "Remember how every Christmas and Easter, no matter how little we had, she would buy us a new dress, even if she bought secondhand. And we always had an Easter basket and a Christmas tree, with presents underneath?" I shared a little secret with her, "A few weeks before Christmas was 'clean up' week; everyone could throw out all their junk for the garbage. You were sleeping, and Daddy stayed with you, while Mommy and I went up and down the streets late one night, rummaging through the trash. We found a doll carriage, dolls, trucks and other toys and brought them home in Old Nellie (the name for our old wooden wagon).

"Mommy had written a letter, pretending it was from Santa, stating two of his elves were ill and he asked me if I could help him fix the toys. Of course I was so honored. So for several nights when you went to sleep, we would wash, mend, paint and fix up these toys for Santa. On Christmas morning, to my surprise, there were a few new things, but most of the toys we fixed were under the tree! Hanging on the tree was a note from Santa saying that I did such a good job, he wanted to give me his best toys for helping!"

We continued to relate good things about my mother. How she would make us brush our teeth twice a day. We laughed as we recalled how she would show us her two rotten front teeth and say, "If you don't brush your teeth, God will punish you, when you wake up yours will be all rotten like mine!" She always made us go to Dr. Stampion, the dentist, for checkups. This was a true sacrifice for her, because we had no dental plan. I remembered bringing him a two dollars once in a while to pay on the bill. (Until this day—thank God and… and our Mother—Mary Jane and I have beautiful, strong white teeth.)

Mary Jane said, "Remember how Mommy would always take us to the eye doctor and for checkups with our family doctor?" We both agreed, although our mother had her very *strange moments* she did her very best to take care of us and she loved us. We loved her too and realized you never really know how much you love someone until you may lose them. Finally, Dr. Marmo came out and told us my mother was going to live, however, she would never be the same again. She would be unable to walk and maybe not even speak. We didn't care… thank God she was alive, that was all that mattered!

Although my mother stayed with her brother Andy, her sister Rose, and a nursing home for a while, she lived with me for twenty-eight years. My mother became my "baby," and we became closer than we were when I was a child. In 1994 she had another stroke and almost died, but thankfully, she recovered. With the last stroke, she needed much more care than I could give her. Reluctantly, I allowed Doctor Salko to find a home for her in his nursing facility, located very close to my home. I am able to visit her on a daily basis at Osprey Ridge, and although she has trouble speaking and is paralyzed on her right side, she is still spunky, remembers everyone and has her wonderful sense of humor.

My mother remained in the hospital for over six months. Although she could not walk, she understood and knew what she wanted to say; however, all that would come out was, "Nurse nurse, nurse, nurse, nurse." I would go visit her several times a day and this I found strange—although she was able to say only "nurse," she could sing! We would enter the hospital ward, hearing her singing … "Rock of Ages"!

We finally had given up my mother's apartment, dividing her furniture between myself and John's sisters. Mary Jane moved in with me. My mother had been in the hospital for so long, the doctors felt there was nothing more they could do for her.

In those days they didn't have the knowledge and medications they have now. If a person has a stroke today, they need get to the hospital within two hours. If they do, in most cases, medication can given to be greatly improve, or even reverse the terrible damage.

I was told I had to take her home because her insurance was running out. I had no choice but to take her to live with me. It was very stressful trying to care for a baby and my mother in a three room apartment. All the while, trying to save my marriage… and I also found out I was pregnant again!

My cousin, Nancy, was dating John's brother Paul. Nancy had been living with me for a while, until they eventually got married. Mary Jane had been skating with Nancy and Paul. There she met Fred Cramer (Buddy). He seemed like a nice enough boy, who reminded me of the singer Glen Campbell. I worried that my sister was much too young to date, but who was I to talk? Mary Jane and I got into a few small arguments over her dating. She accused me of not wanting her to go out because I only wanted her for a babysitter. This was true to a point; she was very helpful to me and watched Mary Ann; however, I truly worried about her and didn't want her to get hurt, or make the same mistakes as I did. Everything was changing, it seemed for the *worse*, including the close relationship I had always had with Mary Jane.

After a few months, my mother became ill and had to go to the Scranton State Hospital. I felt guilty about it, but it relieved some of my stress. When she was able to return home, unknown to me, her brother Andy picked her up from the hospital, to take her to live with them. He also took Mary Jane— unfortunately no one *told* me! I waited for her to come home from school; when she didn't, naturally I panicked. All of my phone calls were fruitless. With Mary Ann in tow, we headed to the police station. They told me that she wasn't considered a "missing person" until she was missing for twenty-four hours. I spent a sleepless night in speculation and worry.

The next day my Uncle Andy called, telling me that the day before, he picked up Mary Jane from school and she and my mother were going to live with them. He also stated that he was coming down for their bankbook. Both Mary Jane and my mother had been receiving a Social Security check, although I did use some of my Mother's for living expenses, most of it, and all of Mary Jane's was in the bank. What hurt me the most is that he was so sneaky about everything. All he needed do was tell me that Mary Jane was going to stay there and save me all the grief and worry. In fact, I was happy I didn't have the responsibility of taking care of my mother, with all I was going through.

When I finally spoke to Mary Jane, I learned she was in the dark about the whole thing, just as much as I was. She was walking home from school and Uncle Andy pulled up with my mother in the back seat of his car. He told her my mother was going to live with them and she had to help him take care of her. I had mixed feelings. I was hurting because not only did I miss Mary Jane's help, I just missed *her*! She was my little sissy, and she was always there for, and with me through all my troubles. She was growing up now, and not only was she turning into a typical teenager in love, it hurt that she didn't seem to want to be around me anymore! I actually felt *jealous,* because not only was she no longer in my care, she had a boyfriend and loved and needed somebody else besides *me*!

John started staying out late again, drinking most of the time. When he did come home, he was usually in a bad mood. Getting that awful feeling in my stomach, I sensed that he was seeing someone else. My girlfriend Margie and I took our babies and went on a spying spree. Just as I figured, he was going out with a girl named Beverly, who he worked with! Heartbroken, I couldn't understand it. What did he see in her, that he didn't in me? She had long red hair, green eyes and was just a wee bit overweight. To be honest, actually she looked quite a bit like me! When I confronted him, naturally, he denied the whole thing. That is until I actually caught him *kissing* her, right in her back yard! Like a lunatic, I emerged from the rose bushes where I was hiding, waving Margie's new Ginsu kitchen knife at them! Beverly started crying, denying that she never even knew he was married. With all the commotion, the porch light came on and out came her father... the minister of the Presbyterian church! John yelled at me to go home and he would explain everything to me.

My pain was unbearable. John didn't even know that I was pregnant again yet. I cried so hard that I got the hiccups. All I ever wanted was someone to love, and for them to love me. Was that so hard to achieve in life? Finally, he came home and unbelievably, he started yelling at me for getting the *poor girl* in trouble with her father! I yelled back and started to scream all the things a person would normally say in a situation like this. When I least expected it, he punched me right in the face! Mary Ann started screaming, and I begged him not to punch me again, because I was pregnant. A strange look came over his face, and he yelled, "I can't take your shit anymore!" and he stormed out the door.

I picked up my baby, we were both were crying hysterically. Kissing her, I became terrified as I noticed her blanket was stained with fresh blood! Relief flooded over me when I realized it wasn't coming from her; it was coming from my mouth and nose!

My husband didn't come home for two nights. I was worried sick and brokenhearted. All I had to do was look in the mirror at my bruised face and my left eye that was almost swollen shut, to help make my heartache turn into anger and fear! The phone rang, it was John on the other end. "Are you still mad at me?" he said in almost a childlike voice. When he came home, he looked at me with disbelief. "Oh my God, baby… I can't believe I did that to you! Please forgive me! I swear to God I will never hit you again! Baby, I love you so much. Bev means *nothing* to me. I was just feeling *trapped* with all the responsibilities of a family, and just made a little mistake! It will never happen again!" He held me tight, and once again, my anger and fear melted. Once again, like the big idiot that I was, I forgave him.

I must say, John was true to his word. He came home right after work and stopped drinking, just like old times… for a while anyway. Little by little, he went back to his drinking, late nights and God only knows what else. I took my solace in my dear old friend… food! One of the neighbors worked in The Community Bake Shop, and he would stop by with pies and cakes that were left over that day. I would cook supper and set a place of honor for the man of the house; however, most of the time there was an absent honoree. I would feed Mary Ann and eat my dinner. After she was in bed I ate another dinner. When John was still not home, I would cut a huge slice of cake, then another. Sometimes, I would end up eating a *whole* pie, slice by slice! Surely, it wasn't because I was hungry… for food anyway. Food was my comfort and substitute for love. I began gaining weight. I tried to fool myself that I was getting fatter because of my pregnancy. Naturally, some of it was due to that reason; however, unless I was pregnant with an elephant, I wouldn't have gained those thirty some pounds by my fourth month!

I never really caught John with anyone else again—well, not unless you want to count that knock at the door one summer night. There stood two men and this girl, with *big* hair; they were looking for John. I was sort of afraid to let them in, since they were dressed like bikers from a Hell's Angels gang. However, I was more interested in hearing what they had to say, than in my safety, at that point. One of the guys looked me up and down and proclaimed, "I'm Mike. He's Chuck, and that's Angela over there. You must be his sister-in-law, Hanna?"

The girl was dressed in a very short leather skirt, and looked like she could handle herself in a major fight. She lit a cigarette, and said, "When do ya think he'll be home... he owes me big time!"

Standing there dumbfounded, I finally asked them what was this all about. The other man said, "I'm sure he didn't he tell you about my sister here... she's pregnant with his kid, well she *was* anyway. Now he has to give her the money."

My heart sank and I started to shake. I said, "What makes you think I'm his sister-in-law?"

Angela spoke up, "Well maybe it's because he said he lives with his brother, and his wife. Does that answer your question? He didn't think we'd find out where he lives, but ya can't hide from us!"

They all laughed... and I started to cry. "No, I'm not his sister-in-law; I'm his *wife*." I sobbed.

"Get going!" said Mike. "Hey, we didn't know. He never said he owned a wife!"

I looked up and asked, "What do you mean you *were* pregnant?"

For the first time her face softened as she said, "Hey, sweetie, we don't mean you no harm. Looks like you have one in the oven yourself." I nodded, feeling sick to my stomach. "Just tell him I *took care* of the matter, and we're looking for him." Then they let themselves out, and were gone.

I don't know how long I sat there staring at the door. I could have told them that John was only two doors up, tending bar at the VFW. The same VFW where my daddy used to tend bar. How I wished my father was still alive to stick up for me. I rose, picked up Mary Ann and headed to the bar. I entered the place, knowing John would never do or say anything bad around all my father's friends. "I need to talk to you... *now*!" I said.

He came out from behind the bar and I blurted out the whole story. "Oh my God!" he said. "Baby, please believe me, it was a lie! Those jerks claim I cheated them in a card game. They said they would get even with me! I never got her, or anyone else pregnant, except you, my baby." He held me so close and tenderly, that I didn't know what to believe. All I knew was that it didn't hurt anymore, and I didn't know how much more pain my heart could hold, so true or not... I believed him.

My mother was acting awful at my Uncle Andy's house. He wanted to bring her back to me, but I told him that I was moving and since I was pregnant again, I couldn't take her at that time. So he sent her to stay with their sister Rose. My Aunt Rosie did all that she could to take care of her. She wasn't there long, when I went to visit. My mother started crying, and tried to say that she wanted to come home with me. She actually climbed out of bed and crawled after me. I didn't own a car, so my Uncle Butch drove her to my house. I felt sorry for her, and was angry with her at the same time. My life was in a turmoil and I needed a bigger place. Now all of a sudden, she only wanted me. I needed this situation like I needed a hole in my head!

My mother was stuck on the couch since I couldn't lift her, so the guys from the VFW came to my rescue. They were getting us a wheelchair. I guess with all my stress, I needed a good laugh. Proudly, they carried this huge, old monster of a thing, into my little apartment! It was made of rattan with an enormous back, giant wheels and was so cumbersome and BIG! I would struggle to get her in the chair; however, we couldn't go far. The darn thing was wider than the doorway!

I was washing clothes in an old wringer washer with a broken leg—the washer's, not mine. Under the broken leg I had to place an overturned bucket. Mary Ann was crying to get out of the crib, my mother was yelling for me and the phone was ringing. I tried to pull the diaper through the wringer faster so I could answer all my calls, when the leg slipped off the pail, and the washer tipped, spilling soapy water all over! "This is it! This is really, really it!" I screamed. Tears streaming down my eyes, I started laughing like a banshee. I propped up the washer, climbed over the wheelchair to get Mary Ann, and yelled at my mother, "What do you want *now*, Miss Molly?"

My mother smiled at me and said, "Moke, Joann. How 'bout it, one moke ok?"

Living with my mother was like a constant game of charades! When she first had the stroke all she could say was nurse. Although she could say a few more things now, if you didn't know her, you probably wouldn't understand what she wanted. I lit a Newport and took a long drag myself. Handing her the cigarette I said, "Here is your moke; are you happy now?" I felt like I was giving candy to a baby. I know that she shouldn't be smoking, but what else did she have?

"I *love* you" she said.

"Oh, sure you love me now, but if I didn't give you a moke you'd call me a *bitch miser*, right?"

She giggled.

I was on my knees, sopping up the water and said to myself, "Come hell or high water, we're moving to a bigger place, and I'm getting another washer!"

Chapter 16

The Haunting

I begged John to find us another place, but he was no help. It was really getting difficult to care for my mother. I explained to her that she was going stay in a nice place, just for a little while. I felt so bad, and guilty, especially when she cried because she didn't want to go. But I felt I had no choice. The only place Medicare would pay for was Clark Summit State Hospital, a facility for mentally ill people. However, they also had a nursing facility for the elderly and handicapped. What really bothered me, and made me feel especially troubled and guilty, is that I had to sign her into a place that was commonly referred to as "The Nut House!" I also promised her that I would visit often. I knew that promise would be almost impossible to keep, since I didn't have a car, and I had to depend on one of my uncles to drive me there. Thankfully, after she got used to it, she really liked it there. In fact, she had the staff wrapped around her little finger!

Mary Ann and I set out to find another apartment. After searching for several days, I found a half double on Samson Street. The landlady and her grandson lived on one side and she rented out the other. I entered the apartment; it was old and beautiful. It had stained glass windows, an open staircase and all the original woodwork. There were three rooms on the first floor and the same on the second. All the rooms were large and bright. I couldn't believe how inexpensive the rent was, with heat and water included! As I walked around the upstairs hall, suddenly, I felt a chill and got that funny feeling in my stomach, but it passed and I overlooked it. It was probably all the anxiety and stress of finding a different place to live.

Some of John's friends helped us move to the new place. I missed the old apartment, even before we were gone. His buddies did a great job. Nothing got broken, and they put the furniture in all the right rooms. After several hours, we were finally all moved in. John said he was taking his buddies for a few beers to thank them for helping us. I got a funny feeling again and begged him to come home soon.

Mary Ann and I sat on the front porch and waited for John to come back. We talked with the old landlady who told me to call her, "Grandma." Her grandson, Paul, who was about twelve years old, came outside and joined us. He seemed very nice, in a *peculiar* way. I was so relieved, John kept his word and came back early.

The next day I started to unpack things and get settled. I don't know what it was, but I felt *something*. I just couldn't put my finger on it. That evening I was in the kitchen cooking and I thought someone had come up behind me, but when I turned around no one was there. After supper I was sitting in the living room and I heard a crash. I flew into the kitchen and all the dishes that had been drying in the dish rack were all over the floor! A few other little strange things occurred over the next few days, so I called the priest to come and bless the house. When Father was leaving he made a strange statement, "You are not going to stay here long, are you?" I said that I didn't know. He looked at me as if he wanted to say something, then changed his mind. Now that strange feeling in my stomach became stronger. How I hated that feeling! I don't know if it was my imagination, or what, but in two places in the house I could swear it was cold, although the rest of the place was warm. Also, on a few occasions when I was in the bedroom, I could swear I heard footsteps on the stairs; when I looked no one was there.

I took Mary Ann to a store up on Main Street. The smiling woman behind the counter waved and cooed to Mary Ann. She complimented me on how beautiful my baby was, and asked me if we just moved in the neighborhood. I thanked her, told them that I did. "Where did you move?" the storekeeper asked. I told them the address, and she gave her husband a strange look and said, "How is *everything* there? You know, that house is always empty; people move in, then they move right back out again. No one ever seems to stay there very long. Is *everything* ok?"

Feeling very uneasy, I said, "What do you mean, they move in, then they move right out... why would they do that?"

She said, "Oh, it's just a rumor, and I don't want to upset you, so I won't say."

I thought to myself, "Boy, I just love it when people do that! They start to insinuate something, and get you all riled up, then they leave you hanging!" I wasn't about to let her get away with it, so then I said, "Oh, you are not telling me anything new; I know *all* about the rumor. But I simply don't care."

After looking at me with surprise she stated, "How can you not care, especially since you have a little child? Aren't you afraid living in a house that is… *haunted*?"

I felt just a little weak and couldn't wait to get outside for some air. I pushed Mary Ann as fast as I could, while talking out loud to myself, "What in the hell is the matter with my life anyway? Was I born under the wrong star, or was I cursed or something? What, what… *what* else is going to go wrong? Yoo hoo…Where *are* you, God?" A few people had walked past me while I was venting; I'm sure they thought I was off my rocker!

I spent most of the day pushing Mary Ann up and down the streets in her stroller. Later, I sat on the front porch talking to the landlady and her grandson. How I prayed that John would come home. As the hours passed, I knew he wouldn't be home until very late, or maybe, not at all. I never knew where he was, or what he was doing these days. Finally, I decided that all this talk was silly, and that we needed to go to bed.

I got Mary Ann all tucked away in her crib, and then got into my bed. I actually felt frightened and pulled the covers over my head like a little kid. In an old house you sure hear all kinds of creeks and bumps. But somehow, I managed to doze off to sleep. I was awakened by the sound of the piano playing next door. I remembered seeing the magnificent grand piano in their living room. The music sounded so soothing and was so beautiful. It must have been Beethoven, or one of those composers' pieces that was being played. It was so beautiful! I started feeling very relaxed and soon fell back to sleep.

The next morning I awoke to a beautiful day. The sun was shining through the windows and I felt so good. How silly I felt, for being afraid in this lovely old house. After we ate breakfast, I took Mary Ann outside for some fresh air. Soon, the landlady and her grandson joined us as we sat on the porch swing. I loved listening to her deep accent, and enjoyed her stories about her childhood in Poland. I spoke up and said, "By the way, which one of you play the piano? I awoke last night to your beautiful music." The old lady turned a little pale, and quickly got up from the swing, mumbling in Polish as she went into the house. I said to Paul, "Did I say something wrong?"

He just leered at me, with a weird smile and said, "My grandmother don't play the piano, and neither do I. It's my father's piano."

I said, "Oh how nice; tell him how much I enjoyed hearing him play. I really would love to hear him play again; classical music is one of my favorite types of music, that and country and western. Classical music always sounds so soothing, especially when played on the piano!"

Paul said, "Oh, I would if I could, but I can't, so I won't... he's dead!"

I got the tingles from my head to my toes, and said, "Dead? What do you mean he's *dead*? How can he be dead; I heard him playing the piano, with my very own ears!"

Paul's grin became wider, making him look a bit sinister, for a little kid. "You heard me right... he's dead! Lots of other people hear him play too, since he died." Both of us just sat there, and didn't say another word. After a long while, I finally got up and went into the house, and started re-packing my things. Some of the boxes were still sealed up, and not even opened yet from the recent move. I was only in the house for less than a month and I didn't know where or how, but I was moving out! I put all of our personal belongings in the front room, to be close to the door.

Mary Ann and I and stayed away from the house during the day by walking around and visiting people. I bought the newspaper and searched the ads, and in less than a week, I found a place in Scranton. The rent was really inexpensive; the people were moving out of town because of a new job. They were trapped in a lease, so they were forced to sublet their apartment. I went to see the apartment, and had to walk up five flights of stairs, but I didn't care! The apartment was really huge. It contained six rooms and a large bathroom. The floors were hardwood, and there was a balcony. I couldn't believe my good luck, for a change.

John was seldom home to experience anything weird. He must have thought I'd lost my mind. "We just moved in, now you're telling me we're moving out!" he yelled. I tried to explain to him what had been going on, however, as usual he wouldn't listen. I was too tired to argue, and too frightened of the house, to be afraid of him! I told him with great confidence that I was going to move, and I didn't care if he followed us or not. I threatened to hire a moving van, and write out a check to pay for it. And I didn't care if it bounced or not. So he'd better get his brother and a few friends to move us, because I was leaving... ASAP. "It must be those damn hormones!" he muttered. "Either that, or I married a complete nut!" By the end of the week, we were residents of Scranton, Pennsylvania.

Monroe & Pine

What a project! It seemed like we took a million trips up and down the steps of our new residence, on the corner of Monroe and Pine Street. By now I was about eight months pregnant, and weighed a whopping 255 pounds! This made it hard for me to breathe, especially that last flight of steps. I still wanted to blame it on the pregnancy, but I knew in my heart I gained almost a hundred pounds because of my constant eating binges. If John didn't come home... I ate. He'd give me a slap in the mouth... I'd shove food in it. When I'd find strange phone numbers in his pants pockets... I'd mix up strange concoctions to stuff myself. So on it went, substituting food for comfort and love. John pulled one of his fast ones again. After we had finished bringing up all our belongings, he plugged in the refrigerator and stated that he was going out to get milk for Mary Ann, and a pack of Pall Malls for himself. Promising to be right back, he asked if I wanted anything. I wanted to scream, "Do I *want* anything? Yes! I want a thin body, a faithful, loving husband, and enough money to pay our bills! I want a whole *new* life!" But all I said was, "Bring me home a Hershey bar, with almonds." Giving us a quick kiss, he stated that later on we'd go to The Stop and Go (a fast food hamburger place) for supper. As he left, I remember hearing his footsteps fade away, as he descended the many flights of steps in the main stairwell of the building. We didn't see him again for three days.

The apartment was so large it actually had an echo. Upon entering you faced a long hall. There were three bedrooms on the left side of the hall and a large bathroom, on the right doors led to a large formal room with a balcony, then the living room and dining room. In the back of the apartment was a fantastic kitchen, with swinging doors that led to a pantry. The pantry was a little room itself. Three walls were lined with work counters and cupboards from ceiling to floor. There was another swinging door directly across from the door to the kitchen, this was the entrance to the dining room. I noticed that the former residents had left a whole box of Swiss Miss cocoa mix on top of the counter. I told Mary Ann, "When Daddy comes back, I'll make us a nice cup of hot chocolate." I tried to work the gas stove, however, I couldn't find any matches to light it. So we waited for John to come home. The minutes turned into hours. I rummaged through some of the boxes marked "kitchen stuff," and found some juice for Mary Ann. I also dug up a jar of peanut butter, and fed it to her, right out of the container, with my fingers. Pulling a blanket from another box, I covered my child and rocked her. Soon she was fast asleep and

I laid her on the couch.

I was all alone again. Playing the same old game of wait for him and wonder were he was, feeling the same old heartache. My unborn baby stirring inside me. "Mama is hungry too, little baby. If your Daddy ever gets back we'll get something to eat." I waddled out to the pantry and pulled out the box of Swiss Miss. I looked high and low again for some matches to light the stove, but my search was useless. Then I went out on the little porch off the kitchen and tore open the package of cocoa, eating it dry. My apartment was on the top floor of the building and the lights from downtown Scranton looked so beautiful. Tears were streaming down my face and I wondered where he was, out there among all those lights. How could he do this to us? He knew we were in a strange place and nothing was unpacked. If he didn't worry about me, wasn't he concerned about his little girl? My baby started kicking, and I started to sob loudly. Soon I will bring another child into this world and what kind of a life will he have! I started blubbering to myself, "Joann, you dumb, *stupid* idiot! You promised yourself that you would never marry a man who drank, like your father! He'd be someone who would love you, and be kind and good. You promised that you would never be poor, and that you, and your "Prince Charming" would never fight. He would never yell, hit you, and your children would *never* be afraid!" I looked up to the heavens and cried out, "Dear God, please, please show me the way! I'm sorry I got us into this mess! I don't know what to *do* to make anything better!" As I sat there, all of a sudden, I knew my Lord was listening. I could feel His presence, and received inner strength, giving me a glimmer of hope! I recalled the day He spoke to me when I was little. Feeling a little calmer, I spoke softly to my unseen God, and said, "Well, I know you called me to make this world a happier, better place and so far I'm not doing such a good job. So whatever it is… sock it to me, Jesus, I'm ready for a little happiness!"

I must have sat there for about an hour, then I finally got up went into the bathroom. Looking at myself, I got such a laughing fit! My face was all streaked with brown lines from my tears and the dry cocoa. "You are cracking up, Joann!" I stated to the person in the mirror, "Crying one minute, and laughing the next… You must be a manic-depressive, with a schizophrenic overload!"

Another Haunting?

The mattress was leaning up against the wall, so I dragged it into the living room and plopped it down on the floor. I placed my sleeping baby on the mattress and lay next to her. Glancing at my watch, I saw it was almost one a.m. Maybe I was dreaming, but as I started to doze off I heard something. Sitting up, I listened… there it was again! "Oh my God!" I thought, "It sounds like a… *ghost*!" Shivers sent goose bumps all over my body. I heard it again " Whooo, whooo," then a tapping sound, first on one end, then on the other. I also heard what sounded like "little tiny people" scampering above me, and then that ,"Whooo whooo" sound again! The hair on the back of my head stood up. I was wide awake now and I knew that I wasn't dreaming! "This is actually happening!" I said out loud. "My God… spooks are following me from one house to another!" I picked up my sleeping daughter, and struggled to carry her. She was about eighteen months old, and with myself being so pregnant and overweight, I found this task very difficult. My heart was beating so fast as I carried her out of the apartment into the main hallway of the building. I stood there shivering in the corner, praying to St. Michael the Archangel. I felt like I was in a Stephen King movie!

The door to the next apartment opened. There stood a girl, maybe a few years older than me, in a green nightgown. She had a cigarette dangling from her mouth, and a rolling pin in her hand. "Who's there?" she cried out.

"It's only me… your new neighbor. We just moved into the apartment next door," I said in an unsteady voice.

"What in the *hell* are you doing in out here in the middle of the night, anyway?" she stated.

I didn't answer because, what could I say … "*My apartment is full of ghosts, and little people, and I'm afraid*?" I know she would have thought I was a weirdo, or something. Maybe she would even hit me over the head with her rolling pin, and call the cops. So after a minute or so of silence, she finally said, "Well get in here so I could at least see *who* I'm talking to." I followed her into her apartment. It was a bit untidy, but not really dirty. Seeing the toys laying about, I knew she had at least a little boy. "I'm Elaine Gibbs; who might you guys be?" she said.

I told her our names and for some stupid reason I quickly followed with… "I'm so fat because I'm pregnant!"

She put on the kettle, and pulled cups out of the cupboard and said, "Coffee or tea?" As I told her I would love a cup of tea. I couldn't believe how kind she was and how easily she took a stranger into her home. She was rough and tough, and sort of reminded me of a gangster's girlfriend, but in the middle of the night she was an angel. I was touched by her kindness and generosity, and made a mental note to show such kindness to someone else someday.

Elaine just took Mary Ann from my arms, and laid her on the couch, then she came right out asking me personal questions. But for some reason I didn't mind sharing my life with her. I knew, right then and there, that I could trust her, and it sure felt good confiding in someone. "Now tell me, why in the hell were you hiding out there in the corner?"

I thought, "Oh well, if she thinks I'm crazy… then she thinks I'm crazy!" So I explained all about my other "haunted house" and now, I think this place was *haunted* too.

She looked at me comically, and lit up another cigarette, and said, "Come on, let's go over there and confront this… *ghost!*" As we crept into my apartment, I told her to listen carefully. "There it is… hear that spooky noise?"

She held out her ear and listened, then looked at me and shook her head, saying, "You are such a dingbat! Haven't you ever heard pigeons before!"

I said, "Pigeons? What do you mean pigeons?"

Elaine laughed, "Just where in the world did you come from, girl? We are on the top floor of the building, and the pigeons live in the rafters, under the roof. You know… pigeons, they fly, shit and make *cooing* sounds… just like the sounds you're hearing!" Since the apartment not set up yet, the empty spaces made the sounds echo, and really sounded weird.

With much relief, I said, "You're right; I *am* a dingbat!" But under my breath, I thanked God that I didn't live in another haunted house!

Learning from True Friendship

Elaine turned out to be not only my friend, but mentor and teacher for the year I lived in the apartment. The next morning she came over with her kids, a pot of coffee and donuts. Her youngest was a little girl named Cathy. She was only two years old, so Mary Ann had a playmate. Together we put the furniture in place, opened boxes and put things away. At supper time she threw a pot on the stove, boiled pasta, threw in a jar of Ragu, and had a meal ready for us all, in no time. I never met anyone like her before! She was funny, tough and told it just like it was, no holding back! But she certainly had a heart of gold.

My sister, Mary Jane, came up for a few days to help me, and she too, was amazed at all Elaine did to help us. Elaine brought peanut butter and jelly sandwiches over for the kids, and warned them to play nice, in the front room, while we worked.

The people we sublet the apartment from left the phone on for us. So we could use it until we got it changed over in our names. On the second day after the move, John called to say he was so sorry, and he would be home in about an hour. Then came his barrage of excuses: got involved in a poker game, didn't realize the time, it went on all night... blah, blah, blah. I thought, "Who cares!" This was the first time that I *really* didn't care if he came home, or not. Mary Jane, Elaine, the kids and I, were actually having a great time... and we sure didn't need him to ruin it!

Elaine also had her share of heartaches in the past. Now, she was involved with Tony, a "garbaligist"... her fancy name for a trash collector. He seemed nice guy, and he didn't mind at all that she was helping me. Of course, he wasn't there all the time. Every now and then, they also had their disagreements, however, she didn't stand still and take it, like I always did. She told me, "Honey, if you want something done, do it yourself! By time you wait for a man to do it, things will never get done!" Elaine showed me how to cover my kitchen chairs to hide the holes, and we made perfect sized curtains for the bathroom window, out of an old bedspread.

I shared with her more personal things about my life with John. He could be so caring, and even funny, when he wanted to. It was only when he drank that he would get violent. Afterward he would always say how sorry he was, and promised never to ever hit me again. I actually think he meant it at the time, but there would always be a next time. I told her that maybe it was *my* fault. Besides, although he had hit me, he was a good father, and never mistreated Mary Ann. Elaine surprised me by saying, "Get the hell out of here... good father, my ass! Why are you making excuses for him? He left you and your baby all alone in a strange house with no food, and that's a good father? What the frig is the matter with you, girl? If he were my man, I'd kick his balls across the room and throw him down the stairs!"

Shocked, Mary Jane and I looked at each other, and we all broke out in laughter! It felt so good to laugh! So there we were, sitting around like three kids, making up stupid ways to hurt your man, the way he hurt you... and make him suffer! Of course, I really didn't want him to suffer, no matter what he did. To be honest, I felt sorry for John. I don't think he knew what he wanted in life. He had no goals, and lived with a "come what may" attitude. I honestly believed, in his strange way, he really did love me. He never said anything about my weight, except that I always felt so warm and gushy to hold, and make love to. Many times he would take the hairbrush and brush my long hair, saying how beautiful he thought it was. He'd always kiss me hello, and goodbye, (well most of the time) and he always said, "I love you, babe." I loved him too, I only *hated* the way he acted most of the time. Sometimes, I actually thought he was possessed by the devil!

It wasn't until the third day after we moved that John finally came home. He acted as if I just saw him an hour ago. Carrying in groceries, and smiling, he handed me a large Hershey bar. There were other two guys tagging behind him. He acted like "Mr. Wonderful" and stated, "Hey, baby, I'm home with the groceries! I brought along my friends to help us move the furniture and empty the boxes." He didn't even realize that everything was all done already.

I learned so much from Elaine... how to make it through a bad situation, how laughter made things a little bit easier, and especially, to stand up for myself. Mostly what impressed me, was what a good, true friend she was. The way she freely shared the gifts and talents God had given her, asking nothing in return, to make my home a happier, better place to live. I truly believe God placed her in my life, so I could learn these important things.

Just like when I was a little girl in school, I was so caught up in my own troubles, that I was forgetting to see the world around me. I was doing the same thing again, until I met Elaine. I vowed from that time on, I would look beyond myself and my own needs, and do whatever I could to share my friendship, gifts and talents to make this world a happier, better place to live in, and to help others... even a stranger. (Whatsoever you do to the least of your brothers, know this... you do it to me! Matthew 25:40)

Dominic

I had to hurry to the hospital... he almost arrived in the cab! I remember the day, it was raining, my spirits were dark and drab!

John was off somewhere again. I called all the bars, and then, my mother-in-law's house, of course he wasn't anywhere! My mother-in-law, Helen, said she would come and take me to the hospital, however, I really didn't think I could wait that long. Elaine wasn't home, so grabbing Mary Ann, I waddled down the steps and got in the waiting cab. The poor driver, I thought he was going to have a heart attack! "Hey, lady don't have your kid in my cab! I never delivered a kid before... and I don't want to start now!"

I was frightened out of my wits, and in severe pain, as I dragged both of us into the hospital. The staff couldn't believe that I had no one with me. They were even more surprised that one of *them* had to stay with my daughter, until my mother-in-law got there. Mary Ann became hysterical as they took her from my arms. They took me immediately into the labor room. (Well not *immediately,* they asked what kind of insurance I had first!) The labor pains were becoming more severe. And my anguish over poor little Mary Ann being pulled away from me, and not knowing where she was, only added to my suffering. They left a young student nurse with me, who was more upset than I was. She said she never saw a baby being born before. I told her that she better get the doctor, because I could feel the baby's head. She took one peek and gasped! After frantically ringing the call bell, she ran into the hall yelling, "Help! Somebody *please* help! We need a doctor in here, right away! Dear God, hurry, we *need* help!"

I didn't have time for the doctor, the nurse and I were the only one. In that little room, on October 20th, there was a miracle— the birth of my son!

Taking matters into my own hands, I got up on my knees and grabbed on to the guardrails of the bed, and taking hard, short breaths, I started to count backwards. With every contraction I pushed as hard as I could and... boom, out he came, screaming like a little trouper! I picked his beautiful, warm, wet body up from the bed, and laid him in my lap, just as the doctor arrived. I cried, "It's a boy! I just knew he was a boy!"

I cried through tears of joy... "I knew he was a boy! I bought all his clothes in blue, long before he was ever due!

The staff came running in, and actually applauded! The poor student nurse looked like she was about to faint. "You did a mighty fine job, young lady," the doctor exclaimed as he checked me out. "Why, you don't even need any stitches! Maybe we should have all our new mothers deliver their babies this way!" he joked.

The nurse cleansed my son, and weighed him. "Wow! This little fellow weighs a whopping nine pounds, ten and a half ounces!" Then she placed him in my arms.

He wasn't little and delicate as I pictured him all this time. He was big, chubby and beautiful... and every inch of him was mine!

As I traced the features of his little face lightly with my fingers, I thanked God for this beautiful child, my son. I shared with the nurse that I was born in this very same hospital, and my mother always told me, all she did was push, and boom, out I came... just like he did. The doctor asked me if I had a name picked out for him. Without hesitation, I said with tears rolling down my cheeks, "Yes! His name is Dominic John, after our daddies!"

I could feel my father's presence, I could also feel his love and joy...

His shall be called, Dominic... after his grandfather, thus I named my newborn baby boy!

It was a day or so later when my husband finally showed up. He was all smiles and full of charm. "I love you, baby!" he said, handing me a box of candy, and half wilted flowers. Of course he made his excuses while kissing my face and hand. I really didn't have too much to say to him, and he *knew* I was upset with him, but he continued to carry on, and act so thrilled over the birth of his new baby. He just kept right on talking and talking, but I barely said a word. About fifteen minutes later he said he was leaving to pick up Mary Ann at his mother's house. He kissed me goodbye, and started to walk out the door, but stopped. I couldn't believe my ears when he turned around, and said, "Hey, what did you have, a girl or boy?"

Chapter 17

On the move again

Soon, my sub-lease would be up on the apartment, and I would have to pay the full amount of the rent, which I knew we couldn't afford. John was only working part time here and there, so I had applied for welfare, something I was so embarrassed to do. My case worker told me about a new government housing development that was about to open in Old Forge. She had me fill out an application, saying she would push it through. Since I was a former resident and soon could not afford the rent where I was living, I had a great chance to be eligible for an apartment. How thrilled I was to be able to move back to my home town. I prayed so hard that we would be accepted.

We all cried together as our families hugged and kissed each other. Leaving Elaine was very difficult, she and I had grown so close. "What will I do without you!" I sobbed.

"Come on now, girl, you can do it! Just remember what we talked about, believe in yourself and you can do anything!" We promised that we'd call and visit each other often.

The housing projects were beautiful, brand new, and there was only *one* flight of steps up to the bedrooms! The apartments were half double houses, or four family units. There was a row of houses on Dunn Avenue in the front and another row in the back, on Kohler Avenue, with a huge space in between. Many trees surrounded us, since it had been built on a site that was formally a wooded area. I had a roomy kitchen with a new stove and refrigerator. There was also plenty of cupboard space, plus a walk in pantry. The living room was also large and bright. Upstairs were three bedrooms and a full bath. Everything was freshly painted and clean. The heat, electricity, water and gas were included in the very reasonable rent.

Looking out into the backyard, I noticed new clotheslines swaying gently in the breeze. The air was fresh and clean, and I was back *home* again. The yard was so large, with grass and trees, that it reminded me of my childhood, and the field in back of my old house on Moosic Road. I got a warm and peaceful feeling, thinking of how happy and safe my life was at that time. John interrupted my thoughts saying he was staying home to help me, then, later on we can call Revello's or Club 17 for pizza. God, with all this, I thought I died and went to heaven!

New... Old Friends

We were one of the first families to move into the development. Our address was 512 Dunn Avenue. I was unpacking when I heard a knock on the back door; It was my new neighbor. To our surprise, she turned out to be an old friend... Jeannie Diaz! John had been friends with her and her ex-husband, Sal, for several years. Many times we would visit them in West Scranton. She just moved in the day before with her two sons Sal and Isadore.

Soon, the development started to fill up. Two apartments up the street, Dorothy Stroke and her husband moved in. They had lived right next door to me, before I got married, on Hickory Street! She eventually started a daycare and took care of my children if I needed to go anywhere. Eventually, several other people that I knew when I was younger moved in; I was in my glory!

I also met many new friends. One of the families were Mario and Mary Lou Panunti and their five children... Marty, Dianne, Roseanne, Mary Anne and Luanne. We became fast friends and are still very close to this day. Across on Kohler Avenue I met Geraldine Mc Donald and her son, David. She would come over and help me with the kids, and even the household chores.

Another neighbor I became very close with was Josephine Decker. She lived in the apartment to the right of me. I sort of looked to her as a mother figure.

Living in Old Forge again made me so happy. With everything but the telephone included in the rent, I was finally able to pay my other bills and get back on my feet. I had friends, and John was staying home more often. We would play 500 rummy, or visit other people in the neighborhood. Life looked like it was going to take a turn for the better... WRONG!

(I must warn you that the remainder of this chapter contains language

and violence which is graphic. It should not be read by minors, and might be offensive to some adults. However, it must be told in this context in order to express the reality of what happened. Please use your discretion, whether to continue reading it, or go to the next chapter.)

Old habits die hard. Little by little, John started his going back to his former ways. I decided that I wasn't going let him get me down anymore. I was going to make something of my life and my childrens'! I went on a strict diet and exercise program, and started to lose weight. It was also a fun time for the kids; they really enjoyed exercising and taking long walks with me. I had to purchase *new* clothes from Sally's (the Salvation Army), but I fixed them over, and they looked good. I had my long hair layered and wore a little makeup, I also had a new attitude and outlook on life!

At first John was real proud of me. He would whistle at me and call me his "sexy baby." Although he never said it, he must have been ashamed to be seen with me before. He would always go out by himself, leaving me home with the kids. With my new look, he would sometimes even take me out to the bars with him. However, after his friends made a few remarks about how lucky he was, and how great I looked… things changed fast!

One night at the VFW, a buddy of his who was sitting way across the bar, gave us the thumbs up and stated, "Looking good, honey!" Before that, John and I were talking and having a good time. He was making me laugh with his silly joke scenarios about some characters called *George* and *Liza*. Suddenly, he became very quiet, and gave me *that* look. His jealousy was very apparent and his anger not only took me by surprise, it frightened the heck out of me! He grabbed my arm and said, "Come on… were out of here!"

We no sooner got out the door and he pulled my hair and started slapping me in the face! "You rotten, no good bitch! What were you doing leading him on? I saw you giving him secret messages. You want to screw him, don't you!" he growled. I was so shocked, because I had no idea what he was talking about, and there was not a word of truth in his accusations. When I tried to protest, he only hit me harder. As we walked down the side roads toward home, he continued to punch me. When I tried to yell out, he covered my mouth with his hand. His attack was so violent, I became nauseated and vomited. I cried that he was killing me. He stopped hitting me, although he continued to curse at me as he dragged me down the dark street. When we got home he started again! The babysitter got so frightened that she ran out of there without even getting paid. He continued to strike me on whatever part of my body he could reach with his fist, and said, "Tell me the truth, bitch! You want to screw him, don't you… tell me now!" I was crying and telling him it wasn't true, begging him to stop. He only became more angry and stated, "Oh… it isn't true? Well then, you must already be screwing him, right, bitch?" Pulling away from him, I ran upstairs into our bedroom. I tried to shut and lock the door, but he was right after me, and pushed it open, almost knocking me over as the corner of the door hit my head. Once inside, he grabbed my hair, twisting it around his hand. I tried to climb over the bed, but he jerked me away, actually pulling some of my hair from my scalp! We struggled, as he forced me to the floor. Climbing on top of me, he continued to cursed and slap me. To my terror, he started to choke me, saying all sorts of perverted, disgusting things about me and his friends. He was hurting me so bad, that he forced me to say, "Yes! I want all your friends to make love to me!" Slapping me again, he sneered, breathing heavily, "You're not listening to me, bitch! That's not what I told you to say! Now say it right this time, like a good girl!" His hands tightened around my neck, and I actually thought he was going to kill me! He loosened his grip again, until I finally chocked out, "Ok," I whispered, "Yes! I want all your friends to screw me!" This made him so sexually excited that he ripped my clothing off, and attacked me violently! He went on to say all sorts of disgusting things and forced me to repeat them. I felt so degraded, like I was being raped by a total stranger. To add to my torment and shame, my babies were awakened by all the commotion, and were crying. Poor Mary Ann was banging at the bedroom door, screaming out, "Mommy! Mommy!"

This was a dark side of John I never knew, and it terrified me. What scared me even more, I don't think he even knew this side of himself before either. The next day I was bruised, battered and aching from head to toe. Usually I hid our arguments from the neighbors, however, with the paper thin walls, I am sure everyone had heard what went on. I felt so embarrassed, and ashamed to face anyone.

As usual, but in tears this time, John begged my forgiveness, rocking me in his arms. He kissed my bruises, and made his empty promises to *never*, ever do it again. I believe he really meant it at the time, and if he could stop, he would. However, of course there was always a next time. Sometimes it was for a few weeks, other times, the peace only lasted a few days.

This stirred up some kind of beast in John and started a whole new chain of abuse. He would accuse me of all kinds of horrible things, forcing me to say it was true. Then he would become extremely aroused and then physically and sexually torment me, sometimes for hours. He would make me go with him to the bars and ask me about some stranger. I made the mistake of pleading with him not to force me to say such terrible things; crying that it was a *sin*. Then he would torment me with: "Hey, bitch, you're going to *hell* for wanting to screw my friends... then you'll have to screw the devil!" I learned the hard way not to say, "No I don't," because this would only make him more angry. He derived great pleasure out of degrading me and would make up all sorts of perverted scenarios. Then, he'd do whatever he could to inflict enough pain, so that I had to say whatever he wanted about the two of us, and other men and even women! I have marks on my inner thigh where I was burned with a cigarette. My face bears the scar where I was punched so hard my lower lip was actually hanging down, needing stitches. He hit me so hard in the mouth that two of my back teeth were broken off. It got to a point that I couldn't even look towards the direction of a man without him flipping out and beating me. It would always be the same, this abuse turned him on. The more he hurt me, the more sexually perverted the fantasy, the better he liked it! I couldn't even have girlfriends over any more because he accused me of being a lesbian. It seemed like he actually became jealous of his own fantasies. The next day he would always be sorry and promise to never do it again, but of course he did, so the cycle continued.

John had a split personality, and really needed some kind of help. (We both did.) He would be so nice and kind one minute, then, for no reason he'd become angry. Behind his back I called him Jeckle and Hyde. When John was nice, he was the greatest, however, once his temper flared, all hell broke out! My children and I lived in constant fear, never knowing what to expect. One night he came home and stated that he had something for me, then he pulled out a switchblade knife. "If I ever catch you whoring around, I will stick this in you and rip you right wide open!" he sneered. That knife was used in many ways, on many occasions to frighten me.

My daughter, Mary Ann still becomes emotional when she recalls the time John was fighting with me and he screamed, "You son of a bitch, I'm going to cut you up into little pieces and bury you where no one can ever find you!" I yelled out: "Mary Ann... take Nicky and run out the back door to Gerry McDonald's house!" as I escaped from him out the front door. My neighbor, Josephine Decker, hearing all that was going on, was waiting for me and summoned me into her apartment. Before she slammed her door shut, she yelled to John, "You better get going fast; the police are on their way! Go on... get going!" John, apparently stunned by her threat, actually took off running. I was shaking as Josephine got me a glass of water. I recall thinking, why does everybody always give someone a glass of water when they are upset?

She was saying that I should throw the bum out… when we heard the most heart-wrenching screams coming from outside! Rushing to the door, we encountered the most pathetic sight. There was my poor Mary Ann, on her little hands and knees, crying hysterically. She was digging frantically in the soft dirt with a spoon. I ran to her and scooped her up in my arms, trying to calm her down. However, for the next few moments she didn't even realize it was me. She kept screaming, "Daddy buried Mommy in the ground! Daddy buried Mommy in the ground!" Josephine's son had planted a bush that morning. When Mary Ann came outside to look for me, she saw the shovel against the house and actually thought John carried out his threat!

John stayed away for days. However, instead of relaxing without him around, I lived in more fear, recalling all the other times he would come home and slap me around, demanding an account of my every move when he was gone. He would tell me that I better have eyes in the back of my head because he was watching me, and one wrong move, I was dead! Also, I knew that he was sleeping around with other women from the bars, and I feared contracting some kind of sexual disease from him.

Once he was gone for over a week, but came home in the middle of the night to awaken me with kisses, and a gift box that held a bracelet wishing me a "Happy Birthday," and then he just left again. Other nights he would literally throw me out of bed, cursing and slapping me around, and start his sexual perversions and abuse again. I truly hate to admit it, but I was so desperate, and sure that one day he would go too far and actually murder me. I started to imagine killing him, before he killed me. I recall one night he come home drunk and after hours of tormenting me, he passed out cold. I said, "This is it… now you're the one who is fricken dead!" First I took the pillow and put it over his face and sat on it. However when he began to struggle in his sleep, I got off and took the pillow away. Next I thought I would strangle him, so I wrapped my hands around his neck, like he had done so many times to me, and started to choke him. Once again he stirred and I lost my nerve. Then I grabbed the lamp from the dresser and straddled his body, intending to smash it over his head and crush his skull. I was thinking that I would surely get away with it; this was self defense. As I held it over my head, I tried to bring in down upon him, but I just couldn't bring myself to do it. Then I got a glimpse of myself in the mirror and actually got a laughing fit! There I was, my hair every which way, my right eye almost swollen shut and my nose was dripping blood onto my breasts, holding a green lamp over my head. It looked like a scene from a cheap horror movie. So instead of murdering him, I went to comfort my babies.

Although he never personally abused my children—in fact, he was always nice to them—they were of course, still in danger, and suffering emotionally from all the anger and turmoil. We would never know what he would do from one day to the next. I was also so ashamed for others to know what was happening to me. I made so many lame excuses about my bruises, saying I fell, or bumped into something, I almost believed it myself.

Once, when John was having one of his very few good days, we went out to a party with our friends Mary Lou and Marty. Everything was fine, we danced and everything seemed to be going smoothly, when all of a sudden, I could see he was becoming upset about... I have no idea what. He jumped up and yelled so loud, that the band actually stopped playing. Calling me all kinds of filthy names he pulled off the wig I was wearing and yelled, "Hey, everybody, this is what the no good, bitch of a bastard looks like without her wig!"

I made up my mind that I didn't know how, but I was going to get away from this lunatic if it was the last thing I ever did!

People still ask me to this very day, why did I stay with him so long. To be honest, at the time I didn't know myself. But after researching the subject of spousal abuse I learned there are several reasons for what it is now recognized as Battered Wife Syndrome. At that time there were no women's resource centers or safe houses. In fact, all the many times the police were called, nothing was ever done to protect me and my children. Women were considered their husbands' property and what went on between them, as long as it didn't disturb the neighbors, was their business. I had nowhere to go, since everyone was afraid of him. My sister let me come stay with her for a few days, but he came after me and dragged me home again, threatening my sister and her children. I also had no money to provide for my children.

When a person is degraded and abused, the one doing the abusing somehow makes the person he is abusing feel as if it was their fault! How many times had I heard, "Now, see what you made me do! If you listened to me I wouldn't have to hit you; it's all your fault!" I actually started to believe it! I felt stupid, ugly and thought I had no worth. A person involved in the Battered Wife Syndrome is also made to feel sorry for the abuser: "I love you... I'm sorry... I'll never do it again... I'll kill myself if you leave me!" etc. Because most people, as in my case, actually love the abuser and it is easy to feel compassion for the one abusing them. They also believe that if they can only be a better wife, the abuse will stop.

Then there is the fear factor. Women are afraid. They are warned that if they left, they or their loved ones would we harmed or even killed. "You belong to me! If I can't have you, no one else can! Just try to leave me, and they'll find you dead in a ditch somewhere!" still rings in my ears!

I thank God that now there are safe havens where abused women (and men) can stay and get help. Many times, over the years, I have been asked to entertain for abused women and children's organizations. After I do my show and we have a lot of laughs, I sit down with them and share my story. They are usually surprised to here that once upon a time, I was in their shoes. I share my story with them so my life might be an inspiration to them. I had nowhere to turn and no one to come to my rescue, however, I made it! God was with me, and He is with them too! I tell them I love them, and I believe in them. They are all so special! And if I could make it... they can make it too!

My heart was filled with pain and sorrow when I heard on the news about a young girl, with a three month old baby, who was afraid to seek help, and was actually murdered by her husband.

My heart is also blessed, when I'd see someone a year or so later, and they tell me, "Jo Jo, you were right! I did make it!"

If you know someone who is being abused, please help them. If you are being abused yourself please RUN...there is help out there for you!

The Lost Child

I am very close to my children, and I truly believe it is because of the closeness and bonding we shared while breast feeding. Usually, it is good birth control, since it is rare a mother is able to get pregnant at that time.

One day I felt awful. I had a headache and cramps in my lower stomach. My friend Rosemary Garvin was visiting, and I told her I thought I was getting my period. The bleeding became worse and so was the cramping. I tried to get in touch with Dr. Campanella; however, he was off that night and the answering service told me that Dr. Alexander was taking his calls. I shared with him what was happening and he wanted to see me immediately. Dorothy

Stroke came down to stay with the kids, and Rosemary took me to Pittston, to see this doctor. He spoke with an accent, and had no bedside manor. "You must go straight to the hospital. I'm sorry... I think you're going to have the baby." I looked at him strangely, thinking I must not be understanding him right. I already had the baby; Dominic was over three months old already!

Rosemary informed me that she must drive me to the cab station, because she was afraid to drive up the steep, winding hill to the Pittston Hospital. So there I was in severe pain, weak and nauseated, as we pulled up to the taxi station. I had to wait ten minutes for a cab. Of course, the dispatcher must have thought we were both nuts. Pulling up and parking our car, then yelling for a cab because we had to get to the hospital with this emergency!

The doctor was waiting outside. When he saw us pulling up in the cab he said, "Why didn't you tell me you didn't have a car? I would have called an ambulance!" Rosemary told him that we did have a car, but we left it at the cab station. He shook his head and mumbled in his thick accent, "Only in America!" I know he thought we had lost our minds.

In the emergency room, his voice softened, and with some compassion, he said, "Honey, I'm sorry; you're losing the baby!"

I told him, "No, I'm not *losing* the baby. I already had him."

He said, "You already had him? How do you know that?"

Again, I looked at him strangely and said, "Because he is *home* in the crib."

He looked at me even more strangely, and said, "Honey, you should have put it in a plastic bag and brought it here, so I could examine it, and make sure it was all there!" About that time I thought someone should examine *his* head, to see if *he* was all there!

The next morning, Dr. Campanella arrived. We got the whole matter straightened out. To my surprise, I was indeed pregnant again, and I had miscarried the baby. Since I wasn't the other doctor's patient, he had no way of knowing that I had just given birth three months ago. He thought I was having some kind of a nervous breakdown from losing this baby.

I had to have a D and C, which was considered surgery, to make sure everything was cleaned out of my uterus. Believe it or not, since I was still a minor, I couldn't give my own consent, and they wouldn't do it without my guardian's signature, because they were afraid of a lawsuit. Of course, you know who was nowhere to be found. I ended up staying in the hospital for almost a week. It took two days for him to come down and sign the consent.

If the whole thing wasn't so tragic, it would have been funny. I couldn't believe how much sorrow this miscarriage caused me. My baby was gone forever. What bothered me the most was that I didn't even know he existed before then. How could I have carried a life around inside of me, right under my heart, and not even known it was there!

Catherine

When I came home, all I did was cry for the next week or so. I was so upset by losing this baby. I would rock Nicky and Mary Ann, holding them so tight; I was afraid that I'd lose them, too.

John began staying out all night more often. Sometimes he didn't come home for days. Although I could never prove it, I knew he was seeing someone else. I was actually glad, because then he left me alone. When he did come home, he was usually friendly and *almost* nice to me, too nice sometimes... that was the dead giveaway. Also, he very seldom wanted to have sex with me, and when he did, it was either horrendous and violent, or over with almost as quick as it began... Thank God! I hated it, but I was afraid of what he'd do if I refused.

A few months passed, and I began to feel ill, so I went to the doctor. He took a some tests and called me with the report. I wasn't sick at all; I was pregnant! You would have thought with all I was going through I'd be upset; however, I was overjoyed! I was depressed over my miscarriage, and feeling so empty and barren. This news was just what I needed. Besides, I don't believe in mistakes. No one is here, unless God willed them to be!

John must have broken up with whoever, because he started fighting with me again. This time when he struck me, something deep inside of me came to the surface, and hit him back! I couldn't believe it myself! I yelled, "You son of a bitch, if you ever touch me again, and hurt *this* baby, I'll kill you with my own bare hands!" (Deep down I always believed that I miscarried the previous baby because of his abuse.) He raised his fist to me again and the anger and frustration of all the years burst forth, and I had a fit of my own! I grabbed the kitchen chair, "Come on, you bastard, just try it, and I'll smash this chair right over your damn head!" I yelled. I started to scream at him all the things I'd been wanting to say to him for years! I grabbed anything I could get my hands on, and threw it at him. He looked at me with disbelief, and did I see... *fear*, and ran out the door.

I felt as if I had won the lottery! What a sense of accomplishment! I don't know where the courage came from, but I had enough. From now on, this would no longer be a one-sided battle. He wanted to fight, well I declared war!

John stayed away for about four days. When he came back, he was as nice as can be, and the peace lasted for a much longer time. Although the abuse didn't completely stop, it wasn't as bad. I think being pregnant had something to do with it, Also, I think he knew there was a change in me, and I was no longer his punching bag. I told him once, when he slapped me for no reason, "If you ever hit me again I'll have you arrested! Better yet, I'll have you *disappear* form the face of the earth. Be afraid... I'm Italian, you know!"

I have to say, in his defense, that he never, not even once, laid a hand on his children. In fact, he was always kind and gentle with them. Mary Ann was the apple of his eye. How they loved him when he was good; how they feared him when he was not.

My sister, Mary Jane, had since married, and found out she was pregnant too! We were so excited! Over the years, we had shared so much, now, we would share this wonderful experience together!

We both took the bus together to the state hospital clinic for our check ups. I found out that my blood sugar was very high. The doctor informed me that I had to go on a strict diet. Not only would the elevated blood sugar be harmful to me with my pregnancy, my baby could inherit the disease. I was so frightened for my child, that I followed the diet faithfully. I was losing weight and I felt good. By the time I was ready to deliver, not only didn't I gain any weight with my pregnancy, I actually lost over twenty pounds! When Mary Jane and I walked down the street with our babies, people would come up to her and say such things as, "Wow! Mary Jane, you had twins!"

We always joke about that time. Especially after she did have twins, two beautiful boys, Joey and Jamie, a few years later. " JA, you put the whammy on me!" she'd say.

I was in labor with the most excruciating pain I ever felt. I was in the delivery room all set up, but the baby wasn't coming. The doctor said I was having a problem; the baby wasn't turned in the right direction. He was trying to help turn her. The process left me in unbearable pain and exhausted.

Dr. Zalintimo sat at my head. He asked the nurse for a cool washcloth and wiped the perspiration off my face. He was speaking to me in soft, soothing tones, "Relax, it will be over soon and you'll have your beautiful baby." As he continued to wipe my face and speak to me, I was so touched by his kindness! No man had ever been so sweet, gentle and compassionate to me as he was. I told him that he wasn't really a doctor, but an angel sent by God. "He sends me angels in my time of great need!"

After what seemed like hours, I told him that I knew the baby would never be born, it will remain in me forever. Finally, after many hours of hard labor, we were able to deliver my baby girl. As the nurse laid her in my arms she told me that my little girl weighed 8 pounds, 12 ounces. Her little face was flawless and she had a soft covering of red hair. She was absolutely beautiful! "I'm naming her Catherine Ann... Catherine is for the saint and Ann is after me. All my children are named after saints. My first born, Mary Ann, is named after the Blessed Mother and myself. And my son, Dominic, is also named after a saint... my father!" I said.

I felt as if I were there forever, and didn't even know what day it was. The nurse told me it was August 17th. I had been in labor for almost two days.

Mary Ann and Dominic were delighted with their new baby, although they were little more than babies themselves. Mary Ann had a hard time saying Dominic, so we had started calling him Nicky. The same was true with the name Catherine, so we called "her" new baby Cathy.

Catherine was a good baby, but I think Nicky was experiencing jealousy. He loved her alright and hugged and kissed her often, however, now he clung to me like glue. Nicky had always been close to me... I had to hold him all the time, and he cried if I needed to leave him, even for a few minutes. I knew it was due to all the problems between John and me. But now he wanted my attention every single second of my life. I had to carry him or hold his hand at all times. I couldn't even go to the bathroom without holding him on my lap. I always gave my children much love and attention, for I knew firsthand how it felt to long for affection. I would sing to them and rock them to sleep. But he needed more. I would be washing the dishes or doing other chores and he'd sit on the floor with his arms around my leg and his little head against my leg. I used to tease him when he screamed and cried for my constant attention. Mimicking my mother, with one hand on my hip and my other one waiving in front of me I'd say, "Wait! Wait until you get married and have a baby. He will drive you even more crazy than you're driving me!" Mary Ann used to tell him to be good because he didn't want Mommy to put that "curse" on him.

About two years after the birth of my son's beautiful, redheaded daughter, Brooke, I received a frantic phone call from Dominic. "Ma, do you love me?" he yelled into the phone.

"Of course, you know I love you!" I answered.

He yelled, "Help! Help! Ma, please help me!" he cried.

"What's the matter? What's wrong?" I answered in a panic, fearing something awful had happened.

"Well, if you love me…PLEASE! PLEASE! TAKE THE CURSE OFF OF ME… THIS KID IS DRIVING ME NUTS!" he teased.

Mary Jane and Buddy were living on Williams Street, just a few blocks away. She had given birth to her first child just a week before I had Cathy. Her baby was also a girl, named Lori Lynn. How exciting it was to have my very first niece, I loved her just as if she were my own. I had this huge, old, gray carriage and we would pack all the kids up and go for walks.

My sister and I were always so close. My heart was heavy, not only for me and my children, but also for my sister. Buddy was also starting to drink and it was causing problems in her home. Mary Jane and I couldn't believe the situation we were both in, especially after we promised ourselves that we would never marry a drunk.

John's drinking and abuse was becoming worse again. When I was pregnant, it was mostly verbal, now it was becoming more physical. He would do his old thing again… stay out for days at a time, then come in the middle of the night, slapping me awake and demanding to know what I did every single minute while he was gone. Although I was still terrified of him, I was becoming a little braver as time went on. "What's the matter, you got a guilty conscience?" I yelled. Of course, he would only hit me again for my remark. But now, I hit back every chance I could. Dear God, was I becoming a violent person?

I got a part time job as a waitress at Gino's, a local restaurant on the corner of Main Street and Moosic Road. Dorothy Stroke would take care of the kids. I knew they were in good hands and I really needed to get away for a little while. So this little job not only brought in a few dollars, it gave me a chance to collect myself. John didn't mind at first, especially when I gave him most of my tips. Sometimes he would even take the kids down to the restaurant to see me. To my surprise, he even made dinner on a few occasions!

I should have known that this would only last for a short time; soon he began to have fits of jealousy. He would come in for coffee and stare at me, then accuse me of having an affair with every male customer I served. I tried to reassure him, but nothing I did convinced him. If I made a big fuss over John, he'd accuse me of doing so because I was tipping off my "boyfriend" that my husband was there. If I didn't pay attention to John, he would say that I was ignoring him because I didn't want my "boyfriend" to know I was married. He even started to accuse me of having an affair with the boss.

When I wanted to quit working, John said we needed the money, or that I was guilty of trying to "hide" something, and that is why I wanted to quit.

Nothing I did, or said was right. What I couldn't understand was, how, where and when, was I suppose to be having these so-called "affairs" when he was always spying on me?

I felt trapped, frightened and tormented. I was sure that if I didn't get away from him I might be an obituary in the morning news, someday real soon!

"Dear God!" I'd pray. "Please, please help me! You have to help me; I have nowhere to turn but you. I know you love me and I believe you have a special plan for my life, but I can't do it alone. I need your help! If not for me… for my children!"

I said it before, and I say it again… God sure sometimes answers our prayers in strange ways. My prayers were answered; however, at the time, I thought He went out for lunch and forgot to return!

Chapter 18

The Breakdown

It was my day off, and we were still in bed. I awoke to the phone ringing, It was my boss, Gino. "Joann, I need your help. Carol can't come to work... she is sick and I have no one to help with the lunch crowd!" I started to say that I hadn't had a day off in over a week... but he cut me off. "Please come in and I'll give you a few extra bucks! I really need some help here!"

I felt put on the spot and said with a sigh, "Ok, Gino, I'll be there as soon as I can."

"Can you believe it... have to go to work," I told John.

He sat up in bed and growled, "Don't give me that shit... I saw the schedule; you don't have work today!"

I continued to get ready and said, "I know, but Carol is sick and he really needs me."

As I was about to call Dorothy to keep an eye on the kids, he jumped out of bed and pulled me away from the phone by the hair. His voice was creepy, almost hissing and he said, "He needs you, does he! Well I need you too! You're not going!" I tried to pull away as he started hitting me and saying all sorts of awful things in that strange voice. I begged him to stop and said, just let me call Gino and tell him I can't come to work... that is the last thing I remembered.

Where am I...Who are You?

I was laughing, because all I had to do was walk on this black mat on the floor, and the doors opened all by themselves! We were at the Community

Medical Center in Scranton.. Everything was really different, huge and very strange. Where was I? Who were all these strange people? Why were my head and ribs hurting and my lip bleeding? Where was my Mommy?

For the next six months I lived in the "twilight zone." Between the injury to my head and all the mental stress, after a CAT scan, the doctors stated I had a brain concussion and a form of amnesia.

I truly *thought* and *acted* as if I were a little child about five years old. I couldn't remember what happened... didn't know where I was, and why everything looked so strange. I do remember that all the people and furniture look very huge. After being examined, tested and probed, I was finally taken upstairs, and admitted to the locked, mental health section of the hospital.

I was later informed that since I really believed I was a child, my mind projected everything around me as I remembered them, when I actually was a child. To all little children the world looks much larger.

The therapist would tell me that I was a grown woman with children, and I would cry and wonder why was he saying such dumb things to me! All I could tell him was that there was this bad, bad man in a red shirt who wanted to hurt me.

The nurses told me that I was in a hospital called The Community Medical Center. I didn't recall any hospital by that name. She told me it used to be called The Hahnemann Hospital. For a moment something flickered in my mind, and I asked if it was near Nay Aug Park. The nurse was elated and said, "Why yes it is!" But after that I couldn't remember anything more.

The Woman in the Blue Robe

I was so confused. Since I was living in the past, I remembered how furniture, clothes and even the cars I saw out the window looked years ago; now, everything was so different and unfamiliar! Every once in a while I would catch a memory of something, then as fast as the thought came to me, it disappeared! I also couldn't understand why my mother, father and sister weren't coming to visit me. (I wasn't allowed any visitors yet.) This went on for several weeks. It was like living a nightmare!

One morning I was walking around the lobby of the ward. I noticed there was a door ajar, it led to the laundry room, so I peeked in to see if anyone was there. I was glad to see that indeed, there was a woman dressed in a blue robe in the room. I smiled and waved, instantly, she smiled and waved back to me. I walked into the room to talk to her, and almost had a heart attack! To my shock, I was peering into a mirror that covered the entire back wall of the room. The grown woman in the blue robe was... ME! I fainted right on the spot.

I awoke, coughing to the smell of an ammonia capsule, as someone was shining a light in my eyes. "Oh my God!" I cried. "It's me... I'm all grown up!" Pointing to the mirror I cried again, "Look, it's me... I'm the lady in the blue robe!"

One nurse laughed and said, "That worked better than a shock treatment!" The other nurse said, "Honey, that WAS a shock treatment!"

How strange, all this time everyone and everything looked so big, now everything looked normal to me!

So there I was... a grown up. The only problem was I still couldn't remember anything from my childhood until that very day. It was like most of my life was missing. I didn't know which was worse... knowing I was indeed an adult, or still thinking I was a child.

Mary Jane and Aunt Annie were my first visitors. What a shock it was to see my baby sister grown up! And not only was she grown up, she was pregnant! My first words to her were... "Does Mommy know you are going to have a baby?"

She looked at me strangely and said, "JA, I'm married! You were my maid of honor!"

When the time was right, the doctors said they would allow my husband to visit. My heart was beating rapidly as I slowly walked into the visitors' lounge. John came rushing up to me. He was hugging me and planting kisses all over my face, saying how much he missed and loved me. However, I said to myself, "Who in the world is this guy? I never saw him before in my whole life!"

Over the next few weeks I slowly started to remember things, mostly by association. My son Dominic was the first child I remembered. I was doing my laundry and I noticed that above the knob was the trademark GE. Something stirred in my mind, so I would stand there and just look at the washer. One day after doing so, I lay down for a rest. As I was starting to doze off I found myself in my kitchen. There was a washing machine with the trademark GE. I saw a little boy with blond hair climb on a chair and stick his little hand in the washer.

I yelled out loud, "Nicky! Be careful; you're going to get hurt!" Jumping up from the bed, I remembered I had a son! I was told that this was typical of how people with amnesia would remember. Something would trigger a memory and that situation would be recaptured in their minds.

John would come to visit often. He seemed so nice and kind. I never told anyone that I actually could not remember who he was, or any of my life with him. I was afraid they would keep me there forever! He was sweet and good to me, so it was like starting a new romance.

I was finally going to be able to go home for a weekend trial. I was excited and frightened at the same time. Everything worked out great. He took me out for dinner and we snuggled and watched television. After kissing me passionately a few times he stated, "Baby, I won't rush anything. If you're not ready to make love, that is ok. I'm just so happy to have you home with me again!"

They gave me two more weekend trials. The next weekend before I was brought me back to the hospital, John took me to his sister's house to see my children. Mary Ann and Nicky were so excited to see me; however, my heart broke when my baby girl Cathy didn't even want to come to me! Over four months had passed. The last time I saw her she was about nine months old. She was not even walking yet... I missed her first steps! My baby girl didn't even know me! She clung to her Aunt Marie, and cried. I started to cry myself. Mary Ann took Cathy from her aunt's arms and said, "Cathy, don't be afraid; she won't hurt you. She is our mommy."

Cathy then started screaming. Reaching out for my sister-in-law, with the tears running down her little face she cried, "Mommy! Mommy!" My heart sank as I realized Cathy thought Marie was her mother! I felt guilty and embarrassed. I thought... is there ever going to be something in my life that I wouldn't feel guilty and ashamed about?

That night I cried myself to sleep. I missed my daughter's most important months. She should have been bonding with me, not with her aunt. I was angry with Marie, although I knew none of it was her fault. I was grateful they had someone to take care of them while I was ill.

Finally, John and I had our last therapy session. The weekend trials turned out fine; now I was going home for good. Although there were still some memories I could not recall, I was assured that in time my total memory should be restored. I didn't know if that was a good thing or not, because I still couldn't remember my life with John. However, I sure wasn't going to share this with anyone. After almost six months in the hospital I wanted out!

The first thing we did was to go to his sister's house, in Lake Wallenpaupack, to see my children. The plan was that Marie would continue to keep them with her for another week until I got settled, then they would come back home. I couldn't believe how they had grown in the past few months, especially Cathy. This time she wasn't quite so frightened of me, but she kept her distance. Mary Ann and Dominic, on the other hand, couldn't wait to see me again. It was wonderful to hold my children in my arms again! Even Cathy let me hold her for a few moments before I left.

John was wonderful to me... at first. My children came home and I tried to get into the swing of life. Mary Ann and Nicky acted as if they never left. However, my poor little Cathy still cried for her "Mommy." This truly hurt me and put a dent in my heart that I still feel to this very day! I would hold and rock her and whisper in her ear, "Baby girl... I am your mommy."

They're Coming to Take Me Away

Well the doctor promised that my memory would be restored; however, I didn't think my awakening would be another nightmare.

John was very nice in the beginning, then he started to change. He would lose his temper once in a while and yell, but then he'd calm down again. Sometimes he would become angry for no apparent reason. This went on for a while, then one day he came home and started to become angry over something very trivial. I yelled back at him to stop acting so crazy and calm down. He looked at me and said, "Look who is calling the kettle black!" We got into an argument and he grabbed me and pushed me up against the kitchen wall and started hitting me. My kids were screaming for him to stop. All of a sudden it was as if I was struck by lightning! Everything, all my hidden memories came flooding back. Like a horror movie was being re-played in my mind... all the beatings, all the terror, everything he had put me through and all he had done to me in the past came gushing forth to the present. It was like being awakened from a nightmare and finding out that it was real.

I started crying and yelling, "I know who *you* are! I remember you! Get away from me! I remember *you* now! Oh my God... I remember!"

I think this unnerved him because he stopped and looked at me very strangely and said, "You ARE nuts! I'm getting the hell out of here!" and out the door he went!

I was crying hysterically and hugging my kids. I kept telling them how sorry I was. Finally, I got my book from the closet and called the Community Medical Center. I babbled into the phone, "I remember everything now!" I kept crying and saying, "I really didn't remember him… I just pretended to and now I remember him! Now I know who he REALLY is! You have to help us!" I probably sounded like I had finally really gone out of my mind. I knew I wasn't making sense and the more I cried and tried to explain, the crazier I sounded! The social worker on the other end tried to clam me down, but trying to explain to her I got more excited and only yelled at her to "Please listen to me!" Frustrated, I slammed the phone down in the middle of her sentence.

I sat on the floor with my kids and cried, not knowing what to do next. The phone rang. It was the social worker. "Honey" she said, "Stay calm. We don't have any room here tonight. I called the police and they are coming to take you to Clark Summit State Hospital to see a doctor." That was all I had to hear. Gathering up my children I locked the doors and windows and shut off all the lights. We went upstairs and hid in the closet.

There I was hiding from the police! This was all John's fault; he should be the one the police should be after! My poor kids were scared out of their wits… I was, too. "God!" I prayed "How could you let this happen? I need help! You know I don't belong in Clark Summit! Where are you, God?"

We heard the banging on the front door. They kept banging and yelling out my name. Then there was silence. "Thank God!" I said, "They probably thought we went out."

I heard a loud crash and them someone yelling out my name. Unbelievably, they broke the window to get in! I tried to keep the kids quiet. I was holding Cathy closely, and I could feel her little heart pounding. Their footsteps were heard coming up the steps. I know they were the police, but to me they were the enemy. One officer heard the kids softly crying and opened the closed door. We must have been some sight, all huddled in the corner between the hanging clothes. I noticed his eyes looked compassionate. "Are you and the children alright?" he asked softly.

Another older officer came in and yelled at me, "Come on! Get out of there right now! As we climbed out of the closet he said harshly, "Did you hurt the kids? Did you take anything?" Inspecting my children he said, "Did your mommy do anything to hurt you?"

Mary Ann yelled back at him, "You leave my mommy alone, she didn't do nothing!"

Then Dominic chimed in saying, "Leave Mommy alone!" Cathy reached for Mary Ann and clung to her for dear life.

They marched us all downstairs and my friend Jeannie was standing there. "Jo, are you ok? I was so worried!"

The older officer finished making a call, then he spoke to me like I was two years old, "Now be a good girl. We have to take you to see the nice doctor; he will make you all better."

I wanted to slug him! Instead I said in the calmest voice I could muster up, "I'm ok now. My husband and I just had a fight. Everything is fine. I just want to get my babies to bed; you guys can go now."

He said, "No, you have to come with us now. After the nice doctor sees you, then you can come home again."

About this time I lost it again. "You big dopes! John is the one you should be taking away!" I started my explanation of how I pretended to know who my husband was, but I really didn't, but I said I did so I could come home. But now I do remember who he really is.

The older officer said, "I'm losing my patience with this one, let's get her out of here!"

They were taking me out the door and I was screaming, "What about my kids? Who is going to take care of them?" I was told that my friend will take care of them. Jeannie was telling them that she didn't know who to call and she didn't want to be responsible for them as they dragged me out of the house. While my children were crying, "Mommy, Mommy come back!" and there was nothing I could do to comfort them.

Over thirty years have passed. Every once in a while, I jump up from my nightmare. My children are screaming for me and the police are dragging me away. Although I am awake, it takes a few moments to quiet the sounds of my children's cries from my mind.

Sitting in the back seat of the squad car, I did everything I could to make them understand. I was banging on the screen that separated us trying to explain what was going on. "Please, please!" I cried "Tell me what is going to happen to my kids. Jeannie didn't want to watch them; I head her say that!"

But they just ignored me as if I wasn't even there. I felt like a... NOTHING! Almost as if I didn't even exist. "Maybe I'm dreaming and I will wake up," I whispered to myself.

My mind went back to my school days. I recalled the time in the movie theater when I was asked to go steady. He left for popcorn, but never came back. The next day at my locker all the kids gathered around me and laughed and made fun of me just as if I wasn't even there. The same feeling of embarrassment, guilt and shame washed over me. What even made it feel worse was none of it was my fault.

It was dark as we drove up the long driveway to the state mental institution. The large old buildings looked ominous and spooky. The officers walked me into the building where someone was waiting for me. I spoke to them; however, once again no one paid attention to me. After signing some papers they left, but not before the younger officer turned and said to me, "Don't worry. Everything will be alright."

I was escorted into a room were I was questioned. I felt like a criminal! I again tried to explain to them what happened, but the more I tried to relate to them, the more excited I became. Finally I shouted out hysterically, "I wish I was dead! No one listens to me; no one believes me! Just let me out of here; I don't belong here!" The next thing I knew, someone gave me an injection and led me to a bed to lie down. I became very lightheaded and sleepy and tried to fight it but I couldn't. My eyes became very heavy as I glanced about the room, then I was out like a light... but not before I noticed they put me in a padded cell.

God's Unusual Ways

I was awakened by the loud clanking noise of the large, old door being unlocked. The large stone walls made the sound echo through the hallway in an ominous way.

At first I didn't know where I was, my mind still in a fog like state from the injection they had given me the previous night. However, all too soon the terrifying events that had occurred came flooding back to me. I could not move my arms and had difficulty sitting up; then I realized that I was in a straightjacket. My very first thought was that I was being punished by God for committing my mother to this very place.

The attendant slowly approached me saying, "How are we doing this morning?"

I wanted to scream, "How the hell do you think WE are doing!" Of course, I thought better of it and quietly stated, "I feel ok. I'd feel even better if I could move my arms." Shortly afterward a nurse came in the room and asked the attendant to remove the jacket that bound me. I rubbed my arms and hands, feeling the circulation returning. I realized that if I wanted to get anywhere, no matter how upset I became, I must remain calm.

For the next several days I underwent a battery of physical and mental examinations. Finally, I was called to Dr. Bucksbaum's office, to my surprise there sat my friend Gail Ercoli. "What in the world happened to make them bring you here?" she said. Gail was my daughter Mary Ann's preschool teacher. We had become good friends. In fact, she took me to Channel 16 television studio to audition for Miss Judy, the star of the well known children's program, *Hatchy Malatchy*. I didn't get that part; however, I did get a call about an upcoming show called the *New Zoo Review* and they wanted me to be "Henrietta the Hippo!" Of course John wouldn't allow me to do it. Gail didn't get the part either, but she did open her own very successful dance studio.

What a small world. As it turned out, Gail was a personal friend of the hospital's administrator!

Years latter... "Jo Jo the Clown" actually preformed on several occasions with "Miss Judy" on the Hatchy Malatchy *show! Who knew!*

Within a day, I was told that they would provide the help I needed to get away from John. I was also informed that I could leave in about a week; after that I could leave whenever I felt well enough. However, I chose to stay for a few weeks. I needed the "vacation!" Indeed, it was just like a vacation, not that I ever went on one before. I found out that my mother was in another building, and visited her several times. Of course she didn't know that I, too, was a patient there!

They made arrangements for me to speak to a legal aid attorney. I finally had people who believed in me. There was finally a light at the end of the tunnel.

In the meantime, I was having a ball. I went to dances, did arts and crafts, made things in leather; we were provided entertainment, watched movies, made new friends and most importantly... the food was wonderful! I didn't have to cook, clean, watch kids, and for the first time in God only knows how long, I felt safe and happy! God did work in mysterious ways; this adventure was His way of answering my prayers.

After about two weeks, I found myself leaving the hospital. As I looked out of Gail's car window at the huge, foreboding buildings, I whispered, "Goodbye. I shall not be back here. You will never, ever see me again!"

Driving up the long winding road to Clark Summit State Hospital, many years later, a chill runs down my spine, as I lay my eyes upon those huge, ancient stone buildings once again.

I find myself shaking as I walk up the stone steps to the entrance. The buildings seem to say, "We knew you would return to us someday!" Ringing the bell, I hear the sound of the door being unlocked, and I am summoned inside. There stood Bob Kaylin. "I've been waiting for you. Follow me." I follow him down the long hall to another closed door. He reaches for the key from his pocket and unlocks that door. Then he yells in a loud voice, "Hey, everybody! Look who is here!" As I make my entrance into the cheerfully decorated room, everyone claps and cheers! The DJ announces, "It's our dear friend... Jo Jo the Clown! She is back here to entertain us once again!"

Chapter 19

The Outside

Things were tough for me on "the outside," since John was giving me a hard time about the divorce. He was threatening me with bodily harm, so the hospital had set me up in one room at the YWCA in Scranton to hide out. I had no money for food, so I was receiving "Meals on Wheels." I was embarrassed by the strange looks from the food carriers since I wasn't old, sick or handicapped. John wouldn't move from our apartment. His sister Marie had been taking care of my children and he claimed he was going to get custody because I was insane.

My friend Gail had helped me through some hard times, and I will never forget her wonderful parents. Her father had given me the forty dollars that I needed to give the lawyer. I promised to pay him back; however, he said, "No. You keep it; I don't want it back. Just promise me that if anyone needs help and you can help them, do so, and don't ever ask anything in return." I always remembered his words, and have kept my promise to him.

Danny

I had been at the YWCA for about a week when I heard a knock on my door. Upon answering it, I found a strange woman standing in my doorway. She informed me I had a phone call. I had to go to the pay phone in the hall to take the call; it was the nurse from the Clark Summit Hospital. "I have some news for you," she stated. "We were reviewing your medical records and for some reason something was overlooked. There may be a problem."

I felt my heart pounding and I thought for a moment I was about to faint. "Oh my God!" I said. "Please don't tell me I have some awful disease," I choked out.

There was a silence at the other end, then she stated in a soft voice, "Joann, you're pregnant."

Slightly relieved, I didn't know whether to laugh or cry. "Pregnant?" I finally stated.

"Yes, pregnant," she said. "That is not the only thing; with all the medications you were on, they could have done serious damage to the fetus. We want you to go down the Scranton State Hospital and see the doctor there at the maternity clinic to take another test. Sometimes they are not always correct."

The next day the doctor confirmed that indeed I was pregnant. And he also agreed that the fetus could be damaged. "We could set you up with a therapeutic abortion. It will only take a few minutes since you are not that far along and you could go home in a day," he said. Abortions were not legal in those days. In fact it was a "dirty word" to even mention such a thing. However, it was legal if the woman's health was in danger, or for other medical reasons. He further stated that after all I had been through and the medications that I was taking, it would be in my best interest to *"take care of the fetus."*

It took a few minutes to recover from the shock of his words. I wasn't even quite dressed yet but I was heading out the door. "Stop calling him a fetus! It's a *BABY*! And he is *MY* baby. I don't care if he has ten heads and fifteen legs. God gave him to me and *YOU,* or no one else will take him from me, until he is ready to come out on his own!" I stormed out of the hospital, the very same hospital where I was born, with tears streaming down my face.

Later, lying on my bed in my little room at the YWCA, I patted my still flat stomach and said to my baby, "Don't worry, little baby, Mommy will take care of you. No one will hurt you as long as I'm alive." Every other night I had a hard time sleeping. The emptiness and loneliness inside that small space made me feel sad, and maybe even a little frightened. But that night I wasn't alone; I had a new little life with me. I slept soundly for the first time since I arrived there.

I had a long, hard road ahead. I had to fight to get my children and my apartment back. John fought me in every way possible. However, finally, I was back home with my children. I still had a difficult time with my Cathy.

She really didn't know me that well, and clung to Mary Ann like glue. It broke my heart that she had such a hard time remembering me, and accepting me as her mother.

John begged, threatened, cried, yelled, broke into my apartment and did just about everything to get me to take him back. But I knew that I must stick to my convictions if my children and I were to have a decent life. I met him several times in Scranton so he could have lunch with his children.

After all this… unbelievably, when the divorce was final, he moved to New Jersey and married someone else within two weeks. I never saw him again until more than twenty years later at his mother's funeral.

I was surprised, and thankful that I didn't have any animosity towards him. In fact, I even gave him a hug while giving my condolences. With God's help, I have forgiven him, and I will always be thankful that no mater what we have been through, he gave me my beautiful children.

I had to go on public assistance and food stamps to feed my kids and keep the roof over our heads. I made it through my pregnancy with the love and support of Mary Jane and my friends.

On July 20th my beautiful son, Joseph Daniel was born. He was tiny with light reddish hair. He was small and had some problems with asthma and allergies, and he was a little late in blooming, but every time I looked at him and held him close to my heart I thanked God that I carried him to term.

I had a perfect family… two boys and two girls, all about two years apart. The only thing missing was a daddy for my babies, and someone to love and share my life with. I had a houseful, however, when they were all tucked away, sleeping snug in their beds… there was only me. I felt such overwhelming loneliness and heartache that sometimes I wished John would come back. Of course he never did. In the morning things seemed brighter, and I was glad, once again, that he was gone.

John has moved back to Scranton. Although he has never come to visit his children all through the years. My son, Dominic met his half brothers, John and Paul while managing the Turkey Hill Store, and has been to visit his birth father, on occasion. I no longer have any hurt and bad feelings towards him, and wish him well. I pray that over the years he has changed his ways and heart, and that he has found peace with himself, his loved ones and with God. I am still fond of his family, especially his sisters Marie and Ann.

Chapter 20

Bill from the Country

Life was hard and depressing at times, but I knew I had to keep going and do all that I could to raise my children. I must admit, sometimes I wanted to run away from it all. As much as I loved my children, some days it was really frustrating. I longed to be free of all the responsibilities, and wished I had enough money to go anywhere I wanted to, and that I wasn't tied down *alone* at such a young age. However, with God's help we made it through. We went to church and I taught them about God's love and mercy. Never once did I say anything bad about their father. (Not in their presence anyway.) I tried to use all the pain and suffering I had endured in my life to be a learning experience. I taught them to be fair, and not to lie or cheat, and to forgive. If they were good I praised them and gave them hugs and kisses. If they were not so good, I would correct them, and if they were really naughty, yes, I would yell at them, or even give them a little smack on their bottoms. (Which I must honestly say they rarely needed.) And what I really helped them learn was, I would always stick to my punishment. If they had to sit quietly in their room for ten minutes, they HAD to stay there ten minutes, not a second less. If they pleaded that they were sorry just to get out of the room, I would add on another few minutes. So they learned that goodness brought joy, and being not so good, brought consequences. They learned to share with each other, and with the household chores. This taught them respect, and they learned the fine arts of cleaning and cooking. They all did a wonderful, *perfect* job, too. (I would always wait until they went to bed to redo some of the stuff.) I would try to make life happy and interesting for them, making games out of their chores. I would say, "Whoever does their chores the best will get a big star!" Of course, I could never pick out the best, so they all ran around the house with a big gold star on their foreheads!

I also warned them about strangers, and I may have been a little overprotective. My fear was great, and did all I could to prevent anything bad happening to them, like what happened to me and old Jack.

With all this love, peace and discipline, I must proudly say they were becoming caring and happy little people.

We would make cookies together, and pack up a lunch and take the bus to Nay Aug Park. At that time there was a zoo at the park, and a small amusement area. I would usually go on Monday, which was "Nickel Day"—all the rides were only five cents. Then we would always visit the Everhart Museum.

Of course we'd visit their Aunt Mary Jane, and we'd all go for walks around Old Forge. They also played with my girlfriend Mary Lou's children. They also lived on Dunn Avenue, a few buildings away from me.

Although I had a full, busy life, something was missing. My friend, Susie kept telling me about Bill, her boyfriend Carl's brother. She wanted us to go on a double date. I had always declined, especially after I had some pretty weird experiences with other men I had met. There was the bus driver who was always asking me for a date when I took the bus to Scranton. I would be sitting there with all my kids and he would be making passes. He would even stop and share his lunch with the kids. He told me he never married and was looking for someone like me all his life. Later I learned he was married with seven children! Then there was another person who actually followed me home from the bus stop. We sort of became friends, nothing intimate, just friends; in fact he became friends with my neighbors and other friends, too. To tell the truth, I think he was actually gay. One day I was taking my kids on the Greyhound bus to see my Aunt Parmie's in New York, when I got that funny feeling in my stomach. By now, I knew better not to ignore *that* feeling, so I changed my mind and came home to find a big truck in front of my apartment. There he was in my house with my television and stereo unplugged, and some of my furniture all set to go out the door! He had told my friends that he was having my apartment painted to surprise me. I can't believe he thought he'd get away with stealing my stuff! What I couldn't believe even more was that my friend Dorothy believed him and gave him the key to my apartment! So I figured I was through with any kind of male relationships, until my kids were grown.

Susie kept telling me about Bill, saying how nice he was. She said I didn't have to meet him alone, we'd double date. I swore that after my awful experiences with the few men I did know in my past, I would have nothing to do with them for quite a while. However, she made him sound too good, so after one particularly lonely day, I decided to take her up on her offer.

The phone was ringing off the wall as I ran in the house. I threw off my shoes and picked up the receiver. I was almost out of breath, but I managed to gasp out, "Hello."

The deep, almost stern voice on the other end stated, "I was just about to hang up! I called you several times but there was no answer. By the way, this is Bill, Carl's brother."

Trying to juggle groceries in one arm, a child in the other and the phone under my chin turned unsuccessful. Soon the grocery bag ripped and the contents went crashing all over my floor. A can of peas went rolling under the table and toilet tissue rolled into the living room. Naturally, the dozen eggs fell and broke right between my toes! "Can you call me back in just a little while," I said.

To my surprise I heard rather loudly, "Look, if you don't want to be bothered just say so and I won't call you again."

Trying to keep Cathy from playing in the egg mess I said, "Oh no! I just had a little accident, and my groceries fell all over. I do want to talk to you. I just need a few minutes, ok?"

I thought he wasn't going to call back. I cleaned up the mess, changed Danny and put him down for a nap and made the other kids peanut butter and jelly sandwiches... still no phone call. About an hour later the phone rang and it was Bill. We talked for about a half hour, asking each other questions. Where, How, Who and When! It was almost like a job interview, but he seemed like a nice guy, so we agreed to meet each other.

A week later I dressed in my new green pantsuit (from the Sally's) and Susie, Carl and I walked into the tavern in Moscow to meet Bill. I was so nervous! There he sat in his new shirt and sports jacket. He had a beard and big blue eyes. Bill was so cute and cuddly looking, he reminded me of a teddy bear! We liked each other instantly. After we all had dinner, we went to the Dalton House dancing. The four of us really had a great time. It truly felt so good to relax, laugh and have fun for a change.

Later on I found out that Bill was probably even more nervous than I was, especially after he knocked his glass of beer all over my lap!

He had been through a divorce also, and was raising his two daughters, Ann Marie and Susan. He also had a son Billy, who sometimes stayed with him, but mainly lived with his ex-wife, Peggy. Bill's mother, Marie, also lived with him. He owned a home in Hollisterville, which was near the Lake Ariel... Hamlin area. It was about thirty miles away from Old Forge.

The first time he took me out to meet his family, I couldn't believe how far away it was. Since I didn't drive, and never went anywhere except Scranton, it seemed like hundreds of miles away. I remember thinking to myself, "Thank God I don't live all the way out here in the woods!"

I was so nervous meeting his family. His mother, Marie, was a short little thing, but was very feisty. She took care of everyone. His daughters were beautiful! They were both sweet, with long dark hair. Ann Marie, his eleven-year-old daughter, was very outgoing, and Susie, who was about nine years old, was shy. I was surprised how nice his little home was. As I was given the tour, he explained how he remodeled everything.

After that, Bill called me every day. He was the first man who treated me with so much kindness. He really seemed to care about me and my children. I had to go to the hospital for some tests, and I was so shocked when he send me a dozen yellow roses!

We had only been seeing each other for a few months when he gave me the shock of my life... he asked me to marry him! I was happy, yet confused at the same time. Was I ready for another marriage when I just was getting over a divorce? Bill was a bit older than me, not that it bothered me, age didn't matter, but would my little kids drive him crazy? Did we have enough in common? Would his children and mother accept me? I was only about eleven years older than his daughter... would I know how to take care of older children? A million questions crossed my mind. I shared my fears with him, but he was positive things would work out. He said that he loved me very much, and never met anyone like me in his life. I was funny and made him laugh. He thought I was the most beautiful, *little* woman he ever met... all soft, white and cushy! Just like a woman should look! Most importantly, I was a good Christian woman, with a caring heart.

I thought about my relationship with Bill; I felt I loved him, too. He was a good man, and hard working. My children would have a good home. I cared about his children also. So despite all my fears, I said, "Yes!" We would all be like the *Brady Bunch*.

Bill went ahead and sold his little house and started to build a new one. He bought land and cut down trees, and all of us worked to clear it. I learned how to do the wiring for the electricity, and we hammered, plastered and painted. I thought I knew how to do things just like a man, until this project. I really learned what hard work was all about! I had blisters on my hands, and my black and blue bruises had bruises!

Although John and I were not married in the Catholic Church, Bill and I still had to get permission from the Chancery to get married. I was happy on the surface, but deep down I was troubled. Not only because it was taking so long for the permission papers from the church, but Bill's mother and his daughter, Ann Marie, were not too keen on us getting married. Marie had helped Bill raise his children and now she felt like I was taking her place and pushing her out. Ann Marie was also feeling threatened, not only by me, but by my children. She was not used to sharing her daddy with anyone else but Susie. I tried to make them both feel comfortable and assure them that I was not going to take over, but the tension only worsened. In fact, the day before we got married Ann Marie ran away from home! Later we found out that she was safe at her girlfriend's house. However, she refused to come to the wedding. I knew it hurt Bill, and it certainly didn't make me feel very good.

Another thing that worried me was that Bill would lose his temper with me every once in a while. Sometimes it was just over little things. Of course, I knew he too, was under pressure with everything. Also, he was working nights and trying to get the house done in the day, so I tried to take that into consideration. Even so, I was becoming a little frightened of his temper. I also realized that he was a perfectionist, and I was just the opposite. I could see that this was making him upset. I know he was trying to make everything right for us, so again, I tried to understand. However, I would get that funny feeling in my stomach and I would become very frightened. Sometimes I would think that maybe everything was going wrong because it was a warning. Then Bill would get in a good mood, and I tried to put my fears behind me. When he was happy you couldn't find a better man.

Finally, May 11, 1974 arrived, and we were married in St. Mary's Church in Old Forge. I wore an ivory and blue, floor-length gown, and flowers in my hair. Mary Jane was my maid of honor, my girlfriend Sue was a bridesmaid, and my daughter Mary Ann was my flower girl. The day was beautiful and we had a lovely reception at the Fieldstone Inn, on Drinker Street in Dunmore. The next day my wedding picture was in the *Scranton Times.* Thank God, at least this time I was really married when my wedding picture hit the news!

My sister had entered my name in a contest at the Scranton Dry, and I won first prize... an all expense paid honeymoon for a week at Cove Haven Honeymoon resort in Lakeville! It was located only a few miles from our property. Our house still wasn't finished, so we all lived in my apartment in Old Forge until it was completed. However, we really couldn't enjoy our honeymoon like we should have, because every day we had to go to the house to work on it. It hurt me that Bill worried more about the new house than having a nice romantic honeymoon with me, but I passed it off and told myself that the house did have to get done.

His mother would never come up to see the house. We did everything we could to entice her, however, she would always say, "I don't want to see it, because I know I will never live there!" We thought she was being sarcastic, but little did we know that her prophecy would come true.

Marie would sit outside of our apartment all day long, stating that she couldn't breathe. Finally, we took her to the hospital and found out she had breast cancer. It was really far along; when she showed the doctor her lumpy, misshapen breast, I almost fell over. She did not live long after that, however we did get close at the end. I took care of her and changed her dressings. She would say things like how come I am so good to her when she was nasty to me. I told her that she would do the same for me. She stated that no she wouldn't! I hoped that she really didn't mean it.

Bill and his children were devastated over Marie's death. This all took a toll on everyone. Ann Marie once cried that if I didn't marry her father, her grandmother wouldn't have died. She said that her grandma had a broken heart and gave up her will to live. Although it probably wasn't true, this bothered me for a long time. I kept thinking that maybe she would have gone to the doctor's sooner... maybe she did just give up... maybe it *was* my fault! There I was again with all the *guilt* and all those *maybes* again!

We finally moved to Mountain Crest Development in Lake Ariel. Well, I think it was. At least the address was Lake Ariel. Because although we lived in Mt. Cobb, we had a Hamlin phone number. We also lived right on the border of Lackawanna and Wayne Counties, in Salem township! I was so confused! One thing for sure, I knew we lived in the woods and we were the only house in the whole development. I wasn't only confused, I was very, very lonely. I didn't drive, Bill worked nights and slept during the day, and all I had for company was kids. This also caused much stress because it was hard keeping little children quiet all day long. I missed Old Forge and my family and friends terribly. I couldn't walk anywhere because the nearest stores were in Hamlin, which was several miles away. Very seldom could I call anyone because it was long distance. So I did a lot of crying; behind Bill's back, of course. I didn't want to hurt him, since he said he did all this for me.

Then to add to everything, Bill's factory closed up and he lost his job. I actually thought he was going to lose his mind with worry! He was so upset and worried about the bills, especially with the expense of a new house. I tried to be cheery and talk about how God would help us, but he went through a terrible depression, and either didn't talk, or lost his temper about the smallest things.

Finally, after several months, he heard that they were looking for security guards at Farview State Hospital, so he applied and took a civil service test. Farview State Hospital, located in Waymart, is really more of a prison for the criminally insane. Since it was a tough and sometimes dangerous job, the pay was good and so were the benefits. I did all I could to be encouraging. I prayed a lot, and wrote a letter to Roselyn Carter, the president's wife. We were thrilled and relieved when he got the job!

Things never did seem to go right for us. He still had to work nights, so we were back to trying to keep quiet during the day, which was sometimes impossible. He would wake up and yell that he had to get some sleep. I in turn would yell at the kids to keep quiet and so forth. Many a night Bill stormed out the door with out even saying goodbye. In an argument he actually told me that he thought I let the kids make noise on purpose just to "piss him off,",just like his ex-wife. I have no idea where he thought that one up. In fact, he would yell at me for many things he thought I did on purpose. If I broke a glass, bumped the baseboard with the vacuum cleaner, or when I made his socks pink because there was something red in the wash I didn't notice. The sad part was I truly believe he thought I was doing things on purpose to upset him. Another thing, I was (and still am) a klutz! If there was something to knock over, trip on, misplace or whatever... I did it! When we first met he used to think all this was cute. Now, all this "cuteness" was driving him crazy. I felt like I was drowning. Nothing I did seemed to be right. The more I tried to do the right thing, the more things backfired.

Soon, other people started to build around us. The Durkovics to the left of us, the Brazzos, Goliases and Comptons across from us, and up the road I made a friendship with an older couple, Lydia and Joe Beckett. Next door, on the right, Helene and Frank Stone built a place. Helene and I became very close. Thank God people finally moved close to me, at least I didn't feel so isolated. Helene and I have a psychic thing between us. How many times I would be thinking about something and she would come over and start talking about it. Once, before she moved to Mt. Crest from Scranton, I was dreaming that she was dividing plants and told Frank that she was going to bring me one. When she knocked on my door, I greeted her, telling her all about the dream. She exclaimed, "Oh my God! Look what I brought you, that is exactly what happened last night! Here is your plant!" Helene and Frank were the kind of friends I could call up at two in the morning, saying that I was coming over, and they would say, "Good! We'll put the coffee on!"

Once Helene and I decided to surprise Bill. We moved the furniture and

I put up new curtains. When he came home he would not even talk to me! I kept following him around the house and asking, "Bill, how do you like everything?" but he would not even answer me. I found out later that he was angry because I had no business moving things without his permission! I moved everything back. Bill would either get in moods where he would not speak to me for days, or scream and curse at me. He would call me awful names like he did to his troops when he was a sergeant in the Army! His words pierced my heart and hurt me just as much, if not more, than the beatings John used to give me. He just didn't see that I was really trying to be a good wife and make our home happy. The sad part was, he truly felt that this was the right thing to do. If I was wrong, I should be punished. He honestly didn't know how else to be. Bill had a hard time expressing his love. He couldn't say he loved me and very seldom hugged or kissed me. He felt the way to show his love was to be a good provider and to buy me big gifts on the holidays.

I would always try to understand his moods, knowing he often didn't get enough sleep, and that he had to work with insane people all night. So I tried to make him feel loved. I would write little love letters and put them in his lunch pail. I would try to make jokes when he was angry. I would look into his eyes when he wouldn't speak to me and say, "I see you in there, Billy! Come on; I see your face cracking!" Sometimes it would even work and he'd break out in a big smile.

At Christmas it became an annual event in the neighborhood. I would get all the children, and we would put on plays, and sing songs in our basement. We'd put up a curtain, and have everyone sit in chairs like a theater. I even bought an ancient typewriter at a flea market, and taught myself to type, making up programs. Little did I know at the time, that these little performances were a prelude to my future as Jo Jo. But for the most part, it seemed like he could only see the negative side of things. I became very frustrated and depressed. I started to doubt myself and felt stupid. I actually thought everything I did was bad or wrong.

Although he was very strict, he was a good provider for my children, and never mistreated them personally. He always made sure they had presents for Christmas and their birthdays, and loads of candy for Easter. Of course, everything that went on between us affected them on an emotional level.

To the rest of the world I had it made. A big beautiful house, material possessions, a good, hardworking husband, a large family, I even learned to drive. I had it all alright, everything but love and affection from my husband. I would cry each night, longing for attention, acceptance and unconditional love from Bill. I know he meant well, and he didn't even realize his actions were hurting me. It was just the way things were.

The Pill Bottle

One night after a particular stressful day, I had it! Bill was yelling and cursing at me, and if something could go wrong that day, it did. I couldn't stand myself or anything else any longer. I sat in my bedroom feeling very sorry for myself, and cried for about an hour. I thought of how dumb, fat and stupid I was. I felt that nothing I did turned out right and I was a failure as a human being. I was just no good, why else would all the people who were supposed to love me act this way towards me? John beat my body, Bill beat my spirit. My children were getting older and doing their own thing and didn't even seem to need me as much anymore. Mary Ann was like a little mother to the younger ones, and all the kids were close to each other. I was tired. Tired of fighting, tired of trying to make things better, tired of myself, tired of living. I remembered the little bottle of pills the doctor had given me for my nerves. I had refused to take them and kept them in the medicine cabinet. At first I thought that maybe I should take one to relax. Staring at myself in the mirror, I recall saying, "You are an ugly mess! I HATE you!" Reaching in the cabinet I took out the bottle and held it in my hands. I opened the bottle of my newly filled prescription of tranquilizers and took one of the little white pills and then lay down on the bed. After about five minutes I said to myself, "These pills aren't working!" So I took another, and then another... one by one, until the bottle was empty.

I remembered feeling as if I were floating on a raft in the water, and I could hear Bill calling me from far off in the distance. There was a bright light in my eyes and I seem to recall a man's voice telling me to swallow, I felt this long tube going down my throat, and then there were no sounds, no feelings... and I was surrounded by a peaceful blackness.

I felt a warm hand on mine, and I opened my eyes to see Bill sitting next to me. His eyes filled with tears and he said that he was so sorry. I truly don't know if I was relived or angry that it was the next day and I was still here. I stayed in the hospital for two more days and was released with an appointment with a psychiatrist.

The kids had a "Welcome Home" sign printed up for me, and I was greeted with hugs and kisses. "Dear God!" I thought, "I was so stupid to think that I wasn't loved or needed anymore!" Things seemed to ease up a little at home, and Bill and I got along better. I went to therapy for several months and took medication for depression and anxiety. It seemed like my mind was healing, but my body started to experience pain. It started very slightly in my right side. Then the bleeding began. I bled for over a month, passing huge blood clots. The doctor found I had an ovarian cyst. I had to have surgery to remove the cyst and part of my ovary. However, the bleeding continued, and so did the pain.

I awoke to excruciating pain, in a pool of blood. I arose to go to the bathroom and I could feel warm blood running down my leg, and I almost passed out. The bleeding was profuse. Bill called the doctor, and he told Bill to rush me to the town of Danville, to the Geisinger Medical Center; they had more modern medical equipment. I remember trying to stay awake, but I had this floating sensation similar to the time I took the pills. By the time I got there I was incoherent. I vaguely remember being rushed into the emergency room and the doctors telling me I had to have emergency surgery. I could see Bill's face through a blur; tears were streaming down his cheeks.

Then the next thing I remembered was that I felt like I floated off the bed head first and was rushing down the hall very swiftly. The walls around me were dark and I thought to myself that this hallway is awful dark and narrow for a hospital. I could see a light at the end of the hall and all of a sudden I burst through the light. It was beautiful! I was floating in all this bright, white light, yet there was wonderful, glowing color all around. My pain was gone and I felt such glorious peace and joy. I smelled a sweet aroma that was a mixture of flowers, candy cotton and vanilla, and could hear a soft music from what seemed like a wind chime. All my senses were sharp and the feelings, sounds and aroma were incredible. Then I heard muffled voices off somewhere. I tried to hear what they were saying. Then I heard, "You're *late* for work! Are you ready to finish?" Suddenly, I felt terrible pain, nausea and something like electricity shooting through my body. I tried to open my eyes, but the light was blinding. A woman's voice was calling my name and telling me to wake up. I struggled to open my eyes and saw several nurses, one stated that I was coming out of it. I closed my eyes again.

I awoke the next day to find myself in a hospital room. Dr. Walker came in and asked me how I felt. He told me that I was a lucky girl. "You gave us a run for our money. We thought we lost you for a second or two!" I had lost quite a bit of blood, and they found a tumor the size of a grapefruit. I had to have blood transfusions, and a complete hysterectomy at the age of twenty-seven. I fell back to sleep. I thought I heard music; opening my eyes, there stood Bill. He was holding a music box, there were two figures of a boy and girl dancing. "Look, honey!" he said, "It's you and me dancing!"

It took a while for me to recuperate and Bill was very good and kind to me during that period. I felt depressed that I could never have children again. I had bought a newborn baby doll for Cathy, and I would carry it around the house wishing it were a real baby.

The Religion Teacher

Gradually I healed, and things got back to normal. After a while things slowly became as they were in the beginning. Bill would get into his moods and lose his temper and I would cry and feel useless. It seemed like the only time he could show me love and affection was when I was sick. I think that he wanted to show his feelings other times, but for some reason he would put up a wall. I never knew what he was thinking or what he would become angry about. This time, however, I knew that "*I had work to finish*" and promised myself I would not let his temper and moods get me down. I even started to answer him back. We said some mean things to each other, and I would always end up crying. I told him once, "One thing I could depend on is that you make me cry every day of my life!" I started to drive places and went to Old Forge to visit my sister and friends. Sometimes I would not even come home and stay over night. This made him even more angry and he started accusing me of cheating on him.

My mother had been in the nursing home for several years. So we decided to take her to live with us. Eventually, we converted the garage into a special room just for her, with a bathroom and shower. It was wonderful to have her with me, even with all the extra work to do. Because of her stroke she had a hard time communicating, but it was actually comical trying to decipher what she had to say. We would both end up laughing. Everyone in the house started to "Molly Talk:"

"How 'bout it... too mokes?" (How about it, can I have two cigarettes?);

"Samatter...scusted?" (What's the matter, are you disgusted?); "Hurry...Wheels!" (*Wheel of Fortune* is on television); "Cracky Joann... Honest!" (Joann, you are nuts) were many of her famous sayings.

We all belonged to St. Thomas Moore Church in Lake Ariel. Eventually, I became friends with Ann Hoffman; she was the CCD coordinator. One day while I was picking up my children from religion class, she asked if I would like to become one of the teachers. I felt thrilled and blessed. To be honest, I didn't realize that I had to go for lessons in theology, methodology and scripture. Then I had to be inducted at Mass as a Teacher of Religious Education. Wow... I was a *real* teacher! I felt that I had something real important to do. Maybe *this* is what God wanted me to do.

I enjoyed preparing the lessons, and even got my own children involved with my planning. I made a big production out of it. When the children arrived for their class, I had the Bible opened, and a candle lit. Sometimes I even burned incense. Remembering how the nuns taught us, I had them stand perfectly straight, bow their heads, close their eyes and fold their little hands in prayer. Speaking in a real dramatic voice I would begin the prayers: The Our Father, Hail Mary and the Glory be. Then I would add my own prayers. I would have them each bring in a prayer request, and as each child asked for prayers, I would teach them to always bow their heads when they spoke or heard the name of Jesus. Some of the prayer requests were touching: "Please let Mommy get better and come home form the hospital." The class would respond, "Lord, hear our prayer." Some were thoughtful: "Dear God please let my brother pass his test so he can get into college." And we would respond, "Lord, hear our prayer." And some were dreadful: "Dear God, please let Joey get killed by a car, because he is so mean and I hate him!" And I would respond, "Lord, don't listen to him!"

It really felt good teaching little children about Jesus, and I was excited that I seemed to have a special way with them. Hopefully, I made the lessons fun and exciting. As we would sing songs and do actions to the words... little did I know that God was paving the way for my Christian Clown Ministry!

We had a wonderful Pastor, Monsignor Joseph Mc Donough, who reminded me of... "God the Father!" He had great love and devotion to our Blessed Mother. In May, all the CCD teachers would get the children assembled after Mass, and we would pray the Rosary outside, in front of Mary's grotto. On the last day he would get a helium tank, and we would all say the Rosary holding helium balloons. Then he would tell us to ask Mary to pray to her son, Jesus, for our intentions. Then we would release our balloons.

What a beautiful sight; all the balloons softly floating skyward in a colorful blaze of glory! Monsignor would say, "I know we are praying with balloons, but we are having a celebration! And you should have balloons at a celebration! Look! All our prayers are going up to Heaven, where Mary will capture them and bring them to Jesus!"

Even if the day was warm, I would always get a chill through my body, and a tear in my eye. I thought this was so profound, and I kept that vision in my heart! Somehow, I knew God was calling me to bring about His kingdom, although I didn't know what... with helium balloons!

Bethany Colony

At the end of the year Monsignor McDonough would take all the CCD teachers out to dinner, to show his appreciation for: "All your hard work, dedication and sacrifice." One year he invited us to Bethany Colony, a dinner playhouse next to Honesdale. We were not only going to enjoy dinner, we were also being treated to *Godspell*. It was a play according to the gospel of St. Matthew, with a little twist. It portrayed Jesus coming to earth, actually New York City, in this day and age.

On the stage, performers dressed in black came out singing, then they started fighting. They were representing all the countries, peoples, differences, jealousy and wrongdoing in the world. The lights went out, and everything became very quiet. Then, there was the sound of a horn blowing and a man's deep voice singing, "Prepare ye the way of the Lord!" Another blast of the horn, then again, "Prepare ye the way of the Lord!" The music became faster and more joyous, and the man, representing John the Baptist, entered pulling a wagon. Soon all the actors jumped up and started dancing, clapping and singing, "Prepare ye the way of the Lord!" They danced through the audience, and invited us all to join in clapping. Wow! What a powerful, joyful feeling that surged through my being! The hair on the back of my neck stood up! I had never expected this from a "religious" play. John the Baptist went along baptizing them with a big sponge, and all of a sudden *Jesus* appeared, stating, "I come to get washed up!" He didn't have long dark hair, a beard, big brown eyes and dressed in a long white robe, like almost every picture in the world shows him.

He had an auburn Afro, with big blue eyes, was clean shaven and was wearing a Superman shirt. Jesus represented a… clown! He spoke with such love and joy, my heart jumped! As the play progressed I found myself in awe. Jesus was speaking about love, forgiveness and humility in a beautiful, almost childlike way. Realizing that tears were streaming down my cheeks I said to myself, "Lord, this is the way I always pictured you in my mind!" No, I never taught He looked like a clown, but He showed the love and joy I always felt He truly had! In every story I had ever seen before then, Jesus was always portrayed as solemn, quiet and even stern, but *this* Jesus was the way the *real* Jesus had to be. Full of life, humor, joy and love! I was so excited; my heart was bursting! I felt as if God was speaking, telling me, "Yes! I am the joyful, loving person that you have always suspected I was, Joann!"

I felt compelled, and I knew He was calling me again, but to do WHAT? However, I knew it had to do with love, music and balloons! How could I bring about His Kingdom with these things?

Mercedian School of Nursing

As time went on, things at home became worse. Bill and I would fight, and I would cry every day. I didn't want things to be like this, and I didn't know what to do to make it better. Bill was never shown love and affection by his parents. He joined the service when he was only seventeen years old. Since he was never shown affection, he didn't know how to give it, or accept it. And since he was always "giving orders" to others as a sergeant in the Army, he thought that is what the head of the household was supposed to do.

I, on the other hand, had love and affection from my family, especially my grandparents. We were, and still are, a loving Italian family, always greeting each other with a big hug and kiss. Bill couldn't understand my kissing everybody and I couldn't understand his coldness. He actually felt that if I gave love to anyone else, I was taking love away from him. He couldn't understand that there are many different kinds of love, and that the love a husband and wife have for each other is different than the love you have for your children, friends or even your pet, for that matter. Also he truly believed that if I was married I could not be friends with another male. I was on a committee at church and I became friends with William Gauck and his wife. Bill became very angry and jealous, and started accusing me of cheating. If I spoke to my girlfriends' husbands, he felt the same way. Bill and I were growing further and further apart. We had other differences of opinion about life in general. To me every day was a new beginning. I tried to learn from my errors, and do and learn something new. He never forgot the past and would bring up things that happened years ago. He also felt that what we had was enough, there was no reason to do or learn other things. I would try to explain my feelings to him, however, he wouldn't listen, or talk about anything, otherwise he'd yell and curse, calling me awful names. Some days I actually felt he hated me.

I felt this need to make a difference in the world. My children were growing, and I was very proud of them. They were doing well in school, and were all great kids. So I went back to school and got my GED. Then I took entrance exams for nursing school. I was so nervous when I received the letter from Mercedian School of Nursing. Placing it on the table, I did chores and would glance at it from time to time, I was so frightened to even read it. Finally, I tore open the envelope and read: "Congratulations. You have been accepted as a student." Oh my God, I almost fainted! I had always been made to feel so stupid all my life, that I couldn't believe what I was reading. Excitedly, I read the good news to Bill, and to my amazement, he became upset. "How are you going to get there every day? What about your home? Boy, you'd do anything to roam the damn roads and get away from your responsibilities, wouldn't you?"

I felt like I had been hit. "Bill, you knew I was trying to get into this school; why didn't you say anything before?"

He just scoffed, "I never thought you were smart enough to get in. I just let you do your thing, and you'd get over it!" I don't know if I was more hurt or stunned by his words. One thing for sure, I was angry, and I vowed that I would make it, and show him and everyone else that I was not stupid!

School was really tough, especially pharmacology. I had not been to school since the ninth grade, and sometimes I had absolutely no idea what the teacher was even talking about. I did enjoy anatomy and nutrition, and surprisingly did very well in those subjects. I would use word association, for instance: The term for the fat gland is the sebaceous gland. So I would think of bacon which is fat, and I would remember. I also had much homework to do, and I must admit that I had to study long and hard. This really didn't give me much time with my family. I would go down to the basement after dinner and stay there for hours. Naturally this upset Bill, so this was another thing we would fight about. I tried to explain that if I became a nurse, I could get a good paying job and help out. He said it was just another excuse to get out of the house.

After each few months the school would discharge students that they felt wouldn't make the grade. When this time came around, we were all frightened that our name would be called. When we started out there were about thirty-eight students. When we were half way done, we were down to about twenty-two. The school was very strict and particular, and I was always so sure my name would be called, but to my disbelief, it never was!

The first half was all book work, now we were about to do on-the-job training. We had to work at the Mercy Hospital. I loved being a student nurse. I truly enjoyed helping people, not only easing their physical pain, but also sharing and talking with them, hopefully easing their emotional worries. We even had to sit in on surgeries, babies being born and even took a trip to see autopsies in Philadelphia. I was truly fascinated with all aspects of nursing, and to my surprise nothing upset me or turned me off about the medical profession.

The students were all nervous wrecks! Next week was our capping ceremony; we heard that six more people were not making it, and would be asked to leave. I held my breath and prayed. Again, to my surprise, my name was not called. I returned home all excited, telling Bill that next week we would have a big ceremony at St. Peter's Cathedral in Scranton, and I would be capped by the Bishop! He said, "I'm very happy for you," in a down, sarcastic sort of way.

"Why can't you be happy for me?" I shouted. "This is so important for me! Can't you share in my joy?"

He answered, "Everything is so important to you except me!"

To tell you the truth, I wanted hit him over the head with something, and then shake the hell out of him and scream, "What is the matter with you anyway? I tried and tried for years to show you how important you are to me, but you wouldn't accept anything I did or said! What do I have to do to get you to see I love you... do everything for you, every second of my life?" But I know he would just shut me out and once again I would be wrong. So I just said, "How come everyone thinks I am nice, and they think highly of me, except you?"

His remark was something that I expected, "That's because they don't know the *real* you!"

The following week there was the capping ceremony and a celebration for family and friends afterward. As I sat in the reserved pew, dressed in my white uniform, I would turn around every now and then to see if anybody came to see me. I thought, "Bill will show up, and bring the kids. He might be angry, but he knows this is a big day for me, and he won't let me down." One by one they called our names. As each person got capped the people in the church cheered and clapped. Cameras flashed as family and friends took pictures to remember this moment forever. Finally it was my turn. I felt shaky as the Bishop Timlin placed the cap on my head. I waited, but heard nothing. Finally one of the teachers started to clap, and the rest of the people followed, clapping faintly. No cheering, no flashes from cameras going off to remember my big moment forever. Embarrassed, I walked back to my pew. We all marched out afterward, and as we descended the church steps the crowd cheered again, and more pictures were taken. All my classmates were crying as their mothers, fathers, husband and friends hugged and kissed them. Words of best wishes and congratulations were heard for everyone; everyone except me. Along with all my classmates I was crying, too, but for a different reason.

I felt humiliated and numb at the same time, as everyone celebrated at the party afterwards. I sat in the corner, doing what I did best when I was stressed, eating. Although I need not have been embarrassed, because everyone else was so caught up with their guests, that no one even noticed I was all alone.

It was almost time for graduation, and then on to state boards. We were down to the finish line, and of all my luck, I became ill and landed in the hospital. You could imagine the surprise of one of my classmates when she came into the hospital and was given me as her patient! I was admitted during the night with severe abdominal pains and bleeding. Several tests later, they found a bleeding ulcer and that I was run down and anemic. I weighed 152 pounds, how could I be anemic?

Sister entered my room, asking me how I felt. Then she dropped the bombshell: "I have good news, and bad news. The bad news is, since you will be missing more than a week of school, you won't be able to graduate and take your state boards. The good news is, you can come back again next year. You don't even have to come for the whole year, all you have to finish is the last quarter and you will be able to graduate and take your state boards. God bless you." And she walked out of my room, just like that!

I stared at the door for at least ten minutes, letting her curt words sink in. "Dear God!" I cried, "How could you do this to me? I worked so hard; this can't be happening!" I was crying my heart out when the nurse came in, she listened to my sob story, and asked if I wanted to see a priest, or social worker. Father walked into my room later, and after hearing my story, he offered kind words of consolation. He also told me to put it in God's hands, because Our Lord He has a reason for *everything*! Finally, I felt a little better, and decided that this wasn't the end of the world, or my nursing career. Yes, I would go back next year and be an even better nurse than I would have been this year.

I gasped at the letter I received a few months later. My hands started shaking, then my whole body trembled. In disbelief, I read the words again, and again, making sure what I read was actually true: "We are sorry to inform you that we have not received our certification this year, and due to this, and financial reasons, the Mercedian School of Nursing will be closing its doors forever."

Chapter 21

Send in the Clowns

    I was heartbroken and truly devastated for a while, after the news about the nursing school. Crying out to God, I still couldn't understand why this had to happen. I knew I would have been a good nurse. I loved to make others smile and feel good; hopefully, this aided in their healing process. I continued to teach CCD, and although I loved it, and had my family, I felt like I needed to do more. It was strange, but every time I saw a balloon or clown, I thought of God. I continued to have this feeling like He was calling me to do something.

    God had blessed me with a beautiful gift, I had always been able to compose poetry. So I would write them on my old typewriter in the basement. One day I decided to send some in to the local newspapers: The *Villager* and *Scranton Times*. Well, before I knew it, I was editor of "The Poet's Corner." I also wrote poetry for our church News flyer, *Wings*. Soon I was also writing short stories for the *Villager*. Although I didn't receive any payment for my work, it was truly gratifying.

    Home life was still the same way with Bill and me, but I was learning that nothing I seemed to do pleased him anyway. So I was learning to do my own thing, and not look for his approval. Of course this made him even more upset. I certainly did not want to hurt him, or make him feel left out, however, I was tired of his insults, and getting put down. The kids were growing older, Ann Marie got married, Susan was getting ready to graduate high school, and so forth; life marched on. One day I purchased the *Villager* to read one of my poems, when I spied an ad. It stated that an ice cream stand called That Shake Place was about to open in Mount Cobb, on Route 348. They were holding interviews, so Mary Ann and I went together to try and get the job. We met the owner, a delightful woman named Mae. She was a mixture of Mae West, Dolly Parton and a little girl. She had a beautiful face, big blonde hair, and a childlike quality that made you instantly like her. She hired both Mary Ann and me, which started a long friendship that lasts until this day. Believe it or not, her husband, Michael, looked like John Wayne!

I truly enjoyed working with Mae; she was fun and interesting. We would laugh at the comical ice cream cones we would make. It surly took practice to get that soft ice cream to swirl just right around the cones. Michael was always dreaming up something to make the shop better. Soon, the place became very busy, and Mae hired other people also. One girl, whose name was Joanne Murnock, and I became good friends. Although she was more Mary Ann's age, we got along great.

The fall was coming and the ice cream place would soon be only opened on weekends, so I took a second job at St. Mary's Villa, a nursing home in Moscow. I loved the job and taking care of the elderly, however, I was soon finding out that it took a very special person to work in the medical profession. Sorry to say, I was not that person. You need to be loving and caring, while detaching yourself from the situation. This was something I had a hard time doing. I would get so caught up in their illnesses and sorrows that I would find myself crying over their pain. I would visit them on my days off, and once I even wrote several letters to a little lady, pretending to be her daughter. She had cried to me that she was forgotten, and had not seen or heard form her family in years. I know it was deceitful, but it did make her feel better. I was realizing that God did know what He was doing when I never made it to state boards and became a *real* nurse. Each day I went to work and vowed I would be stronger, but I always ended up the same old softie.

My friend, Ann, from church was really getting theatrical. She would direct shows for the children's church programs, and naturally, I would love all the singing and dancing. Once, I even dressed in a "Miss Piggy" costume, and sang a love song to Father Feldcamp, who was pastor at the time. Of course, he was also in a costume. I loved all the hoopla and fun.

One day she called to say we were going to put on a real big production before Thanksgiving Day Mass. It was a story about a clown named Vladimir. He was a Christian in Russia, and was trying to convert others to the faith. He believed that Jesus Christ was love, and love could conquer all things. Well, I was game for anything. The story went: Vladimir did an experiment in the town square. He brought a mouse, and its natural enemy the cat, putting them together in a large box, separated only by screens. As you can well imagine, the cat hissed and growled, while trying to catch the mouse right through the screen. The poor little mouse squeaked and ran around his end of the box in a panic. Vladimir then put a shade between them, and each day he would bring them food and water. He would remove the shade so they could see each other. Giving food to the mouse, he'd pet it, speaking in soft loving tones. Then he would do the same with the cat. Each day he would move the screens closer so the cat and mouse could get closer to each other. After several weeks the cat and mouse got used to one another, and the cat no longer hissed and growled, and the mouse no longer squeaked and ran in fear. Soon, the big day came when Vladimir would remove the screens. The people watched in anticipation as he fed them, and then slowly took away the barricades. To the amazement of all, the mouse actually scampered up to the cat, and the cat started to purr as she continued eating! The whole town was in awe that the cat and mouse who were natural enemies, became fast friends, even cuddling up with each other to sleep! Afterward, when Vladimir finally released the pair, they stayed together like a family. It is even said that when the cat had kittens, she would actually nurse the mouse!

Vladimir proved that through love and kindness even the worst of enemies could live together in harmony, just as the Lord Jesus had proclaimed! Because of Vladimir's experiment, many people were converted to Christianity. According to the book Ann read, this was a *true* story, and these events *actually* happened!

Ann produced and directed the whole play. She would be the cat; a friend and fellow CCD teacher, Deloris, would be the mouse; and she cast me as the clown, Vladimir. I was so excited to portray a clown, especially after seeing *Godspell*! This made me really feel excited and good deep down in my soul. Well, we all got to work making costumes and props for our play. Ann selected the music. The stage was set before the altar, in front of the church. At first the cat and mouse were pretending to fight and growl at one another, then they got behind their screens and put their backs to one another as if angry. Soon, it was my grand entrance. The song "Peace is Flowing Like a River" played as Vladimir walked up the center isle, and then went from the cat to the mouse, petting each one and moving the screens closer. Soon, as with the real story, Vladimir finally removed the screens and they all embraced. It was all very, very touching. We practiced and practiced so it would be letter perfect. Hopefully, we would get the message across and bring a tear to the parishioners' eyes.

Finally, it was Thanksgiving morning, and my whole family woke up on the wrong side of the bed, including myself! Bill and I got into an argument over something stupid. It had something to do with him proclaiming that the celery for the dressing wasn't cut right. The kids were fighting over God only knows what, and even our little poodle, FiFi was barking and running all over the place. I had to get ready for our play before Mass, and I finally had it! I started yelling at everybody, "Today is Thanksgiving and all of you are acting like lunatics! What is the matter with you anyway? You should be giving thanks to God for all your blessings, not fighting!" I was so mad, and everybody knew it! "I have to go do this play about love and friendship and what do I have to wake up to… a mad house! I carried you kids around for nine months before you were born and *this* is the thanks I get! See what you all did! I am going to call and cancel the play… how can I teach others about love when my own family is acting like this! And it's all your fault!"

Now of course, I wasn't about to cancel; I just wanted to give them a guilt trip, like any good mother would do when her kids weren't acting right. I had a commitment, and I wouldn't break it. However, I was still so angry I could have eaten nails! Everyone became quiet; they knew it took an awful lot for me to lose my temper like that. I marched into the bathroom grumbling to myself, and slammed the door.

Here I am, Lord

I started to put on the clown white and I tell you a *miraculous* thing happened! As I gazed into the mirror just for a split second I actually saw Christ in my eyes! I started to tremble, as the back of my hair stood on end, and all of a sudden my mind was transported back to that rock when I was a little girl, and I was no longer standing in my bathroom. I felt as if I were floating in some beautiful presence, and the same exact feeling I received when I was a little girl came upon me, and I knew that presence was God. And just as He did when I was a child, He spoke to my heart. *"Joann, This is what I have called you to do! Go out there with the gifts and talents I have given you and bring about my Kingdom through laughter, joy and love!"*

I do not recall how long this lasted, however, when I finally realized I was standing by the sink in my bathroom again, my heart was so filled with joy it could have burst! Tears were streaming down my eyes, and I started singing the hymn: "Here I am, Lord! It is I, Lord! I have heard you calling in the night… I will go, Lord, if you lead me; I will hold your people in my heart!" Dancing around the bathroom I exclaimed, "This is it! I absolutely, positively know this is it! Thank you, God! Finally I know what you have called me to do! Yes, Jesus, I *will* go forth and bring about your Kingdom as a err, umm... clown?!" I burst forth from the bathroom singing, "Be a clown... be a clown!" and, "There's no business like show business!" While hugging and kissing everyone! I know my entire family thought I'd lost it. I recall Dominic stating that, "Mommy went nuts! She went into the bathroom mad and come out singing and smooching everybody!"

This was the first day of the beginning of my lifelong career and ministry. From that day forward I vowed to allow God to use me, in this very unusual way, to do great things!

I realize that some people reading my story will not believe this actually happened, but this doesn't matter to me, I know it did! As I said before, to those who do not believe, no explanation is possible, for those who do believe, no explanation is necessary!

I dressed in flowered, baggy pants, a shiny purple blouse and black vest. Then I put on a black curly wig, and a big red nose and... Taa daa! A clown was born! I can still recall the fantastic feeling I received walking up the aisle in church that Thanksgiving morning. The play went as planned, and the reception we received was even better. Every one loved it! Ann decided that we would go into the clown business. We went to Bloomsburg State Collage and took classes for in mime, acting, etc. Purchased books on balloon sculpture, and anything else we could do or find about the art. Ann even went to school for lighting at Penn State. We would have a big production company! Now you must understand, at that time there were no entertainers around our area, with the exception of a few magicians, like my dear friend Damian. So this was a big challenge for us.

We were all set to go, when one day Ann announced she was moving away. I was stunned! Just like that no warning, she was leaving me and our big dreams behind. Devastated couldn't even begin to describe my feelings. She really offered no explanation, other than it was personal, and it had nothing to do with our friendship. I had to accept the fact that Ann had her own life to live, and she had to do what she had to do. Seeing Ann off, all I could do was kiss her goodbye and wish her well. My heart felt abandoned and wounded, and I was certainly confused. I thought my big dreams were over. However, would you believe of all people in the world who came to my rescue... Bill! He never liked

Ann anyway. I guess it is because she took up so much of my time with our church projects, so he was happy that she was gone. He said, "You don't need Ann. You are a very talented woman and can do it by yourself!" I could not believe what I was hearing, and especially WHO I was hearing it from!

There was a fireman's picnic coming up for the Maplewood Fire Company, so Bill went to them and asked if they would like a clown to sell balloons. Bill even used his truck to carry my helium tank (which I was thankful Ann left for me), to the picnic. It went over great! So from there I went to Lake Ariel, Hamlin and other local firemen's picnics to do the same. I loved it and never received so much attention in my whole life! The children just seemed to be drawn to me. I will always be grateful to Bill for this. I really feel that if he hadn't encouraged me at that time, I may have let God down and forgot about the whole thing. I never felt like I could do anything on my own before. To be honest, I was truly surprised that it went over so well.

I decided that I needed to change my image a bit. I had already selected my clown name. I prayed about the name and it came to me. Since I was given the name Joann at baptism, and my patron saint was Saint Joseph, I took the *Jo* from Joann and the *Jo* from Joseph, to make the special name... Jo Jo!

Although my big red nose would make most children laugh, sometimes it would frighten very young ones. Besides I became allergic to the glue used to attach it. So off with the fake nose, and I painted my real one a bright pink, topping it with glitter. I also exchanged my black curly wig for a colorful red one. Jo Jo was looking better all the time. I took workshops in business from SCORE, and also Christian Clowning. I learned that a Christian Clown should have a meaning for their face, so I painted a blue moon on one side and blue star on the other for the universe created by God, a red heart on my chin for love, green triangles over my eyes for the Trinity, and I put a J in the middle of my forehead for Jesus, and on the right temple an M, for Mary and on the left another J, for Joseph, representing the Holy Family. Then the true mark of a Christian Clown, a red dot on the side of my cheek. Then came the day I became a true Christian Clown and was "Knighted" at Marywood College.

I also continued to hone my skills in theatrics and acting. I became involved in several plays and musicals such as *Jesus Christ Superstar* and *Cabaret*. Then, since I had two left feet, I needed to learn the fine art of dancing. So I took dancing lessons from Mr. David Blight himself.

Soon, I felt I was ready to entertain at children's birthday parties. I prayed to the Holy Spirit for guidance: "How should I enter; what should I do first after I arrive; how long should I stay there? Help! I need you to show me the way, Lord!" The first thought that came into my mind was: "This is my commandment, to love one another!" So I realized that I should make the children feel loved! Then the thought came to me that I should be a teacher. I could show them love, and teach them about goodness, honesty, kindness and love without them even realizing it! They will think they are just having fun! Of course I had to find out what kind of fun things I needed to do. I prayed some more and then I thought about the plays I acted in. There was always a beginning, middle and of course an end. My birthday parties would be something really special. I would make a grand entrance... with music and helium balloons. Everyone in house would know I had arrived! Ok, I entered, now what should I do? The Holy Spirit enlightened my mind again... "Use the special gift I have given you!" I recalled all the poetry I had composed for the newspapers. Elated, I sang out: "Yes! I will compose a personalized poem for each birthday child! I'll ask the mother all kinds of questions about the birthday child and make them a poem! Wow! Won't that make them special!" Of course at the end of each I always add the prayer: "And I have some special wishes for you on this day; may all of God's blessings always come your way! May He smile down upon you and protect you from above; May your whole life be filled with peace, health, prosperity, joy and most of all... Love!"

I purchased tapes of children's songs and played them over and over again. What would they find the most fun and appealing? What can I do for all ages? I decided on the *Hokey Pokey* and *Chicken Dance*. After all, even adults do this at weddings.

Jo Jo"s very first birthday party, in 1983! Pictured with Jo Jo and her puppet "Jingles" are: "Jasper" (son Dominic) Mark Boos, the birthday boy and friends. Party was held in Lake Ariel, Pennsylvania.

I Took the Cake

I thought about a birthday cake. I could offer different packages, and offer a birthday cake made fresh from a bakery! However, that little voice inside of me shouted, "No! You will make them with your own little hands!" So off to Lackawanna County Vocational-Technical College, to take night classes in cake decorating. I loved to learn how to mix different ingredients to make my own batter and icing. It was like an art project. We were provided with pastry bags, and several little metal tips, to create borders around the cake. We were also taught how to bake bread, Danish and other delicious goodies. How fondly I recall the night we make several kinds of Danish: blueberry, strawberry, pineapple, cinnamon and cheese. Then we concocted all kinds of different flavored, sweet glazes to drizzle over them! I left for home with them still hot from the oven. Stopping at my dear friend Ann Murnock's house, I carried in the box of homemade pastries. The aroma was incredible. What a fantastic time we had! There we were late at night, like two little kids, giggling, drinking tea and sharing each and every one of them. How we laughed at each other's sticky fingers and faces! We really felt like little kids when our stomachs ached from eating too many goodies.

I felt so proud when I received my cake decorating "diploma"—now I was a *real* baker... clown! When I went home I decided to make my first cake for my family. As I started to add the ingredients, I decided to add my own personal touches... a little extra of this, an extra pinch of that, and my mind suddenly drifted off to the days when Jesus was a little boy. How many cakes did Mary bake for her family? She must have prayed to the Father over her cooking and baking. So as I added the eggs I said a little prayer. "Father, please bless these eggs," then I said the same prayer as I added the flour, milk and other ingredients. I also asked the Lord to "Bless those who eat this cake with good health, prosperity and happiness!" The cake was delicious... I mean really delicious! My kids even mentioned that this was the best cake ever! I knew in my heart that it wasn't only because of my extra pinches of this and that, it truly was because I added my other *secret ingredient*s... love, good wishes and prayers. You don't find these ingredients in store bought cake.

I realized why that inner voice told me to make them with my own hands. From that day forward, each and every cake I have made for my thousands of birthday children has been made with love and prayers. And you can ask anyone who has tasted my special *Blessed* Birthday Cake, they all say... "This is the most delicious cake I have ever had!" Honest, that's what people always tell me, anyway!

The Printer

I worked on making up several "Birthday Party Packages" and took them to John Boos, owner of JRB Printing, located in Mt. Cobb. His mother, Helen, a sweet, older lady, was a friend of mine. After explaining to him about the packages, I shared with him that although I'd had a little clowning experience at picnics and churches, I was a little frightened because I had never entertained at a child's birthday party before. I worried about taking people's hard earned money in exchange for my entertainment. Would strangers feel I was good enough to actually pay me?

John called me about a week later to tell me he had a sample flyer made up and for me to come over to approve it. His work was great, and I actually got a chill down my spine, seeing my name on an advertisement for the first time! Then he spoke to me as a friend, giving me tips about being self employed. Finally, he made me a challenge. Knowing how I was feeling about my first party, he told me we could make a business trade. His son, Mark, had a birthday coming up; I could entertain at the party and in turn, he would give me the flyers. This way, maybe if money wasn't exchanged I wouldn't be so nervous. His jokingly said that his son's party would be my "guinea pig," and if it wasn't that great, so what, he didn't pay me money anyway!

I prayed, and practiced my show over and over again. My poor children had to put up with all this, especially my son, Dominic. He *had* to be my assistant, whether he liked it or not. He wore an old red sports jacket, plaid pants, my old, black curly wig and a pair of dark framed glasses with a large rubber nose, bushy eyebrows and mustache attached. He looked very interesting, sort of like Groucho Marx, in a cute kind of way. I dubbed him "Jasper." Dominic actually was a good sport, for a young man. He was always a very comical child anyway. You know the type, the joke teller of the family. He was also very good at imitating celebrities that were on television; so he fit right in. In fact, I think he was much more calmer than I was over the up coming birthday party. The night before the party I could barely sleep. When I did doze for a few moments, I had nightmares of children throwing things at me... like my homemade birthday cake! Finally, morning came. As I dressed for the celebration, I talked to myself, going over everything I would do at the party, and of course I prayed real hard!

The First Party of the Rest of My Life

I drove up to the house and stared at the front door... my heart was pounding so hard I thought I would be ill! I was almost tempted to put the car in reverse and leave. Then John came out to greet me, saying, "Well, are you all ready for the big day?" I nodded, and quietly handed him the cake. Turning on my music, I took a huge breath, and entered the gate leading into the back yard. I was greeted by a gang of cheering children! Taking one glance at their little eyes looking up at me in awe, and their smiling faces, made my fear melt. In my mind I prayed, "Dear God please help me!"

Not only did the kids have a wonderful time, so did the adults... and so did I! In fact, I think I had even more fun than they did! I felt free, joyful and young, just like a child. Laughing and acting silly made me forget my troubles. When it came time for me to paint their little faces, my eyes just filled up. There they were, all lined up patiently waiting their turn. I held their soft, little chins in my hands and looked into their trusting eyes, and I thought... how wonderful Jesus must have felt when all the little children came up to Him. The joy in His heart must have filled His soul, just like it did mine, right then. I told each one how handsome, or beautiful they looked with their faces painted, (although my face painting left much to be desired at that time) and asked if I could have a hug. I was amazed at how many children readily responded to my show of affection. Their little hugs were strong and meaningful!

Soon, it came time for the birthday cake. We sang the usual... "Happy birthday to you... Happy birthday to you... Happy birthday dear Mark, happy birthday to you!" and the candles were blown out. The cake looked nice, and professional enough, but as I cut and served the it I held my breath, thinking, "Oh please let them like it." However, I should not have worried, everyone complimented me, saying such things as: "This cake is so delicious; what's in it?"... "It is so moist and flavorful; there is something different about your cake!" and, "Jo Jo, did *you* make this cake; what did you put in here to make it so good?" I just lowered my head and smiled, saying, "I made it with my own special… *secret ingredients.*"

As with all good things, the party was coming to an end, and I was actually feeling a little sad to leave. But one thing for sure, I knew that God wanted me to do this for the rest of my life… my very first party was a grand success! I was feeling as high as a kite with peace and happiness. I asked the children to sit down on the soft, green grass, and played the tape "There is Love" low, in the background. I felt elated, as I looked up at the blue sky, dotted with white, puffy clouds. The air was warm and fresh, and I could hear wind chimes tinkling softly. (I had to actually choke back the tears thinking of the day in the hospital when I floated to a beautiful, bright place, and I heard wind chimes.) I shared with them that they were all wonderful and important, and there was no one in the whole wide world exactly like each one of them. They were all precious treasures. And that if they loved one another and shared with each other the world would be a better place… just because they were in it. Then I said goodbye, and told them that I loved them. As if to read my mind, they ran up to me for a hug goodbye, saying, "This was the best party ever!" Playing my ending song, I made my grand exit waving and blowing kisses.

John, along with his wife and mother, met me outside the gate, "Jo Jo, you were fantastic, the kids loved you!" he said, as he handed me an envelope with money. His wife and mother both agreed with him.

Surprised, I stated, "What is this? We have a deal—you don't owe me anything!"

He said, "Oh, yes I do. So please don't argue with me and take this. Just be happy and proud; you *earned* your first pay!"

With a grateful heart, I thanked them, and my soul sang out in praises to my Heavenly Father. We had a group hug, and waved our farewells. As I drove away John yelled out, "Jo Jo, this *was* the best party ever!"

I have heard that same saying at almost every birthday party I have celebrated, so by popular opinion, I adopted it as my slogan on my van, flyers, cards etc… "Have the best Party ever, filled with the love and excitement of Jo Jo the Clown!"

My Costume Designer

My business really took off! I placed ads in the local newspapers and passed around my flyers. Mae suggested that I should also give the Shake Place's phone number, so if I were working, people could call me there. Mae was even more excited than me, when people called there to book parties. Also, by the end of the year, I had been invited to the birthday party of almost every child that had attended my very first one.

Although I had changed my looks a bit, I knew I needed a new and different costume. My made up one was fine for a while, but now, I had started to become a real business person. I wanted a special costume to reflect Jo Jo's personally. Since I didn't sew too very well, I had asked Mae if she knew of anyone I could hire to make a costume for me. Immediately she said, "Joanne Murnock's mother, Ann, sews beautifully!" I asked if she thought she would be interested in helping me make a new costume, and she stated that Ann was such a wonderful, kind person she would do anything for anybody. I cornered Joanne, asking her all sorts of questions about her mother's sewing abilities. She told me that her mother made all her clothes when she was little. And she still sewed for everybody in her family. I was so excited. When her mother came to pick her up after work, Mae introduced me to her, telling her all about my being a clown and needing a new costume. Ann was even more beautiful and sweet than Mae had said. Without even meeting me before, she made a date to meet me, so we could go shopping for material. This was the beginning of a long, wonderful friendship. (Years later we found out that we were actually distantly related!)

Ann and I met the following week, and went to the Scranton Fabric Center. Both of us hit it off like we were friends all our lives. I felt good, and comfortable around her. We spent over an hour looking through patterns, trying to figure out which clown costume to make. In the end, we didn't like any of them. I wanted a costume with puffy sleeves, and also baggy bottoms to hide my chubby little legs. We found puffy sleeves with straight legs, and straight sleeves with baggy legs. But no pattern with both. I also wanted the costume to have a fitted waist, to accentuate the only small part of my body, besides my wrists and ankles. Everything else in between was naturally padded. No pattern came with a vest... I wanted a vest. Ann wasn't satisfied either; she didn't want me to have the "regular ole clown look—she envisioned me in beautiful flowers, with ruffles and lace on my collar and cuffs. So finally she said, "We will make our own pattern!" We purchased a blouse pattern for the puffy sleeves, a jumper pattern with a fitted waste, a clown costume with baggy legs and a vest pattern for the vest. "There!" Ann said triumphantly, "We have everything we wanted!" We took another hour looking for just the right material. I also bought lace, and sequins to make it sparkly.

Ann amazed me as she took my measurements, cut out the parts of all the different patterns and came up with one costume. I couldn't believe how wonderful and talented she was. Instead of me, an almost stranger, being an invasion, she made me feel like one of the family. Ann worked for days on the costume, almost like she was driven by, do I dare say the… Holy Spirit? She wanted it to be just perfect! When she had finished her creation, it was! It had baggy legs and puffy sleeves, a fitted waist with a satin sash that matched the satin vest. The collar and cuffs had ruffles, lace, bows and sequins. I sewed a shiny string of sequins all around the edge of the vest and wrote "Jo Jo Loves" on the back. We even bought red shoes and glued bows on them. As I gazed in the full length mirror, I heard a gasp from someone who I realized was myself… Jo Jo the Clown was beautiful! From that day forward, Ann has become my personal costume maker. She does this with zeal and joy, never, ever accepting any payment (we've had many friendly arguments over this one) except for my love, friendship and an occasional performance at a church function.

As time went on, my wigs became longer, pink and more feminine. I added a feather and curly ribbons flowing down the side, and of course my ever noticeable extra, long eyelashes.

After years of desperately trying to undo the back zipper every time I had to go to the bathroom, I changed from the baggy pants to a ruffled petticoat, covered with a flowing skirt. The rest of the costume remained the same.

THEN: The photo with the short black wig and red nose is the first actual picture of ...Jo Jo the Clown!

NOW: Jo Jo is pictured with her dearest friend, and costume designer, Ann Murnock. Notice the big changes to wig, makeup and costume.

Mary's Poem

Ann had become all excited and wanted to "show me off," she was involved with the Diocesan Console of Catholic Woman, and they were having a meeting. She absolutely refused to accept any payment for her expertise, and long hours of labor in creating my costume. She suggested that if I would compose a poem about The Blessed Mother, come to the church meeting and read it, that would be payment enough. Of course all the money in the world couldn't be enough to me, for all she had done, but I happily complied.

I sat down and prayed to the Holy Spirit to enlighten my mind, and soon, I was composing a beautiful, heartfelt poem all about Mary. I decided that just as with a birthday party, I must have a special program. This was to be a beautiful tribute to Our Lady, and also to Ann. Finally, I came up with a plan... Dominic dressed as "Jasper" would enter the room, pushing a broom, while the song from *Godspell*, "Prepare Ye the Way of the Lord," would be playing. Then I would make my entrance, carrying a bouquet of blue and white helium balloons. As the music become faster, I would dance about, randomly passing out the balloons to the women. After the song was finished, the *Ave Maria* would play softly in the background, and I would recite my poem. I had also made copies of the poem, rolling them up like a scroll, and tying them each with a blue ribbon. Later I would present one to each of the women.

Needless to say, my program wasn't long; I didn't eat fire, or walk on my hands, however, simple as it was, it went over fantastic! God was truly using me! Ann then told them all about my clowning, and asked me share the meaning of my face. I, in turn, shared all about how Ann made my new costume... and the women loved it! They were handing me pieces of paper, with dates of special events that would be going on in their church, and they all wanted me to do the same performance. Ann then became not only my dressmaker, but my "church agent!" She assisted Jasper and me to the many different churches, and would give me a much too wonderful introduction, and then play the tape recorder. Although I was a Knighted Christian Clown, this was truly the beginning of my Clown Ministry. God really works in mysterious ways!

From then on I added on to my programs. Performing songs with my puppet monkey, "Jingles," adding other songs with audience participation, and of course my poetry. All the priest, minister or even yes, rabbi had to do was give me a theme, and the good Lord and I would produce a beautiful program to fit the occasion.

The Healing

One of the ladies, Vicky Ross, was from my hometown of Old Forge. She was so excited about a huge event called the Bafonna, an Italian festival that was held each year at St. Mary's Church. She was thrilled with my performance, and wanted to make arrangements for me to entertain. At first, I was so thrilled and honored, however, as the day came closer, I was beginning to have doubts. My mind would recall the days of my childhood, when I attended St. Mary's School. Maybe I would see some of my old classmates... maybe they would laugh at me, or even walk out! Maybe I wasn't good enough to entertain there...maybe, maybe, maybe... here come all those maybes again! All my self confidence that took me years to build up, was suddenly falling down. My mind would play all the unkind things some of my former classmates did to me over and over again, like a tape recording. In my self pity, I was beginning to dig up all the old junk in the back of my mind, that I thought was erased. However, there they were, still tucked away in the cobwebs of my past. Feeling frightened, and so unsure of myself for the first time since I started my clowning, I made the decision not to go. I realized that I was not only letting the church down, which had greatly advertised the event, I was letting myself down too...but my pain was too great, and my self esteem too small! No way; I just couldn't do it!

Ann would not hear of it. "You go out there and shine!" she exclaimed. "I will be with you, and so will God!" Of course, although it took some doing, she talked me into it again. I was so frightened as I carefully prepared for the program. At the last minute I composed a poem; it was all about me going to St. Mary's, and a tribute to our late pastor, Father Guroix.

As I waited in the wings to be introduced, my heart pounded, very reminiscent of my very first birthday party. The large auditorium was beautifully decorated, and filled to capacity with anxious guests. They were all awaiting this new and different type of entertainer. Vicky made the announcement, and "Prepare Ye the Way of the Lord" began playing. Jasper entered, pushing his broom, and I finally entered carrying a bouquet of colorful, floating helium balloons. I was shaking so hard that I actually thought I would have to make a beeline for the ladies' room! Thankfully, I made it to the brightly lit stage. I recall thinking the last time I graced this stage was for my eighth grade graduation. I began my performance, praying harder than ever. I asked God for his guidance, and to allow my show to give Him the honor and glory.

Calming down a bit, I continued; all was going well. Usually when I preformed, I looked into the audience, trying to make eye contact with as many people as I could, but that night, I just looked past the audience. Did I perhaps fear looking into the laughing face of an old classmate? Finally, the end of the show was nearing, and with the *Ave Maria* softly playing in the background, I began to recite my poem… "I used to walk these very halls, when I was a little girl, I wore a blue and white uniform, a beanie on top of my head of curls…" As I continued, for some reason I finally had the nerve to actually look at the audience. I noticed my Aunt Annie, my Aunt Marie, Mary Jane, Ann and yes… there they were, my old school mates! They seemed to be looking at me in awe and wonder, trying to figure out just WHO was this clown!

(*When I went to school Father Guriox forbade anyone from calling me Joann. He would state, "Your name is Joan… there is no St. Joann," however, he had a favorite nickname for me.*)

My eyes returned to the poem, as I ended the reading… "Well, Father Guriox, I am back here at St. Mary's tonight, and I just want you to know… I'm am not here as Joann, or even Joan, but your dear old friend… Jo Jo!"

Everyone just stared at me… no applause, no booing, no nothing! Then a buzzing sound went around the room, as they began talking among themselves. Finally, someone shouted out… "Well, tell us …WHO are you?" I stood there frozen on the spot! Others chimed in… "Who are you?" "Tell us your name!" My Aunt Annie finally stood up and said, "She's my niece, Joann!" Lowering my head, and anticipating the worst, I heard my voice speak into the microphone, "Um… my name is Joann Scorzafava." Then I heard it… the laughter, they were all laughing! But wait; it wasn't laughter; it was applause! They were all clapping louder and louder, like thunder across the sky! Soon, they were all up from their seats, cheering… my God, they were giving ME a standing ovation!

As I exited the stage, classmates, friends and even teachers came rushing up to me. We were hugging, kissing and crying. The very same people who had once called me names were now giving me compliments and praises. I couldn't believe it! All my pain and suffering from my childhood school days, melted right away with my tears.

You could not even imagine the happiness this event bestowed upon me. No. It was not because I *showed* them that I made something out of my life, this had nothing to do with that. This *showed* me that children grow up. And I learned another one of life's valuable lessons… I was the only child who didn't grow up! All those years I held on to the pain because of my own self pity. I was the one living in the past, my former classmates were adults now, and they grew up to be caring, wonderful human beings. I saw them all in a new light. And my anger turned into love for each one of them.

I'm still in touch with a few of them from time to time: Dr. William Belcastro is a fantastic dentist, who has his practice right here in Carbondale. I spoke with Lorraine De Angelis on the phone, and it was just like old times. I see Jackie Reveillo, Corrine Cologero, Rosina Edmondson, Rosemary Cuccio, and even Mrs. Angellia, my old teacher called me one day.

Yes, I grew up physically in a little town of Old Forge. However, years later, in that same town, I grew up emotionally and spiritually. That night I was healed!

In the Spotlight

A local television show just hit the air. It was hosted by Sam La Sante and his son. It was called *Spotlight Talent Showcase*. The program featured local talents. Children and adults would come on the program and show off their stuff. One day I received a phone call inviting me to make a guest appearance on the show; of course I said yes! I had just finished several programs in New York. My Aunt Parmie had made arrangements for my Clown Ministry in several churches in Long Island. My cousin, Mary Ann dressed up and became my assistant. We even entertained at a few birthday parties.

The day of the taping for *Spotlight* finally arrived, and I was amazed that although excited, I wasn't nervous, or even frightened of all the lights and cameras. Sam gave me a beautiful introduction, and I performed two acts. First I danced to a song called "All for the Best," from the play *Godspell*. Although it was religious, it was also a funny song, where at one point I had to dance extremely fast. Immediately afterward Sam came up to talk to me about my Clown Ministry, and to my horror, as I spoke… I couldn't catch my breath! As Sam asked me a question, I tried to answer, then just gasped for air, as I held up my hand and choked out, "Wait…I have to stop a minute." Oh My God, how totally embarrassing! I could not believe this was happening to me in front of what seemed like the whole wide world! God love Sam, he just kept on talking all about my "tour" of New York, and after a few minutes asked me if I were ready to go on. Very nonchalantly I said with huge "clown actions"... "Oh yes! I just had to run after, and catch my breath for a moment!" as I pretended to catch the air and put it in my mouth I stated, "And here it is; I'm fine now!" Sam introduced my next song... "Here I am Lord," which I preformed in interpretive dance. Despite my embarrassment, I began to feel wonderful! I was praising God, and it was being witnessed by thousands of television viewers. My heart was brimming with joy!

It wasn't until days later that I finally had the nerve to watch the videotape of the show. I couldn't bear to watch the awful moment when I lost my breath! Well lo and behold, to my amazement, I actually covered it all so well, it looked as if Sam and I planned the whole thing, so he could go on to talk more about my other shows! (Thank You, God!) Hey, as they say, the show must go on!

This led to me becoming a regular guest on Sam's show, which lasted for over eight years. I would take children from the neighborhood or birthday parties, and even from contests I held, on the show. They would gather at my house and I would teach then songs, usually about Jesus, and if not, at least about goodness and kindness, and we would entertain on *Spotlight.* How they would love to practice, and put on their little productions that always turned out beautiful! Most of the children never had any professional lessons, so they probably would have never had the opportunity to appear on television. However, you would never know it. Each one was truly wonderful. They were all my prodigies. Even my granddaughters Sarah and Tammy, and twin nephews Joey and Jamie made their debut on Sam's show. This only proved my point, that we are all blessed with special gifts and talents, even if we don't take lessons!

Late at night, when I can't sleep, I make myself a nice cup of tea, and pop in one of the many tapes of Sam's show. These children are all grown now; some have children of their own. However, as I watch, tears stream down my cheeks... they are still my little blessings, giving honor and glory to God, and I am so very, very proud of them! (Am I a big mush, or what!)

He Can't Hear You

As I was entertaining at a birthday party, I noticed a little boy sitting all alone in the corner of the room. At first I just thought he was just shy, so when the opportunity arose, I went over to speak to him. He looked at me, but didn't answer, then he lowered his little head. Another child came over to us and said, "Oh, that's just Kevin; he can't hear you." I felt like someone slapped me in the face. This poor child was missing out on all the fun, just because he couldn't hear, and it was hard for him to understand what was going on. I leaned over so he could see my face and with a big, goofy smile I waved to him. Then I made some comical faces, causing him to break out in a little smile. Then I put my arms around Kevin, and just held him, soon I felt his little arms slide around my neck. I pointed to my lips making a smacking gesture and then to my cheek. This time he gave me a huge grin and planted a kiss on the side of my face! I also pointed to him and then to myself waving an "Hello." At first he waved back, then the next thing I knew he was signing to me a mile a minute! His mother, who was watching the whole episode, came to my rescue, interpreting what he was saying. This not only touched my heart, but taught me one of my never ending lessons in life. How many people are left out in the cold because they can't understand, or are misunderstood!

Two weeks later I found my self at Scranton School for the Deaf, taking a course in sign language. Although I can't sign as fluently as I would like, at least I can communicate with hearing impaired children. It is such a joy to see their little faces light up when I sign… "Hi, my name is Jo Jo the Clown; what is your name? How old are you… where do you live… are you married?" Now, I simply take a little child by the hand if I know they have a hearing loss, and bring them into the circle, and as I speak, I also sign. I have also noticed that this action also makes other children interested in signing, so they too can talk with their "new" friend.

I also love to use sign language to perform songs in my Clown Ministry! This truly adds to the beauty of the performance, and I feel as if I am giving praise to God… twice!

Another lesson I quickly learned was when I was asked to entertain for the Blind Association. They were adults; some had very limited vision, the rest had no vision at all. Since they couldn't see me, I had to accentuate things that could be appreciated by their other senses. They could hear, so of course I would use music, but what about myself… "I know; I will put bells on my costume, so they could hear me as I pass!" Then I thought… they have the sense of smell, so I'll douse myself with Emeraude perfume.

Making my entrance with music, I did the show as planned. Then I explained to them what I looked like: "I have a fluffy, red wig, a blue star and moon on my cheeks, very long eyelashes," etc. then I went around to allow them to feel me. I was told I *looked* beautiful! I also did my skit… *Take me out to the Ballgame,* in which I play an imaginary game of baseball, in slow motion. My assistant, Rainbow, narrated my actions, while everyone sang along to the popular song. Later I blew up long balloons, asking them what color they liked best, and twisted them into their favorite pets. We had a marvelous time together! Since that day, the Blind Association has called me back every year to entertain. The jingle bells and perfume have been made a permanent part of my costume.

The Media

I was amazed how things just fell into place. This only assured me that this was surely my calling from God. Agents… Ed Curry, Harry Meier, Cosmic Productions and Spotlight Entertainment were just a few of the many talent agencies that contacted me. However, Mr. Ed Curry became my main agent. He worked diligently to get me high quality jobs, for good pay.

How surprised I was to hear from the Chancery. The Bishop's office called to say they wanted to feature my Clown Ministry on their television program, *Real to Reel.* The taping took several days, as they followed me into my dressing room, showing me applying my makeup, while I explained the meaning of my face. Then I went out the door and into St. Thomas Moore Church, where I preformed a program about the forgiveness of Jesus, and the love He had for us. My daughter Cathy was my sidekick. Afterwards, they interviewed some of the children, asking them what they learned. Happily, they truly got the message. The next day, the camera crew filmed me at a nursing home. I belong to an organization called Serving Seniors, formally Interfaith Friends, where I volunteered to entertain at different centers each week. The sweet elderly people had a grand time, singing and clapping with me! Although I receive no payment, the joy and satisfaction I receive is worth more to me than gold!

One December day I paid a visit to his Excellency, Bishop Timlin. I just walked into the Chancery and asked to see the Bishop, surprising him with a song called "Violets in the Snow," depicting the birth of Christ. He was touched by the song, and we became good friends. He has given me permission, and his blessing to go about spreading the Good News of Jesus, through my Clown Ministry.

I was really surprised when my agent, Ed Curry got me an engagement on the nationwide television show the *700 Club*! I had to drive to Virginia Beach for the program. My main sidekick, Rosie, accompanied me on the trip. We were put up in a fancy Holiday Inn, and given the royal treatment, all expenses paid!

All my other television experiences were taped, and shown at a later date, however, this was a live broadcast. Dressed in my costume, we spoke of my life and how and why I became a clown. I feel it was a fantastic tribute to God. For weeks afterward, I received many, many letters from viewers, sharing their problems of abuse in their marriages. One was even from a husband who was being abused by his wife. They told me that my story was an inspiration to them, giving them hope that with God's help they could make their life better.

Soon, I was becoming an old pro at television appearances! WNEP-TV contacted me for several programs. I was a guest on a popular children's show called *Hatchey Melatchy*, with Miss Judy. I was also asked to co-host *PM Magazine*, with Jane Adenezio and Harry West. Each year I am asked to the *Jerry Louis Telethon*, where they televise at the Steamtown Mall. WYOU-TV also dedicated me as one of their Local Patriots. They filmed me at ABC Academy, a child care center in Old Forge, doing a program about the Desert Storm War. The next thing I knew, I was appearing on WVIA-TV for telethons. Meanwhile I was still appearing regularly on Spotlight Talent Showcase, and other television shows.

Radio shows were also becoming popular for me. I was a guest on several programs called *The Talk of Warmland*, with host Ron Allen. Also, I have made several commercials for such businesses as The Honesdale Dime Bank, Allstate Insurance, in Hamlin, and of course Spotlight.

One day the *Scranton Times* called me up to make an appointment for a photo shoot. "What is this for?" I asked. I was told that I was chosen that week as *Northeast Woman*. They did such a beautiful, huge write up I was embarrassed... well almost.

I had dislocated my shoulder and was in a cast when I was notified about receiving the Franklin Delano Humanitarian Award. They were holding a big ceremony, and the Mayor of Scranton would be presenting me with a plaque. In my poor, unfortunate condition I was unable to don my costume. So my sidekick, Bubblegum, accepted the award in my place. I didn't know it would be televised; they showed her accepting the plaque, however, I was surprised and touched when they presented an old clip of me performing somewhere else. It was truly a beautiful tribute.

I was flabbergasted when newspapers from all over: *The Scranton Times, Weekly Almanac, Wilkes Barre Times Leader, The Wayne Independent, The Villager, The Tri-Boro, The Advantage, The Catholic Light etc.* were asking me for interviews about my life, after all I was just a clown!

I always prayed for God to keep me humble, always knowing that I can do nothing by myself. Whatever talents I had, were given to me, on loan to use for Him. Most of the time I truly do feel humble. But you know, I am very human, and every so often I do get just a little puffed up with all the attention. One fine summer day I was entertaining for an event before a large crowd at The Viewmont Mall. The people were laughing, clapping and having a good ole time. One little girl, about five or six years old, climbed onto the platform, and was looking up at me with her sweet little face. I could hear the remarks from some of the audience: "Just look at that little girl; how she adores Jo Jo!" and, "My goodness, children just love Jo Jo; look at that child staring up at her!" Now I must admit that I too, noticed this child, and was feeling just a little *too* important and proud! Soon, the little girl pulled on my costume and whispered, "Jo Jo can I tell you something?" By this time I was thinking I was really a *big shot.* I just knew she was going to say something wonderful about *me!* So naturally, I took the opportunity to make a big deal about it and spoke into the microphone, "Attention everyone! This darling little girl wants to say something, let's give her a big hand!" Lowering the microphone for her to reach, I said, "Now speak real loud so everyone can hear you, honey." I stepped back smugly, awaiting the wonderful praises I just *knew* she was going to give me.

"Is this loud enough Jo Jo?" she yelled into the mike. I nodded. She spoke loudly alright; I think the people in the parking lot could hear her! "Jo Jo, why do you have all those ugly, black hairs up in your nose? They really look yucky! And you have a green bugger up there too!" Naturally the crowd roared with laughter. The little girl's mother grabbing her child, was totally embarrassed, as she whispered apologies to me. But even without the microphone we could hear the child's cries as the mother scolded her, "Mommy, why are you so mad? Jo Jo did have black hairs and a bugger in her nose! They were yucky, Mommy, honest!"

With my big ego deflating, no one was more humiliated than me! Laughing along with the crowd, I stated, "Well, folks, there you have it! I always ask the good Lord to keep me humble; do you think that's humble enough for me today?"

Last week I went up into the attic, and pulled down several boxes. To my amazement, I counted over three hundred newspaper articles about Jo Jo the Clown. Over a third of them were on the front page. She was even on the cover of Feature, Sports and Fashion Magazine. They were all about Jo Jo—none were about Joann! I said out loud, "Oh sure, look... everybody likes Jo Jo better than me! Whenever she goes anywhere, everybody gets all excited and rushes over to her, nobody even notices me, or writes anything about me! It's always Jo Jo... Jo Jo... Jo Jo!" As I walked down the steps I declared, "God, now I know I must be going off my rocker! I'm jealous of myself!"

Chapter 22

The End of a Marriage

My life as the *famous* entertainer, Jo Jo the Clown, was wonderful, fulfilling and blooming, but my marriage was dying. I was a *star* to everyone except my husband, the person who mattered to me the most. Things went from bad to worse at home. In the beginning of my career, Bill was happy for me that I had a little business to keep me occupied, but things changed. No one knew that my popularity would grow so rapidly, and I would become such a huge success. I tried to make him feel important and loved, but I guess it wasn't enough, because he was becoming bitter. I wanted him to feel my joy, and share my success with me; however, it didn't work out that way. I was beginning to get tired of hearing, "Well, I see you're getting ready to ram the damn roads again!" I guess Bill was having a difficult time accepting what was happening to me. Before, when he became angry, I felt belittled with his name calling. I would cry and feel worthless, now I just ignored his hurtful remarks. I would try to reason with him, explaining that this meant so much to me. Entertaining made me feel so happy, and I was doing what God wanted me to do... bring happiness to other people. His response was, "God wants you to take care of your family, not go all over hell's creation, and love everybody else!" I guess he couldn't understand that I could love and care about my family, and still love other people; there are all different kinds of love. The name calling became worse, and he would be so cold and angry all the time, I hated to come home. Everything I did or said, seemed to be wrong in his eyes. Days would pass by when he wouldn't even speak to me. Sometimes I would follow him around like a little puppy, begging him to speak to me.

Thinking about it now, I guess he felt if he stayed angry long enough, I would stay home more often. He didn't seem to realize all he had to do was take me in his arms, and tenderly show me love and affection. If he could have just expressed that he loved and needed me, and how much he missed me when

I was gone, maybe I wouldn't crave the love of the public so much. For some reason, Bill remained cold, and couldn't show his love and affection. This was breaking my heart, and killing my Spirit. I know that if he did, it surly would have changed things.

I wanted to understand his feelings and would tell him that I loved him. I'd also tried to express that we could still have a good marriage, and I could have a successful business too. For some reason, Bill always thought that whatever I said had another meaning. He would say with contempt, "I know what you *mean*, alright! Boy you'd find any excuse to ram the roads and get out of responsibility around here!" Then we'd have another one of our all too frequent arguments. I'd say that I *hated* it there and I couldn't wait to get out the door for parties! He'd say the familiar, "You are nothing but a thorn in my side, get out and stay the hell out!"

It got to the point that I actually thought he was driving me away purposely. I guess he was hurting just as bad as I was. Although he never showed me this side of him, so I truly didn't know. I would very often believe he showed me no tenderness and love because he was actually trying to chase me away with his cruel words. There was a big age difference between us, and it certainly didn't bother me, but at the time I thought maybe he felt I was too immature for him, and he was sorry he married me.

Each day became worse than the day before. I was so depressed that I couldn't sleep, ate constantly and cried all the time (I must have become tired, fat and wet) However, when I put that costume on and went out into the public, a miraculous thing happened; I was loved, if not downright adored by the children! The people out there thought I was wonderful, smart and beautiful. I surely didn't feel useless and stupid with strangers. At home, I felt like I was a nothing.

My children were getting older. Ann Marie and Mary Ann were already married with their own homes. Dominic was in the Navy, serving on the ship the *USS Sampson*. Susan had a daughter, Sarah and lived in her own apartment. The only children still home were Cathy and Danny. Bill would say so many things like, I cared more about other people's kids than I did about my own. He would also say other negative statements, that the two youngest were beginning to believe it. I would take both Cathy and Danny to parties, not merely to assist me, but to make them feel a part of what I was doing. After Bill and I would argue, and he would express his negative feelings about me caring more about other people than I did my own family, after a while they no longer wanted to come with me. Especially Cathy; she and I started to have disagreements over this issue. This really tore at my heart. My children were the most important thing to me; I lived for them when they were little. Now they were older and didn't need me looking after them so much. Cathy had a boyfriend, Carl. He was a nice young man that she knew from school. I also knew his family, so I felt she was safe when she was with him. Danny had his friends, and loved to spend time at Mary Jane's, because he was close to his cousins, Joey and Jamie. He was old enough that he didn't want his *mommy* hanging around him all the time. I felt as long as I showed them I loved them, and took care of their basic needs, I wasn't hurting them with my career.

I don't know... maybe I was wrong, and Bill was right. How many things have we all done in our lives that we wish we could go back and change, or repair? If this did hurt them, and I could go back in time....

One of Bill's famous sayings was, "This is *my* house! If you don't like it... there's the door!" I was so tired of hearing this threat, and he said it more and more as time went on. After a while that door looked very tempting to me!

Things could no longer go on this way, for everyone concerned. I had a huge decision to make. I would either have to give up my work to have peace at home, or stay in business and live in turmoil. As I would lament over this, the more I thought about it, the more I realized that things were not right from the beginning. When Bill became upset, he always yelled and called me names, even before Jo Jo was born. That is why I threw myself into the business so passionately in the first place. How many days had I come home from working at parties, and just sat in the driveway, dreading to go in the house? I never knew what I would come home to. Bill would either not speak a word to me, or would make crude remarks. It became a vicious cycle... the more he was silent, or yelled and carried on, the more jobs I accepted. The more jobs I took, the angrier he became. We were on a merry-go-round, going nowhere fast!

I finally decided that there was so much turmoil in the house even before I had my business, and clowning seemed to be the only happiness I had. Besides I believed that this was truly my calling from God Himself. Bill would just have to understand and come to terms with it.

Let me be the first one to tell you, I was *far* from perfect. I sure made plenty of mistakes... on several occasions I turned his socks and underwear a lovely shade of pink, by washing them with the burgundy towels. I accidentally dropped his mother's favorite drinking glass, which he rightly so, treasured, as it slipped from my soapy hands and went crashing to the floor. I would sometimes knick the woodwork with the vacuum cleaner, and God knows how many times instead of walking *properly*, I ran up the basement steps, once falling and giving myself a concussion! I also totaled the car he just had painted when a Mac truck almost ran me off the road. There were times when I got so caught up composing my poetry, that I would make supper late (like I am doing now writing this book). I also talked too much, and my English sometimes left much to be desired, like when I would say, "Outen the lights." Then there was that clothing bonfire! I was going through what I call my depression cycle, and clothing from nine people just got piled up higher and higher next to the washer on the basement floor, so by the time I finally got to wash them they were moldy!

I am a very gentle, non-violent person. To this very day I speak softly, and rarely raise my voice, even when I become angry and upset. However, I was getting really fed up, and started yelling back. Bill and I were shouting some pretty awful things to each other. I despised myself for swearing, and also taking God's name in vain; something I *hated* to hear other people do. But he would make me so angry sometimes! I didn't like the person I was becoming. In fact, the situation between us caused a rift between Mary Jane and me.

My mother was always trying to find ways to give us presents. She would go about the house with her walker, and pick up little things that were of the least importance: a half roll of toilet paper, an almost empty bottle of cologne, a little unwanted knickknack that was thrown in a junk box in the closet, my ripped, used underwear, and the like. Although my mother's apartment was connected to the house, she had her own outside entrance. Mary Jane could come up to visit her, even if we I wasn't home. My mother would proudly pull out all her *treasures*, giving them to Mary Jane. I could have cared less; in fact, I knew this made my mother happy. Mary Jane would always tell me what Mommy had given her and we would get a kick out of it. I told her jokingly she could keep my underwear since they were full of holes anyway! Once, Mary Jane and I had a really good laugh... she had given me a bottle of Emeraude for Christmas, and although it was almost empty, Mommy wrapped it up in toilet paper and presented it back to Mary Jane!

This was so amusing, I thought I'd share it with Bill. I should have known better. He became instantly upset, saying that he didn't want my mother rummaging through his things and he didn't want Mary Jane in the house when we weren't home. "God only knows what else your mother is *stealing* to give away!" he declared. On this one particular day, Bill and I were in Hamlin at the grocery store, and my sister's friend, Nancy Rivello, had driven Mary Jane up to see my mother. When we got home, Bill was furious, "How many times have I told you that I do not want *your* family in *my* house when we are not home!" he declared. Naturally, we got into one of our ever occurring arguments. Then he went stomping into the house. Of course he wouldn't speak up and say anything; I had to do the dirty work!

So to spite him, and trying to convey to Mary Jane that it was *Bill* who said it, I marched right into my mother's room and angrily shouted loud enough for Bill to hear… "Mary Jane! Bill does not want you in *his* house ever again, when he is not home. He is afraid you're *stealing* his precious stuff!" Well, poor Mary Jane left in tears! And my mother starting hitting me with her good arm, calling me a "selfish bitch!" Of course, Bill carried on about making him look like the bad guy, claiming he didn't tell me to throw her out.

My temper made me cut off my nose to spite my face. I didn't stop to think that Mary Jane might take my angry words to mean they were my *own* feelings!

It wasn't until many years later that Mary Jane confided in me that after all this time, she kept the hurt from that day locked in her heart. She couldn't believe her "Big Sissy," whom she adored and looked up to, didn't stick up for her. My actions made her feel that I didn't trust her. Although I did it to get back at Bill, my sharp words cut through Mary Jane's heart, all because of my big mouth! Another lesson learned, *almost* a little too late.

What really used to gall me was why I got all the blame for everything. When Bill and I were first married, I honestly did all that I could to make a happy family, and have a successful marriage. Especially after we both had already gone through a divorce. I wanted to live in peace. He was the one always yelling about this or that. Bill claimed that he had to be stern to "teach me right from wrong." And he yelled at me because he cared. More often than not, I felt like I was in the Army, and he was my commanding officer. The sad part was, since Bill was a good provider, and a faithful husband, he honestly believed that was all it took to be a good husband. Showing love, attention, forgiveness and respect for his wife had nothing to do with it. He truly felt that I was the one who was totally wrong. I think much of the problem was we were just two different people. Coming from a large Italian family, I thrived on hugs, kisses, noise and conversation. It didn't matter to me if the house wasn't always perfect, and everything was not all lined up, or if something got broken. It was only a material thing. A new one could be bought, or mended. However, a broken heart took a long time, and sometimes forever, to mend! Bill seemed to put too much value on material things, not that they were not important, especially if you worked hard for them. But others' feelings were far more important to me. Bill was a good man in many ways, but his stubbornness, temper, coldness and unforgiving nature were not what I needed to be a whole person.

Soon, I started to neglect my home, since I felt nothing I ever did pleased Bill anyway. I'd come home from an engagement, and instead of preparing dinner, I prepared for my next show. The house became dusty, chores were left undone, and I did the laundry only when desperately needed. Sad to say, my beautiful house, that I helped build with my own hands, the house with seven large rooms, a finished basement, and two grand fireplaces… which stood on almost two acres of beautifully landscaped grounds, was a place I associated with anger, sadness and threats. It all didn't mean anything to me anymore. I just figured, "What's the sense?"

The only person who seemed to care and understand was my mother. I would go into her room and tell her all about my day. How I made the children laugh, and the excitement of hearing people cheering me. Her face would light up, and she would say with a big grin, "See Lord, Jo Jo Famous!" I would think, "Yes I am famous alright, famous for having bad marriages!" My business phone was installed in her room, so I could spend time with her as I made my phone calls to book parties. I would keep my helium tanks and balloons in the corner of her room, and she loved it. Each morning I would bring her in toast and coffee, and then fill the balloons I needed for my parties. She would come sit by me, and hold out her good hand. As I filled a balloon I would hand it to her, until she held a colorful bouquet. I would tease her and tell her that she was going to float to the ceiling. How excited my mother would become when a new shipment of balloons came in. She would enjoy putting them away in their color coordinated boxes. This made her feel useful, needed and she shared a part in what I was doing.

Although she had a nurse come in to take care of her personal needs, and a housekeeper would come in a few days a week to tidy up her apartment, I felt guilty that I wasn't there to keep her company more often. All she needed and enjoyed was for me to bring us in a cup of tea, and she would tell me all about the soaps she watched that day. I am ashamed to say, in my state of mind at that time, I was even neglecting my mother, the only person in the house who gave me encouragement, and actually loved the work I was doing.

My marriage was on the rocks, and of course according to my husband, I was the culprit… the *only* one who ruined it. The sad part was that Bill really believed it, and convinced others it was so… even my children and friends. Of course my good friends, Helene and Elaine knew how things were, they would stick up for me.

I continued to throw myself into my career, taking each and every opportunity to work, be it paying, or volunteer. I worked diligently on skits for nursing homes, put together programs on reading, safety and energy conservation for schools and excelled in giving glory to God in my Christian Clown Ministry. Learning new songs and dances, I composed a show for every religious and national occasion and celebration. This caused me to become even more popular and successful. To everyone else, I was the happiest person on earth. People thought I had a wonderful life, with no problems or troubles. And to tell you the truth, when I put that costume on, all my worries, aches and pains did disappear! Jo Jo the Clown had no problems!

This photo was taken in the 3rd grade, at St. Mary's School, on Grace Street in Old Forge. See the long curls that were made by setting her hair in "Rags"!

Will the Real Joann Please Stand Up

A very strange phenomenon began to occur, I actually started to become two different people. There was the happy, joyful, beautiful laughing clown, and then there was this sad, depressed, ugly, stupid woman. I actually *hated* Joann, but deeply *loved* Jo Jo the Clown. As a guest speaker I would say, "I love being a clown; I could get away with anything! Why, I could go into the largest city in my costume, and go up to everyone I meet saying, 'Hi. How are you… God bless you!' and everyone would come back with a similar greeting, laughing, hugging and getting all happy. If I did that in my street clothes they'd put a net over me and take me away!"

I would find myself speaking about my alter ego, as if *she* were another person! Pathetically I would feed my face, and sit alone watching television programs I had been on and say, "Wow! Isn't *she* wonderful! Why can't I be more like *her*?" I actually wish I could have been *her* all the time. *She* was the one that could do everything right. *She* was the one called by God to make the world a better place. *She* was charming, bright and intelligent. While I was a total mess of a human being, who had no talents or self esteem and was a terrible mother, wife and daughter!

One Sunday I was visiting with my good friends Elaine and Al Ullner. I looked forward to visiting them each Sunday after Mass. Elaine always had a warm welcome, a cup of coffee and a shoulder to cry on, waiting for me. My children also enjoyed playing with their daughter, Laurie, and son, Paul. Al also had a special place in my heart. He was always making furniture, or building something. This brought memories of my father, giving me a good feeling all over.

So there I was sitting at their table, with my cup of coffee and my second piece of Elaine's delicious apple cake, going on and on about *her*. Elaine was looking at me sort of funny and finally said, "Her who? Jo, who are you talking about?" I exclaimed, "Jo Jo, who do you thing I'm talking about?"

Elaine said, "My God, I thought you were talking about someone from church, or something!" Jokingly she went on to say, "You know, Jo, you really need help!" I was beginning to wonder if maybe she was right. Was I really beginning to think Jo Jo was not really me, but someone else?

When I arrived back home again, my heart was breaking over all that was going on. I *should* be the happiest person alive, with all I had going for me. Would I ever find peace and contentment in this life? All I really ever wanted out of life was for someone to love, respect and accept me for who I was, not for what he thought I should be. Was this too much to ask... doesn't everyone want that? I didn't want my marriage to break up, yet it couldn't go on the way things were. I was feeling a terrible guilt, because here I was a devout Roman Catholic, and I was already heading for a second divorce. I had begged Bill to go for counseling, but of course he wouldn't, so I went alone. This made him feel even more animosity towards me. He said I was *airing my dirty laundry* to our priest. Maybe Bill was right... maybe I was a horrible person. Maybe this, maybe that, maybe this other thing ... I was so full of doubt, anger, fear and especially self pity that it was sickening. I was even upset with God. Why did He allow me to get so far in my career, a career that brought me and so many other people so much happiness, only to let it get in the way of my personal life? I begged my Lord to show me the way, before I lost my mind... forever, this time!

After much lamenting, sleepless nights and prayers, I came to a heartbreaking decision, after almost twenty years of a stormy marriage, I was leaving. I still cared about Bill, and I think he still loved me too. We had been through so much together: raising children, loss of income, illness, death of loved ones... and we made it through. All these things should have brought us closer; unfortunately we only grew further apart. I realized things were never going to change, and if they did, it would only be for the worse. I could no longer live like this. It was not fair to me, or to Bill. I took a good, long look at myself in the mirror and said, "Joann, or Jo Jo, whoever you are, take a stand... it's time to go!"

Chapter 23

The Photographer

I had hired a photographer named Dennis Jordan; he had taken photos and video for several of my promos. I had been employing him for a year or so, and we always had strictly a businesslike relationship. I was to be a guest on the *700 Club*, and he had come to the house to take photos in the yard, among the beautiful trees. For the program, they wanted me in costume, however, they wanted an eight-by-ten photo of my *real* self, to show on the air. My pictures should have been delivered several days before, so I called Mr. Jordan to inquire about them. To my surprise, he stated that they weren't ready yet. I could feel myself becoming upset, and trying to keep my cool I said, "What do you mean, they are not ready yet? I hired you several weeks ago, I need them *now*! I am leaving for Virginia Beach in two days! What's the problem?" Although I did not raise my voice, I couldn't help the sarcasm; by this time my nerves were frayed. Mr. Jordan apologized, explaining that his work was way behind, because he'd had surgery, and he was unable to get to the lab. However, he ordered all of them made up, and he just had to pick them up. Well naturally, he was behind on his work... I felt like a horse's behind! "Me and my big mouth again!" I scolded myself.

We made arrangements... since the lab was not too far from his home, he would get them that afternoon. I offered to pick them up at his apartment in Moscow, so he didn't have to drive all the way over to my house, especially in his condition. I scribbled down the directions, agreeing on a time to meet.

Driving to Moscow, as usual my mind was on my problems. How I wished I could get my life straightened out. I felt like a hypocrite; in a few days I would be traveling all the way to Virginia Beach to be a guest on a Christian television show. I would be telling the whole nation about my happy, wonderful Clown Ministry, when my real life was a wreck. My thoughts were distracted while I looked at the paper for the photographer's address. Finally, I found the place, and knocked on the door. There was no answer, so I knocked louder. I was about ready to leave, thinking he wasn't back from the lab yet, when I heard a weak voice, "Just hang on; I'll be right there." Opening the door, he was bent over, and holding his side. He was explaining that he had a hard time descending the stairs.

I was shocked! After seeing Mr. Jordan several times for our different photo engagements, I knew that he was a slim person. However, he looked so thin and gaunt, I actually thought he was at death's door! I was so surprised by his condition I just blurted out… "Oh my God! Mr. Jordan, what happened to you? You look absolutely awful!"

As he struggled back up the steps, he said, "I told you before, my name is Dennis; Mr. Jordan is my father."

Climbing the stairs close behind him, like an idiot I repeated, "Oh my God, Dennis, what happened to you? You look absolutely awful!"

He went on to explain that he was going through a rough time of it. He not only had surgery, but his wife left him. He was all alone with his cat, Tiffany. He said that he wasn't feeling too well, and his incision hurt like hell. In my concern, I started asking him all sorts of questions, which were none of my business. His family lived in New York, and he had only one friend, Dave Medici, that he could count on. I had shared with him that I went to nursing school, so with a helpless look upon his face, he said, "Would you take this the wrong way, if I showed you my incision? It's really hurting; I think something is wrong."

I told him to let me take a look. As he lifted his shirt, I gasped: "Oh my God ,Mr. Jordan, err I mean Dennis, you have an evisceration and it's infected!"

He said, "I have a what?"

I guess it was my professional nurse voice that caused him to quietly obey my orders. I went on explaining that his incision had opened up and his insides were hanging out, and had gotten infected. Getting a warm washcloth I gently patted the wound, and put on some antibiotic ointment on it. Then I insisted that he make an appointment with the doctor ASAP. I also asked him if he needed anything from the store. After some coaxing he said, "Well, if you're sure you don't mind, you could get me a pack of cigarettes and some cat food."

I declared, "I'm sorry, but you need much more than cat food and cigarettes, you need some decent food!" I ran across the street to the Turkey Hill Market to pick up a few things. When I returned, my photos were all laid out on the table. Dennis must have thought I was as conceited as the day was long. Picking up each photo, I couldn't believe that the photos were actually of me! They were beautiful! The only time I ever looked good in pictures was when I was in costume as Jo Jo. I always hated myself in photographs, however, these were different. I was leaning against the red maple tree in my front yard, wearing a teal green dress. The sun was highlighting my red hair in soft, shiny waves about my face and shoulders. I exclaimed, "Wow! I look *so* beautiful in these pictures! What kind of lens did you use? I never look good in pictures!"

Dennis said, "I didn't *do* anything; the camera only takes what I see. That's how *you* look."

Of course I didn't believe him, he had to *do* something to make *me* look like this! I was so thrilled, and said, "I love them! I don't know what photographic tricks you pulled, but I look beautiful! Thank you so much!"

Dennis wished me well on the *700 Club*, and said he'd tape the show for me. I happily took my photos, promising to check up on him when I returned in about a week. Driving home, I realized that instead of dwelling on my own heartaches, I was thinking about someone else for a change. Here was my own photographer going through all this, and I would have never known if it weren't for my pictures. I promised myself that I would keep in touch, and help him if I could. I wondered how many other people I knew who were suffering in some way or another. It made me realize that I should look beyond myself and see what was happening to others around me.

I kept my promise to Dennis. A week later, dressed in my costume, I kept repeatedly knocking at his apartment door. However, there was no answer. His red Cavalier was parked in the driveway; so I figured he had to be home. I began to get worried, thinking, "What if he fainted! What if he is too ill to answer! Oh no; what if he's...dead!" On the ground floor was Carmel Ardito's Dance Studio, so I entered her place to see if anyone could help me, but no one was there. So I took the privilege of using her phone, and called Dennis upstairs. I could hear his phone ringing through the walls, then I got his answering machine. I yelled into the receiver, "Dennis, are you there? Yoo hoo... Dennis, are you ok? Please tell me you're not dead!"

Rushing back outside, I noticed on old, wooden escape ladder; however it was too high for me to reach. So I climbed on his car roof, and jumped on to the ladder. It was real shaky as I climbed to reach his window. Well, all the cars passing by on Main Street below must have thought seeing a clown climbing the side of a building was a very amusing sight. Cars and trucks beeped their horns, and yelled out to me as they passed by. I noticed one lady hanging out her window, taking a picture! But I didn't care; I was a clown on a mission...

I must save my photographer's life! Clinging to dear life myself, I peeked into the window... imagining that I would see him sprawled out on the floor, like in the movies with the chalk line all around the body. I knocked on the window, yelling out his name. I jumped, almost off the ladder, when I heard a man's voice yelling up to me, "Hey, what in the hell are you doing up there? Do you want to kill yourself?" Now I was in trouble; it was Paul, the landlord!

Yelling down to him, over all the car horns, "I think there is something wrong with Dennis! I can't see or hear him; I hope he's not dead in the bedroom!"

Paul yelled back up to me, "He's not dead! His friend, Dave, took him to the doctor's! Now get down, you idiot, before you fall and find yourself dead!"

As he helped me down, I got the, *"Don't ever let me see you doing something like this again"* lecture. As usual, I felt silly and embarrassed, but at least this time I got a lot of attention from the public!

"Paul never yells and is really a nice guy," said Dennis, as we laughed over my escapade. But through the humor of the situation, Dennis was really touched that someone cared enough about him to go through such lengths. I also had the opportunity to meet his friend, Dave. He was a really great guy and nice to talk to. I shared with him what a good friend Dennis thought he was, and although I wasn't family, I appreciated what he had been doing to help Dennis. The three of us still remain very close friends today.

My sidekick, Rosie, also lived in Moscow, and several times we would stop and visit Dennis on our way home from a party. We would bring him Burger King and other goodies to make sure he was eating. Rosie said once we fatten him up a little, he'd be kind of cute. "Hey!" I said. "Maybe I could fix you guys up!" We laughed, and I said that I didn't think her husband would appreciate that.

Bill and I were finally speaking decent to each other, however it was all about our breakup. He acted really surprised when I said I thought that we should get a divorce, although he did agree that things could not go on the way they were.

I needed a good lawyer, so I was referred by a friend to Attorney Zacharellis. I was informed that he was a fair, just and kind lawyer. How nervous I was for our first appointment, but I soon relaxed after meeting this fine gentleman, knowing my friend was right. He was the kind of person that I felt comfortable putting my life in his hands.

Looking through the newspaper for a new place to live, I was starting to feel guilty. I didn't want to hurt Bill, and was hoping this was the right thing for both of us. Later that evening, I was visiting with my friend, Helene; I found out that

Bill and her husband Frank had already gone to talk to a lawyer over a month ago, to find out his rights in a divorce. I said to Helene, "And he accuses me of keeping secrets!" However, I was glad that I wasn't the only one that felt we needed to separate.

Dennis and I would talk frequently on the phone, and became good friends. He would share with me about his work, hopes and dreams. After a while, he felt comfortable enough to share some personal problems, including his failed marriage. I did the same. He was very surprised to hear I, too, was having marital problems, because just like everybody else, he thought Jo Jo the Clown had a perfect, happy life. He said, "It is really so hard to believe! When I came to your house to take pictures, I was sure you had it all: a beautiful home, a successful business and a loving family and husband... I would have never guessed!"

I found it so easy to talk with Dennis; he was concerned and a good listener. Soon, after a busy, hectic day, I found myself looking forward to venting with him on the phone. He would make me laugh and feel good about myself. One day we met for coffee, and I found myself feeling a twinge of jealousy, after the waitress flirted with him. "Be careful!" I scolded myself.

Moving out of my house in Mountain Crest was very painful... full of tears, regrets and fear of the unknown. At first I got a double wide mobile home, and rented a piece of land, on my dear friends, Millie and John Morgan's property, about a half mile away. I loved Millie, she was an older woman, who had three sons, John, Bob and Paul, but never had a daughter. She actually wanted to adopt me if anything happened to my own mother. I also loved her husband, Jack, fondly referring to refer to him as my daddy.

Millie and I were not only very close, she became one of my sidekicks... Aunt Millie. I became really close to Brother John, and he is still like one of my family. In fact, his wife, Sherry's mother, also became my number one sidekick... Bashful. She is with me today, almost twenty years later! Bob's wife, Rose also worked with us for a while. Why we were just a big family of clowns!

I lived there for a while, however, I soon became so confused, and filled with guilt and anxiety, depression set in so hard, I couldn't even go to work. For the first time in my career, I canceled parties due to illness, mental illness that is! Dennis would come and visit once in a while, so he knew the struggle I was going through. I cried to him about all my negative feelings, and he did and said what he could to try to help me. Believe it or not, after putting everybody through all this... I went back home again! Bill also wasn't feeling that well, so I figured we could help each other. We really tried to iron things out again, but needless to say, within a few months things were heading back to the same old thing, and I was looking for another place again.

Dennis and I continued to remain friends and would talk on the phone. Some days after work, Rosie and I would meet him for coffee. Sometimes after dropping Rosie off, I would meet him alone at the Acorn restaurant, on the way home. I felt he was my best friend, and could talk to him about anything. Soon, I began having feelings I had no right to feel. Although Bill and I were talking divorce, I was still married. Besides, even if I were single, he was my friend and photographer, nothing else. I wasn't even his type; he went for those tiny, little things. Besides, I knew he had been in serious relationships since he was only seventeen, and he was enjoying his new freedom, going out with Dave and his buddies whenever he liked.

The more we talked, the more we found we had in common. Dennis came from Brooklyn, New York, and I would tease him about his accent. He was also married twice before, and both were named... Joann! The only difference was, we all spelled our names differently. We both shared poor childhoods, our fathers were alcoholics, we also both attended Catholic school, and even came to find out we were actually taught by the same nun! I was made fun of because I was fat, he was laughed at for being too skinny. Dennis had the same birthday as my first husband, and my sister's twin sons, Joey and Jamie. We both enjoyed country music and scary movies. I found Dennis to be a kind, sensitive, warm and caring human being, who loved his friends and family, especially the apple of his eye, his daughter Mary Patricia... Trish, for short. And he also thought Jo Jo the Clown was the greatest!

The Race Car Driver

Dennis was telling me all about his great love for NASCAR. With great enthusiasm, he shared with me all about the races, and his favorite driver, Richard Petty. It filled me with joy to see a grown man as excited as a child, anticipating the upcoming race at Pocono Raceway, in Long Pond. I had never even heard of NASCAR before, and I certainly didn't know who any of the drivers were, however I enjoyed listening to him, and sharing in his passion for the sport. Then he said to me, "I would give anything if I could get to meet Richard Petty in person!"

So not knowing just how important this driver was, and how difficult it would be to walk right into the pits to see this man, I said, "I can get you to meet Richard Petty. I'll compose him a poem, and present him with a Balloon-a-gram. You accompany me as my photographer, and take pictures; it's as easy as that!"

Dennis looked at me jokingly, but with hope in his eyes and said, "Jo Jo the Clown, can I hire you, for a change… to do a balloon delivery for King Richard Petty?" I said of course I would. Dennis then stated, "That sure would be a dream come true, but no one can just walk into the track without buying a ticket, and even if you had a ticket, they won't just let you into the pits without a pass. And… even if you did manage to get into the track, you would *never* be able to even get near him!

I looked at him rather smugly and stated, "Blah, blah blah… is that so, Mr. Jordan? Don't you know that you are dealing with the *great* and *powerful* Jo Jo the Clown?" We both broke out in laughter.

With a glimmer of hope in his voice he said, "If you really think you can pull it off… you're hired!"

Dennis related all sorts of dates and figures about Richard Petty's wins, trophies, tracks and all sorts of trivia, while I jotted everything down. "Are you sure you can make up a poem out of all this information?" I told him not yet, because now he had to share what was in his heart. I needed to know what he would say to Mr. Petty, if he met him in person. After that, then I would be able to compose the poem.

The day of the Pocono Race finally arrived, and we drove up to the speedway. As we neared the track's entrance, Dennis worried that they might not let us in. "Just relax, and don't fear a thing!" I said with confidence.

I pulled up to the gate and was greeted with, "Hey! It's Jo Jo the Clown!" The gated opened immediately, and I was escorted right in.

A few people came over to me and I said, "I have a Balloon-a-Gram for Richard Petty!" A gentleman in an orange vest pointed and stated that he was out there, practicing on the track, but we could wait for him in the pits.

Dennis was elated and couldn't believe what was happening! He said in a silly, childlike voice, "I'm going to meet Richard Petty!" He then went on about all the drivers and their statistics.

I noticed a tall, thin man wearing a cowboy hat, walking across the lot, and from the photos Dennis showed me, I knew it was him. I floated up to Richard

Petty and announced, "Richard Petty, I have a very special message for you!" as I handed him the bouquet of balloons. Dennis was having a field day snapping pictures right and left. Richard Petty just stood there as I read him his poem. When it ended, he said in a strong southern drawl, "That was mighty nice of you... You touched my heart, darlin'!" I noticed that his eyes were actually misty. "I'm going to put this in my museum, back home," he stated softly.

Dennis was grinning from ear to ear, as he offered Richard his hand and said, "I'm the person responsible for this Balloon-a-Gram!" Mr. Petty gave Dennis a strong handshake and thanked him from the bottom of his heart. Dennis was like a schoolboy! He hugged and kissed me saying, "I'm never going to wash my hand again!" In his excitement he also stated, "Jo Jo the Clown, I *love* you; you made my dream come true!"

A man was waiving and calling me over... "Hey, you... clown, the NASCAR officials want to speak to you!"

I said, "Uh oh, I must be in trouble!" To my relief and Dennis's glory, they wanted me to come back the next day. NASCAR was sponsoring a special event from an organization called, Happiness is Camping, a camp for children who were suffering from terminal cancer. These children were being treated to a special autograph session with all the drivers, and they hoped I would volunteer some time to entertain them.

The very next day, I was hugging and kissing these beautiful, precious children... and those handsome NASCAR drivers! We were hanging out with such celebrities as Richard Petty, Ricky Rudd, Dale Earnhart, Dale Jarred, Darrel Waltrip and the whole gang! A few let their hair down and even got their faces painted along with the kids! (Too bad I didn't know and appreciate who they were at the time) Of course Dennis thought he died and went to heaven and was photographing all the Angels and Saints!

A year later, as Dennis sat in the grandstand at Pocono International Raceway, he noticed something on another fan's program. Dennis said, "Excuse me; do you mind if I see your program for just a second?" He couldn't believe his eyes; there was one of his very own photographs, printed right there for all the NASCAR world to see, of Jo Jo the Clown and Dale Jarred!

Chapter 24

Don't Toss Us Away

Sam La Sante was having a talent competition, at the Atlantis Casino in Atlantic City. It would be aired on *Spotlight Talent Showcase*. Everyone was so excited when actor Jack Palance agreed to be one of the judges for the event. Since I was *Spotlight's* "mascot," Sam not only asked me to be their guest entertainer, he asked me if I could accompany Mr. Palance into the auditorium.

I met Jack at the door and as he was being introduced, I slipped my arm through his and accompanied him down the aisle, escorting him to his judge's seat of honor. Everyone stood, clapped and cheered him *us*... oh, I mean *him* on, as we made our grand entrance. Of course, my photographer took some dynamite pictures. I mean this in an affectionate and respectful way, although Jack Palance always acted a little *different* than most people, he seemed to be so pleased to be seen with this clown... I think?

How many photos had Dennis taken for Jo Jo with... Bishop Timlin, Senator Mellow, State Representative Ed Stayback, Scranton and Carbondale's Mayors, Jim Connor, Jim Moran and Joe Vadella, Miss Judy from the children's television show, and other personalities from Channel 16, Channel 22, and Channel 28. The Red Barren's Grump, Tux, from the Penguins ice hockey team, Tug Ma Graw, the famous baseball player, Frankie Vallie, lead singer of the Four Seasons, Emmitt Kelly Jr. the famous hobo clown, and countless other celebrities, I truly don't know, but I can tell you, he surely earned his pay... I bet the film could stretch for miles and miles, if he laid it all out! Dennis was always right there for me when I needed a publicity photograph, or a friend. How many times did he video or photograph shows that I was volunteering at, and he would not accept any payment, not even for his expenses. He would say, "If you are volunteering your time and talent to this worthy cause, so can I."

Most of the time when we saw each other I was always dressed in my costume. I used to tease him that if I knocked at the door as the real me, he would probably think I was the Avon lady. On this particular day, I went to his apartment to pick us the photos and video of my family reunion. I was dressed up this time as a real person. When I was leaving, he walked me to the door and said, "You know, Jo Jo always gives me a hug goodbye; how about a hug from my friend, Joann?" We embraced for a moment, then all of a sudden I was kissing him passionately! I don't know what got into me! My heart was racing, and I think I heard bells. His scent, and just his closeness erupted feelings in me that I never knew I had. Dennis was surely taken by surprise, and said, "You really shouldn't be doing this... you're still a married woman!"

Embarrassed by my unplanned, wild show of affection, I said meekly, "I'm getting divorced."

He tenderly looked at me and softly said, "Until then, you are still another man's wife. My wife left me for another man, and I know how it feels. Besides, anything can happen; you are still living under the same roof. What if you change your minds and don't get a divorce... where does that leave me?" Totally humiliated and ashamed of my actions, I was more confused than ever. I didn't know whether to go home, or find a church and go straight to confession!

For days I moped around the house, finding if difficult to cope with my new feelings for Dennis. I had truly never even thought of him as anything more than a dear friend. I also appreciated his excellent gift as a photographer. I didn't have enough to handle in my life, why was *this* happening to me now? How I prayed for guidance and help, trying to rationalize what was happening to me. I would say to myself in the mirror, "Look! You are just infatuated with him... it will soon pass. Get over it... now!"

Although Dennis was seven years older than me, he was slim, handsome and so very young at heart that I actually felt older than him. He was part Italian, and Irish, with longish dark hair, bushy eyebrows, soft green eyes and an impish smile. He also had a dimple on his chin. Dennis always wore jeans, sneakers and NASCAR tee shirts, with several gold chains around his neck. (Bill always called him a Mr. T, wanna be) He had a rough, Brooklyn demeanor and sassy attitude that could easily fit in *Grease, Happy Days* or any gangster movie. However, his somewhat tough look surely didn't match his kind, caring heart. Although this was Dennis's normal dress, when he was working, he had a very different appearance in a suit, then he reminded me of Bogart in *Casablanca*! But no matter what he wore, he always looked fine to me.

Was it because he was the first man who actually cared about what I believed in, or was it because although he was a good conversationalist, he was even a better listener? He felt my dream of making this world a happier, better place through my clowning was beautiful, honorable and good. Not only did he accept me for who I was... he didn't think I needed to change anything about myself. In fact, every time I would talk about Jo Jo in the second person, he'd say, "Wait... you *are* Jo Jo! You are the same wonderful person, with or without makeup!" Even when I shared my feelings about being overweight, and homely looking, he'd stop me and say, "Jo, you are *not* fat! Just look at your tiny waist! You just have large bones, and muscles, especially in your legs, from all the dancing you do! And from a photographer's point of view, you have a very pretty face, with perfect features. Look at your large, green eyes, dainty nose and soft, full lips. And you have the perfect shaped face, that you can wear your hair up, over or anyway you like. How can you think Jo Jo is beautiful, and Joann is not? Jo Jo is just you... with a lot of makeup!" For some reason when he said those things, it made sense; he almost had me believing it was true. I surely didn't know what was happening to my heart, but I would never want to lose him as a friend.

The next time I saw Dennis I promised myself that I would never, ever mention my true feelings. I would simply act just as if that kiss had never happened. He offered me a glass of ice tea, and we talked about the usual, I suddenly burst into tears. "What's the matter? Did something bad happen?" he said.

Sobbing like a baby, I blurted out the words I wouldn't even say to myself, "I think I am falling in love with you!"

Poor Dennis, he didn't know what to do, or say, but I could tell by his reaction that he didn't feel the same way. He held me close to him and let me cry, as I made an idiot of myself, carrying on about my feelings for him. Finally, he said, "Jo, I love you too... like a best friend. I would never want to hurt you, but like I told you before, until you get that divorce, you are still a married woman. I will not be responsible for breaking up a marriage. Besides that, I just came from a broken marriage myself, and I am trying to deal with my own pain and rejection, so I don't want a serious relationship right now. Can you understand that I just want to be *me* for a little while?" Boy, did I feel like a big, fat, stupid fool! He went on to say, "Jo, I will always be here for you, and I will always be your friend, so let's just be happy with that for now, ok?"

What could I say... I came here and carried on like a star-struck school girl, making a complete jerk out of myself. I acknowledged that he was right, with my words, but my heart was in total disagreement. I left there wishing that Christopher Columbus was wrong, and I could drive off the end of the world!

I didn't even bother to go out the door for days. I just moped around in my old flannel nightgown, doing what I usually did when I was stressed out... eating everything in sight. My heart was so heavy, like I swallowed a bowling ball and it got stuck in my chest. "Some clown you are," I said out loud. "All you have ever done for most of your life was cry!" I went over my life... thinking of my childhood, first marriage and all the things that had happened until that present day. Do you know what truly bothered me more than anything? It was that I felt like a big hypocrite! I honestly believed in God, and I would go fluttering about in my costume telling everyone about love, forgiveness, joy and happiness, and I would actually feel happy, and believe it then. I was also a religious instructor, teaching little children about Jesus, and on Sundays I would lector at St. Thomas Moore Church, reading Sacred Scriptures. Out there, I was a good, holy person, who honestly believed in what she was doing and saying. However, at home I was this angry, depressed, hopeless woman, wondering if God had gone away on vacation. Now, look what I had gone and done... fallen in love with someone else, while I was still married. To make me feel even worse, Dennis didn't even feel the same way. In fact, I felt so humiliated that he had very nicely put me in my place. I thought how I had neglected my home and family for the past year. Was Bill right... was I totally wrong? I cried so hard and ate too much. Soon I was such a whining, pathetic, guilt-ridden mess that I was anticipating the door bell to ring, any minute, and a man with a microphone and a camera crew would be awarding me the Sinner of the Year Award! "You make me sick, Joann... with all of your self-pity, tears and... food! I wish I could run away and leave you here!" I said to my reflection in the living room mirror.

I was so despondent and heartbroken, that I taped a country video by Patty Loveless, called "Don't Toss Us Away." I listened to it over and over again. I surely didn't tell my mother what was happening, and Cathy and Danny didn't seem to notice anything was the matter. Probably because they were at the age where they were into their own thing, or maybe it was because they hardly saw me as myself and didn't even know their own mother without a pink wig! Surprisingly, someone did notice something was wrong... Bill. He actually wanted to know what was troubling me. At this point I really needed someone to talk to before I exploded, mentally and *physically*... as I put the chicken leg down. The last thing I wanted to do was hurt Bill, I am sure he was hurting enough, but I wanted to be honest with him. So I told him all about Dennis, and what happened. To his surprise he said, "You mean your photographer, that Mr. T Wanna Be? What in the world so you see in a skinny little runt like him?" I told him that I never meant for this to happen, baring my soul, I explained everything. How I thought I was in love with Dennis. How humiliated I felt by Dennis's response to my show of affection... you know the works. I explained how my heart was breaking, not merely over Dennis, but for all the pain and suffering I had endured all my life, and especially for all the pain and suffering I had inflicted on others. I couldn't take any more. I was sorry for everything and everybody!

Bill really shocked me! He acted very kind and interested, and most of all... understanding! This was a side of Bill I had never seen before. He said jokingly, "Well, now you can tell *me* everything. You don't have to be afraid to tell me anything; I will be your *girlfriend*." We talked for a long time; I couldn't believe how easy he was to talk to, and how well he took my news. Why didn't this happen years ago? But then isn't that the story of my life.

I still had some contact with Dennis, although not as often. We'd talk on the phone, and occasionally we'd meet for coffee, but it was always the same... I couldn't resist the temptation to express my feelings of love for him, and he'd back off saying, "I just want to be me for a while." I would think, "Why was I doing this to him... why was I doing this to myself? Did I have no shame?" I think all my carrying on was beginning to put a wedge between our friendship, because one day he announced that he needed a change, and was moving to Wilkes Barre, a city about twenty-five miles away. Although he said it had nothing to do with it, I knew he was just being kind. If I were *him*... I'd run a hell of a lot farther than Wilkes Barre!

Things must have really been bad for me... I couldn't *eat*! All I did was listen to that haunting song... "Don't Toss Us Away" over and over again.

Chapter 25

Carbondale

Although Bill and I were talking, and finally being civil to one another, our marriage was done with. We both contacted our attorneys. I agreed to accept $20,000 in the settlement and he did *not* have to pay alimony… giving Bill the house, the furniture (with the exception of my mother's hospital bed and the dining room which I was still making payments on), the acre lot in New Foundland, the boat, the truck, the tools, the riding lawn mower, the bank account, his pension, his Social Security… the whole enchilada. After I put a down payment on my house and paid my legal fees, I was left with nothing. However Bill kept insisting that I "raked him over the coals." It got back to me that he was telling others, "I took that girl from the slums of Old Forge; she didn't have a pot to piss in, or a window to throw it out of! I can't believe I had to give her *all* my money!" His remarks really hurt; I was being far more than fair. According to the laws in Pennsylvania, I was legally entitled to half of everything, and if I fought him in court I may have even received more than half. Although I didn't retaliate, my lawyer could have argued that with my mother's money we built on an efficiency apartment, only adding to the value of the property, which he was going to sell. Also, we could have indicated that my mother's monthly income went into the house. Since he never adopted the kids, I was receiving child assistance checks for them, which also went into paying the bills. My lawyer could have also brought to light that I helped build the house with my own hands, even before we were married, saving him thousands of dollars on an electrician, plasterer and painter. I also brought in an income, and he had five tax deductions because of me. And what about my services as a wife, lover, mother, housekeeper and cook, which I was very good at until the last year so. I was greatly urged to take it to court and fight for my rights, but I figured that there was no sense. I also knew that losing his material possessions meant so much to him and would only hurt him more, I was tired of causing others pain. So I let things stand as agreed, and didn't take him to court.

Of course, trusting Bill and being honest with him... he blamed Dennis for the breakup, which we both knew wasn't true. We had been having marital troubles long before Dennis ever stepped into the picture. And Bill also knew that Dennis did not want to have any kind of relationship with me other than friendship, because I was still married. The stories came back to me that all I used him for was to raise my kids, and after they were grown, I didn't need him to support them anymore so I left him for another man. I also heard what a slob I was and never cleaned, cooked or did the laundry because I was busy "ramming the damn roads all day." And of course how I "raked him over the coals." The awful, unkind things Bill was saying about me "raked my heart over the coals!" However, I didn't even say anything to him, I figured if this made him feel better about the situation, more power to him.

The divorce proceedings were approaching, and I was thankful Bill allowed me to stay in the house until I found somewhere to live. However, he kept urging me to get out soon, so he could fix the place up to sell.

My realtor had shown me several houses, but for some reason, I wanted to look for houses in a little city called Carbondale, which was nestled in the mountains. I had been to Carbondale on several occasions, to entertain at birthday parties, and to conduct programs for Sister Eleanor, at St. Rose Church, and also at Our Lady of Mt. Carmel, for Deacon Carm. I especially fell in love with the quaint little place after performing for some new friends, Louis and Claire Gentile. Ann had told them all about my Christian Clown Ministry, and they were having the Rosary and May crowning of the Blessed Mother. Their yard was beautiful, and all set up with chairs, decorations, food and a statue of our Blessed Lady. After the rosary, Claire announced to the crowd that she had a surprise. And I made my grand entrance. How I loved to perform songs about Mary and Jesus in sign language. We all sang, joked and had a fantastic time together. We instantly became good friends.

The realtor showed me books of houses to look at; after turning the pages I declared, "This is it! This is the house I want to buy!"

She laughed and stated, "You have to see the *whole* house, not just a photo! Let's make an appointment!"

Dennis felt that he had made a big mistake moving to Wilkes Barre. With all the traffic, noise and crime in the city, it reminded him too much of Brooklyn. He longed for the peace of the country again, so when I moved out of the double wide on Millie's property, he moved in. Giving him a call, I said, "I'm going to look at a house in Carbondale. Would you be able to come with us? I'd like an opinion of an old friend."

As we pulled up in the driveway of the house located at 18 Chestnut Street, I exclaimed, "Yes! This is it! I *told* you this is the house I want!" Everyone told me to clam down. I might not even like the inside. As we neared the front door, I just knew there would be an open staircase. Oh, how I loved open staircases! We rang the bell, and Dorothy, the owner, answered. I strained to look past her, and yes… there it was, my beautiful staircase! The two-story house had eight rooms and two full baths. The marvelous staircase was made of mahogany, and curved gracefully up the steps and around the top of the hallway. There was so much space in the bright upstairs hallway, that it could be used for a little room all by itself, just off the master bedroom. I could imagine a dressing table next to the window, a special place to apply my makeup for work. As we walked around the rooms, my mind was filled with ideas, and visions of loveliness.

Afterward, sitting in the car, the realtor said, "Well it is old, and needs a little repair and paint, but it has a strong foundation, and it sure has potential." I was barely listening to her. I didn't see cracks in the wall, or the totally yellow kitchen, or the brown paneling with the big, gaudy orange flowers… all I saw was the most wonderful, beautiful house in all the land. My mind was already wall papering, hanging drapes and most importantly, living in peace, quiet and happiness.

As we drove away, I looked at the grand, old house and whispered, "I love you!" I could almost swear I heard it whisper back: "I love you too… hurry home!"

The Wrong Bank

I put a bid on the house and prayed. They came back with a counter offer. And I made another bid… they accepted! Now, the only problem was to get a mortgage. All along I had been working with a mortgage broker, and I was sure having an awful time. No bank wanted to give me a loan. It wasn't because I had bad credit… I had no credit! All the credit cards were in Bill's name. I was given different excuses… one bank turned me down because I was self employed, and my income was uncertain. Another said, since I had my first mortgage with a husband, they couldn't be certain I would pay it on my own, and so forth and so on... one rejection after another. I said more prayers than ever, and I didn't give up, because I just knew in my heart that house on Chestnut Street was mine! How many times did I drive over to Carbondale and sit across the street from the house, and just talk with God: "Please, dear Lord, find a way for me; I love this house!" Then I'd look at the lovely, gray home with white shutters and say: "I love you, house; find a way that we can be together." Why, I could almost swear the house smiled at me!

Each night I would light candles and pray to Jesus, picturing myself painting and wallpapering. I would be arranging furniture, and placing family portraits about. Or else I would see myself outside in the garden, planting colorful flowers and filling bird feeders. I could almost hear the wind chimes I had strung, tinkling merrily as I watered the shrubs in the warm sunshine.

The homestead was situated on the corner of Cemetery and Chestnut Streets. Across Cemetery Street stood huge, beautiful trees, and woods cascading with greenery over the embankment, until it reached the Lackawanna River. The river sounded so soothing, as the waters gently flowed by; it was like a sanctuary! I believed that I wanted that house more than I have ever wanted anything in my whole life. Usually, I do not put so much importance on material things, however, this house represented far more than a building to me. It meant freedom, peace and contentment.

Answering the phone, I heard, "Joann, I'm so sorry, that out of state bank rejected your application for the mortgage. But don't give up; we'll try somewhere else." I wanted to cry, but I said, "No! We won't give up! All things are possible with God!" When I told Bill the news, he said that if I couldn't get a mortgage, rent someplace; he needed me out of the house so he could have some work done.

The following Sunday I was at a birthday party in Carbondale. While there, I met an old friend, Tom Zaccone. Several times I had entertained at a birthday party for his beautiful daughter, Samantha. "How are things going?" Tom asked. I felt comfortable enough around him to explain my dilemma, and he told me that he would try and help me if he could. As it turned out, he was a good friend of the loan officer at the bank, he said that he would speak to him and give me a call. Sure enough, Tom was true to his word. He called, explaining to me that I had a two o'clock appointment with his friend at the bank. Tom had explained my situation to him, and he was expecting me. All I needed to do was bring him my paperwork. I gave Tom the phone number of my mortgage broker, so he could phone her with the correct papers I needed. He wished me luck and I hung up in a mad dash to get dressed and ready to go.

It was almost one p.m. when I pulled up to collect my papers at the mortgage brokers. Debbie was all excited for me. "These are all the papers you need. Now, hurry to the bank, and good luck!" I started to drive away, then suddenly I stepped on the brake, and yelled out to Debbie, "Hey, which bank am I supposed to go to?"

She called out, "The Carbondale bank."

I yelled back, "I know I have to go to the Carbondale bank, but what is the name of the bank?" I could see she was thinking, but had a puzzled look on her face, as she said, mostly to herself, "What bank did he say… humm?" Then turning to me she stated confidently, "You have to go to the Community Bank and Trust!"

Speeding over Salem Mountain, I prayed to Jesus, Mary, Joseph and every Saint in heaven! Finally arriving in Carbondale, I realized I had no idea where the bank was located. I stopped someone on the street and asked directions.

Entering the bank, with not a moment to spare, I said to the woman behind the desk, "I'm Joann Goerlitz, and I'm here to see the loan officer."

The pleasant woman said, "That would be Bill Boyle, please take a seat."

I was so nervous, begging God to help me. I was shaking my leg so hard as I practiced what to say, when I noticed the plant on the table was shaking along with me. The vibration of my leg moved the plant right to the edge and was ready to fall off! Soon, a young gentleman came out and said, "Joann? Please come in." Sitting down in the leather chair with such force, it almost sounded like I was expelling a ton of gas, as I plopped all my papers in front of him and began rattling on and on "Oh thank you for seeing me on such short notice! Oh please, *please* help me; I'll swear on a stack of Bibles that I *will* pay you back! I really *need* this mortgage; you are my last chance; *nobody* else will give me a mortgage; Oh *please* you've got to help me!"

Mr. Boyle looked rather stunned by my appeal, as he flipped through the pages. He stated that everything seemed in order, I would have to answer a few more questions, and then he would have to take it before the board. All of a sudden, I could feel my eyes filling up, and I thought, "Oh no, please… not the tears!" Well the floodgates opened and I started crying and babbling on and on about how many times I've been rejected, and if the bank would only give me a chance, I would never let them down and… sob, sob, boo hoo, boo hoo! To make matters even worse, I got the hiccups. Poor Mr. Boyle was visibly taken aback by all this, and didn't know what to do. Finally, he handed me a box of tissues and called out to the girl in front to bring me a glass of water. Talk about feeling like an idiot! I thought, "Thank God this man is a friend of Tom Zaccone's. Could you well imagine if I just walked in off the street; he would think I was a total nutcase!"

After a few minutes, I calmed down enough to finish the interview, despite a few hiccups between the questions. When we came to the part about my income, he became excited when he realized that I was Jo Jo the Clown. He said, "I know *you*! You entertained at my son's first birthday! We *love* you; you are the greatest!" I suddenly felt the stress leave, as we shared some happy moments over his child's birthday party. Mr. Boyle stated that I had an excellent reputation, and he was in my corner. He promised to do all he could at the board meeting, which was to be held the following Thursday. As he accompanied me out of his office he said to a beautiful woman sitting at a desk, "Winnie, do you know who this is? It's Jo Jo the Clown!" Winnie came up to me with a gracious smile and said, "Hang in there; things have a way of working out!"

I left the bank feeling much lighter and happier than I had in months... maybe even years! The bank was located on Fallbrook Street, just a few blocks from Claire Gentile's house. So I decided to stop in for a visit. She was thrilled to see me. I explained all the commotion that went on over at the bank. She said, "I know someone who is on the board at the Community Bank, and so do you! I'll give him a call right now!" She immediately got on the phone... "Frank, this is Claire; guess who is standing here, next to me? It's Jo Jo! She is trying to get a mortgage at the bank." She went on to explain the situation and then, handing me the phone she stated, "Here, he wants to speak to you." The voice on the other end said, "Is this our Jo Jo that I'm talking to? Don't you worry, honey, I'll tell them all about you!" As it turned out, Frank was one of the regular people who attended Claire's Rosaries, and he greatly admired my work.

The next day was Saturday, and after my parties I drove up to visit *my* house. As I sat across the street doing my usual praying and visualization, an older gentleman came up to my van and asked if I were looking for someone. He had noticed me parked in front of his house on several occasions. I explained who I was, and why I was there. He said, "Well I know *who* you are, your name is written all over you vehicle, however now I know *why* you are here." He told me his name was Harry Gursky, and he and his wife Helene and their daughter, Diane, lived in the house across from *mine*. Harry shared with me that next door to *my* house, lived Joe and Sonja Baldwin, and next to them, was Louie and Barbara Sirianni. He expressed that they were all good neighbors, and most of them had lived in this town since childhood. As he left, Harry said, "Good luck! We'll keep you in our prayers!" I thought, "What a nice man! And what wonderful neighbors, *I have*!" From there I went downtown to McDonnell's Restaurant, on Main Street, for some dinner. Everyone made such a fuss, seeing a clown come in to eat, and I joked around with the people sitting at the tables.

The owner, Jim McDonnell, came up to me later on and said, "Boy, Jo Jo, you really liven up the place! Why can't we have someone like you living in Carbondale?" I stated that maybe his wish would come true, then went on to explain all about *my* house on Chestnut Street, and how I was trying to get a mortgage. Mr. McDonnell broke out in a big grin and said, "Well, what do you know about that! I'm on the board at the Community Bank and Trust, and I believe this town needs a clown!"

Monday morning I received a call from Tom Zaccone. "Jo Jo, What happened at the bank?" he said. I began laughing and telling him all about my crying jag and everything that went on. "Tom, all I could say is, thank God he was your friend, or he would have thrown me out on my butt!"

There was a pause on the other end, and then he said, "Oh, so you *did* go to the bank, after all?"

I proclaimed, "Yes, I did make it to the bank!" and went on to tell him all the other news. "Since I was on Fallbrook Street, I ran up to see Claire Gentile, and she knew Frank and..."

Tom interrupted me in mid sentence, "Hold on... wait a minute! You went to the bank on Fallbrook Street? What bank did you go to?"

I answered, "To the Community Bank and Trust!"

I could hear Tom break out in laughter, and he said, "To the Community Bank and Trust? Why did you go *there*?"

I came back with, "What do you mean...why did I go there; you sent me there!"

Tom continued, "Jo Jo, I didn't send you there... you went to the *wrong* bank!"

My blood pressure shot up and I began laughing and crying all at once! "You've got to be kidding!" I said, "You mean I went to the *wrong* bank? The Community Bank and Trust is the *wrong* bank? You mean to tell me that Bill Boyle is *not* your friend, and I was a stranger who just walked in off the street into the *wrong* bank?"

He repeated, "Yes, I'm afraid that's what you did, alright; you went to the *wrong* bank!"

I repeated in disbelief, "You mean I cried, hiccupped and pleaded at the *wrong* bank?"

Tom finally said, "Jo Jo, it doesn't matter how many times you say it, when it all boils down... you went to the *wrong* bank!" Oh my God, talk about feeling like a clown!

The very next phone call I made was to Debbie, asking her why did she send me to the Community Bank and Trust? I told her that it was the *wrong* bank! Debbie said, "I could have sworn that Tom told me to send you there! You mean it was the *wrong* bank? My God, I am so sorry! I honestly don't know why I sent you to the Community Band and Trust... I can't believe that I sent you to...(and we both chimed in)... the *wrong* bank!"

I said, "I might still have a chance at the *wrong* bank, I know of at least three people who want to give me the mortgage."

I stared at the phone on Thursday, hoping that it would ring, then again hoping that it wouldn't. I yelled at the phone: "Come on already; the suspense is killing me! Either you gave me the damn loan, or you didn't... just ring already!"

My mother looked at me and said, "Cracky Joann, honest!" I waited all morning, then all afternoon, but no phone call from the bank. Every time the phone did ring, I was disappointed that it was just a call for me to entertain at a party.

It was almost four p.m., when the call came in. Picking up the phone, I said, "Hello?" It was Bill Boyle. My heart was banging hard against my chest, and I could feel weakness come over me, as Bill said, "Well we had the meeting, and you know you weren't really that qualified for that amount of a loan. There were many obstacles in the way, and it was a difficult decision for the board to make. Despite everything we all voted the same way. You were approved for the loan... Congratulations! You got your house!"

I realized I was holding my breath the whole time he was speaking. Letting out a huge sigh of relief, I finally spoke, thanking him over and over again. The tears began flowing, the hiccups started, I dropped the phone on my big toe and knocked my mother's ashtray all over her bed... but who cares! "Thank you, Jesus! Thank you, Mary! Thank you, Angels and Saints... I got my house! You didn't send me to the *wrong* bank after all!"

Chapter 26

A New Beginning

My heart was racing, and every fiber in my being was fired up, as we sat around a large, long table of the boardroom of the Community Bank and Trust. My attorney, Mr. Zacharellis, sat across from me; he was pulling papers out of his briefcase. Mr. Boyle, and several other bank members, along with the owners of the house on 18 Chestnut Street, were also present. I remember shaking my right leg so rapidly, that the table actually started to vibrate. I looked up, and to my embarrassment, everyone stopped talking among themselves and stared at me with an expression as if to say, "Stop that... right now!"

Never in my entire life did I have to write my signature on so many papers at one time! I didn't even realize I was holding my breath (something I do at lot when I'm stressed) until I let out a huge gasp. Everyone seemed to jump, as they glared at me. I was terrified that *something* would go wrong. I pushed down the negative feelings that shouted inside me, "Something will happen and go wrong... you never do anything right! At the last minute the bank would find some error and you won't get your house! The people will decide that they don't want to sell...!" However, thankfully, no spoke those dreadful words. All seemed to go well!

Finally, after what seemed like a million papers, Mr. Boyle shook my hand, and held up a little ring with three golden keys dangling from it, saying: "Congratulations! You are now a homeowner, and a fine member of our bank and community!"

I stood outside, looking up at the large house on Chestnut Street, and said out loud: "I *love* you, house! You belong to me, and I belong to you!" My hand was shaking so hard that I dropped the keys twice before I could even get them into the door. It swung open, and I stood at the threshold, feeling like a new bide. The beautiful, grand staircase welcomed me, and the large, empty rooms called out to me. I literally ran through the house crying... yes, I was crying again, however this time they were tears of joy. I passionately sang out, "This is the day that the Lord has made; let us be rejoice and be glad in it! Thank you lord, I love you… and I LOVE YOU HOUSE!" I swear to you, that I kissed every single wall, doorway, step and even the floors in the entire house… singing and shouting, "Praise the Lord! I love you, house!" I honestly didn't care if the whole neighborhood heard me and worried that a crazy lunatic had moved next to them! This was *my* house and I could sing, dance and shout all I wanted, and I was mighty *proud* of my behavior, too!

A feeling of peace and tranquility overcame me, and I lay down on the soft, taupe carpeting, right there in the middle of the dining room and just closed my eyes, giving thanks and praise to God. "Lord, you found a way where there was no way! All things *are* possible with you!" I felt so comforted, as if the house embraced me, cradling me in her loving arms, like a new mother. With such peace, happiness and contentment, I actually fell fast asleep… right there on the floor, in the middle of *my* beautiful, old house!

As the days and weeks passed, life was becoming good, and I could feel the pain and stress slipping away. Almost immediately, I started my redecorating projects. Just as I had envisioned, I fixed, painted and wallpapered, making the inside even more beautiful, cozy and personal. The small corner lot soon became a yard filled with flowers and wind chimes, beckoning birds and butterflies. The statue of Our Blessed Mother, that my son Dominic bought me for my birthday, was set in a place of honor, in the front corner. I planted pink azaleas and rose bushes around her. I placed a statue of The Sacred Heart of Jesus, in the back corner, and surrounded it by assorted plants and flowers. Of course, I also planted grapevines, and underneath, in a special area is a statue of St. Francis of Assisi. (I make homemade grape jelly every year, and share it with the neighbors.) We had two decks built and I planted a fruit tree, which rewards me with plentiful, juicy peaches. To remind me of my grandmother's yard, I planted a fragrant lilac tree. The whole yard is surrounded by lovely green hedges. One day I heard a happy, soothing sound, and I realized it was coming from me; I was singing!

I wanted to make it really nice for my mother. The room next to the upstairs bathroom was hers, and I fixed up the adjoining bedroom into a living room. I also had a special shower installed in the bathroom. I know how much she loved her efficiency apartment in Lake Ariel, and I was trying to recreate it for her. One day I heard a happy, soothing sound, and I realized it was coming from my mother; she was singing!

Danny claimed the room at the top of the stairs (it is now my office where

I write this book) and of course, I took the large master bedroom in front. As I planned, when I first looked at the house, I placed a lovely, antique dressing table, that was given to me as a gift by Dennis's cousin, Vito Cutrone, in the large hall, next to the window. A rocking chair was placed in the corner, and a hall table and mirror was set at the head of the stairs making it a bright, perfect dressing room. Each day, as I carefully apply my moon and star, becoming Jo Jo, I enjoy the beautiful mahogany staircase that gracefully curves around, making my special area warm and cozy.

Dominic was still in the Navy at the time. He was stationed on the *USS Sampson*, in the Persian Gulf, fighting in Desert Storm. One of the happiest days, as you can well imagine, was when he returned home from the war unharmed! I had been volunteering at schools, talking to children about the fears of war. One pre-school, ABC Academy, located in Old Forge, had been sending Dominic letters and cards. WYOU-TV did a special on *Local Patriots,* and had named Jo Jo as one, for the work I was doing. When he returned home, the television station did a follow-up story showing Dominic with the children. Of all the many dozens of tapes I have about me and my work, this is absolutely, positively my very favorite!

Since the house was so large, Dennis moved in with us. He had the room off the dining room. At that time we used it as a bedroom, later on, we took out the window and put in French doors, which open onto the two large, split level decks we had built.

Dennis and I become inseparable. He helped me in my business, becoming my manager. Not only did he build my confidence up, he actually became an assistant when Rosie, Rainbow, Bashful or Patches were unable to work.

I opened up Jo Jo's Party Palace, on Main Street. Dennis worked very hard, along with Tom and Damien Hodgens, turning it into a true palace, complete with a knight in shining armor, cartoon tapestries, ballroom lights and a golden throne, where the birthday child would be crowned the Birthday King, or Queen of the Palace! There was a hidden bubble machine hidden in the ceiling, and at that perfect moment, the chimes sounded and the horns blew, Sir Kevin would appear, carrying a purple pillow with a gem encrusted crown on top. Jo Jo would place the crown on the birthday child's head, adding to all the music and excitement, an array of sparkling bubbles floated from the heavens, as the guests cheered and applauded.

My landlord, Ronald Konosky, was the best! He operated an antique store with his son, Kevin, right down the street. He was like family, allowing me to do anything I wanted to dress up the place. I loved his wife, Maria, and their beautiful, blonde daughter, Laura, who of course I celebrated birthdays with.

The building was large, and located on the corner of Main and Salem. The Party Palace was located on the lower level, which was great because it was huge! I was able to make three rooms and a kitchen area. It also added to the mystique and intrigue, as the children descended the stairs, which were covered in colorful lights and helium balloons. They would be welcomed by the delicious aroma of freshly popped popcorn. I would make my grand entrance, after my number one kitchen helper, Kim, served the pizza and goodies, singing my own (personalized for each child) song: "Welcome to Jo Jo's Party Palace!"

After the Crowning Ceremony the show would begin, the guests would share in the fun and entertainment and face painting by Jo Jo and her Palace Sidekicks: Chi Chi, Bows, Rosee, David, Happy, Dancer or Patches! Then they would be treated to a magical performance by the fantastic... Derius the Magician! (Derius—Joseph Vargo—had a brilliant mind; he set up many special surprises and features, including a wonderful sound and lighting system.) Afterwards, we would have another ceremony to present my own special "homemade" birthday cake!

I always strived to make each child's birthday celebration a wonderful, happy and positive experience, which would hold loving memories hopefully, lasting lifetime.

The Grandest Opening

Subway sandwich shop had moved in upstairs to the left, and to the right was a dress boutique, owned by Cindy Wilce. We all became like one great big happy family. We shared in the Grand Opening, and believe me it was the Grand!

We engaged two DJ's, and the popular radio station Magic 93, broadcasted live. Besides all my own sidekicks, many local entertainers came, not only to wish me luck, but to also add their talents to the day's entertainment... Sam Lasante from *Spotlight Talent Showcase*, Timbo the Clown, Cosmic Louie, my beautiful and talented friend, Gail Barbrie, with the young ladies from her modeling agency... why we even had a visit from that Purple Dinosaur, Santa

Claus and the Easter Bunny!

The ribbon cutting was presided over by Mayor John Moran, city council members Mary lil Hazelett and Francis Lagana, along with my dear friend, State Representative Edward Stayback, among others.

We held contests and gave out prizes. Our friend John Morgan must have grilled *millions* of hot dogs, which were freely given out along with candy, popcorn and balloons!

The cast from the play *Godspell* honored me by attending (in full costume) my opening, after they heard my story of becoming a clown, and how the play affected my life! We all danced outside, and I was thrilled to join them in singing "Day by Day" from the play! The highlight of the day for me was when our friend, and pastor from St. Rose Church, Monsignor Feldcamp, came and gave the blessing.

Wow! I can safely say that most of the town of Carbondale was there! The police had to actually close off one lane on Main Street!

Of course, Dennis took all the publicity photos. Through it all, my friendship and working relationship with Dennis brought us so much closer. We had a chance to learn everything about each other, both positive and negative. Thankfully for us, we admired and respected all the good things about each other so much, that we didn't even recognize the bad. Since he lived in our house, my family and friends had a chance to get to know him. He tried to be a friend to my children, helping and advising them whenever he could. I was able to go off to work knowing Dennis was in the house with my mother. How she used to tease him about being "skinny," and beg him for "two mokes!" Dennis enjoyed having her around, especially when everyone else was gone.

I couldn't believe how my life turned around! I loved working with the children. Be it at the Party Palace, or a birthday party in their homes. I wanted each child to feel *loved* and *important*. When I used to put on that costume and go out among the people, I always felt so *loved* and *important* myself. Now, I noticed something changed… when I'd come home, away from all the limelight, and took off costume, I *still* felt loved and important!

Chapter 27

The Joining of Two Hearts

By this time, I am sure Dennis was just as much in love with me, as I was with him. And although we had grown close, he really didn't like to "be put in a box," as he would call it. So I never pushed him to say or do anything that would put pressure him. I was finally becoming very happy with my life, and content with the relationship we had. We were talking, and all of a sudden he became very emotional. Dennis held up my hand and told me that his heart was in it. He shared that he not only loved me, he was *in* love with me, and he also *liked* me very much! "Jo, you can put me in a box and put the lid on it, because I never want to leave!"

The next day I was sitting on the sofa reading, when he came in the door calling out, "Lucy, I'm home! (He had long ago started calling me Lucy because of all the silly mishaps I have, and all my accidental stunts I did.)

I yelled back, "Ricky, I'm in here!" He entered the living room, got down on his knee, pulled out a box containing a diamond ring, and asked me to marry him! Of course I accepted, and we hugged, kissed, cried… and all that other mushy, good stuff!

His dream was always to open a photography studio. Since he was always there for me, I wanted to do something special for him. We turned the back room of the Party Palace into a photo studio. Now, he could not only help me with my business, I could assist him when he was taking pictures. We thought long and hard to pick out the perfect name for it, finally it came to us… We would take the *Jo* from Joann, and the *Den* from Dennis and add an R in the middle, thus christening our new studio… JorDen Photography!

If I was named Mary, Sally, Zelda, Hortense, Alice, or any other name… likewise, if his name was George, Stanley, John, Tom, Oscar, or any other name it wouldn't say JorDen. How ironic is that, since both our last names would soon be… Jordan!

The wedding day was approaching, and Dennis and I made fantastic plans.

We were to be married in Saint Rose Church, by Monsignor Feldcamp. I had purchased a gorgeous, pale pink, lace and satin wedding gown. It featured a fitted waist and full skirt and a long train. The people at the Bride and Boutique, in Mount Cobb, where I bought the gown, made a beautiful long, matching veil.

Everyone was going to be in the wedding! Mary Jane was my matron of honor, my daughters Mary Ann (she would carry my one-month-old granddaughter, Samantha in her arms), and Catherine, along with Dennis's daughter, Trish (who was pregnant with our grandson, Johnny), and my godchild Jackie, were my bridesmaids. Our grandchildren Paula and Tammy were the flower girls. My son-in-law, John, was an usher, and Dennis's son-in-law, Anthony, was his best man. And my sons Dominic and Danny would walk me down the aisle. Several friends, including John Morgan and Joe Vadella, (soon to be Mayor of Carbondale), were ushers and drivers. Dominic's wife, Tammy, and Dennis's sisters, Maureen and Linda, would carry up the gifts at Mass. His niece Jessica, and my dear friend Ann Murnock, were to do the readings. (I thought there would be more people walking up the aisle than there was sitting in the pews!) Everyone was so excited!

I made all the favors myself, for weeks and weeks and *weeks*... I made little clowns with glittery, lace collars. With all the people we wanted to invite we needed to have two receptions! The first would be at my Party Palace, where we planned on decorating it with pink bows, flowers and helium balloons, with our names and wedding date printed on them. I looked forward to making my own three-layered wedding cake, complete with white pedestals and pink flowers. At this reception we invited everyone who would attend the church service, and distant business acquaintances and friends. It would be beautiful, intimate and fun.

The second reception would be held in the evening, at a very elegant place called Fiorellis. It was located in Peckville, a town not too far away from Carbondale. The Fiorelli family are also very good friends of mine. How many special events and parties I had celebrated and entertained at in their beautiful reception center, I couldn't count. Although they were
catering my wedding, and promised to give me a reception that was fit for a king and queen, they were also my invited guests!

The music would be provided by our dear friend, Jeremy Pribulla (he has since been called home to heaven), his talent and great personality were sure to make the celebration lively and fun.

Everyone was excited and looking forward to the big day. I felt just like a little girl looking forward to Christmas. My wedding party chose navy blue, velvet dresses, which would compliment the pink flower girls' dresses and my wedding gown. It was a wonderful mix of excitement and stress, scrambling to go for fittings, chose hair styles and find satin shoes that *fit*!

Dennis and I grew even closer, if that's possible. He loved me just the way I was, and never tried to change me, as others had tried to do. Dennis thought everything I did was wonderful, from my work as Jo Jo to my decorating skills. Of course, I thought he was pretty perfect, too! In my entire life, no one had ever given me so much affection, understanding, encouragement and love... everything that I always *longed* for!

Dennis and the guys stayed at Maryann's house the night before the wedding, and the girls stayed with me. Their gowns were not even finished yet! So to the rescue came Ann Murnock, staying with us all night (free of charge of course) doing the alterations! How many times through the years had I told her that she was so good and kind, that when she dies and goes to heaven, her crown will be so big that a thousand angels will be needed just to hold it up!

Finally, November 25, 1995 arrived, and what a fantastic confusion there was! You can well imagine the scene with nine females, including a one-month-old baby, all trying to get ready at the same time! Everyone was scrambling for their showers and... dresses, strapless bras, slips, pantyhose, shoes and diapers were all over the place!

Mary Jane and I were alone in my bedroom, for a little solace amidst all the commotion. She had tears in her eyes as she lovingly looked at me and said, "Big Sissy, I never saw you so happy and radiant in all your life. You and Dennis are soul mates, and were meant for each other." As she lovingly kissed me she whispered, "Out of all the husbands you ever had... this one is the best!" We both burst out in laughter.

I was extremely proud of my *size ten* wedding dress. As my official matron of honor, Mary Jane helped me dress. Placing it over my head, I stood before the mirror as she fluffed and fixed in into place, then she zipped it up... well she *tried* to zip it up! "Oh my God, Jo," Mary Jane frantically stated, "what happened? I can't get the zipper up! It zipped up at your last fitting three days ago! What in the world have you been eating?" As usual, I was already running late, so in a panic she called in the troops, and as I sucked in my stomach and held my breath, all the bridesmaids did everything they could to hold the back of the gown together, until she finally managed to zip it up! We all got a laughing fit, imagining as I was walking down the aisle, the seams popping open and my two *girls* falling out!

Now, most brides are fashionably late by a few minutes, however, I was almost a half hour late, by the time we arrived at Saint Rose Church, and I only live about three minutes away! I remember worrying that no one would show up at the church... so I peeked in the door, and to my joy, the church was full of people, even townspeople who weren't invited came to see Jo Jo the Clown's wedding!

The music began, and my Folk Group director, Mary Ann Demark, started singing... "Here I am, Lord." She is blessed with the sweetest, most beautiful voice I have ever heard. Tears were streaming down my face, as Dominic and Danny escorted me down the aisle to be united with my *Prince Charming*! I was so used to seeing him in his jeans and NASCAR tee shirts, that when I saw him in his tuxedo, he looked so handsome, the sight of him actually took my breath away!

Our ceremony was so beautiful and holy. Elaine Dux played the piano, accompanying Mary Ann, as she sang all the songs we had chosen... "Ave Maria," "The Irish Wedding Song," "Let there be Peace on Earth" and "Hail Mary Gentle Woman." The last song I placed flowers at the statue of the Blessed Mother's feet. Then turning around, as Mary Ann sang the words, I also preformed it in sign language. (I heard people blowing their noses, so I guess that seeing a bride doing this really touched them.) Monsignor gave a heartfelt sermon, speaking of the love and friendship we have shared over the years. Everything was perfect, especially at the end when he proclaimed: "Ladies and gentlemen, I present to you for the first time... Mr. And Mrs. Dennis Jordan!" What a fantastic feeling his words sent through my heart and soul! Then everyone cheered and applauded as Beethoven's "Joyful, Joyful We Adore Thee" (the first song I learned to play on the piano) boldly sounded as we exited down the aisle!

As we waited to greeted people in the reception line in back of the church, I realized why everyone broke out in laughter as we left the altar... the members of my wedding party had all put on big, red clown noses!

Both of our receptions were even more wonderful and exciting than we had expected. It was so remarkable sharing one of the most important days of our lives with family and friends. The next day Dennis and I left for a honeymoon in Niagara Falls, Canada... the same place my mother and father went on their honeymoon. Dennis was not only my best friend, he was also a romantic, tender, fantastic lover!

As the years have passed, God has blessed our union, and Dennis and I have grown together as children of God. We have deep love and respect, not only for each other, but also for our children, grandchildren, families, friends, neighbors. We attend Mass regularly, and pray out loud together each night, before we fall asleep in each other's arms. There is harmony in our lives that we both have never experienced before. Both Dennis and I have the child within us, and receive the greatest pleasure out of not only helping others, working together, but enjoying the simple things like hanging out together watching television, playing board games and camping with our neighbors Joe and Sonia, from next door. Although we may have a little disagreement every once and a while, we never let it get out of hand. I can honestly say that we have never, ever had a *fight*. We both agree that with the love and respect we share for one another, we would never let any disagreement go that far. I can depend on Dennis for anything, especially his love. I always call him... "My hero!"

My business also continues to grow and prosper immensely. In fact, the Purple Dinosaur, The Power Rangers and the like, may come and go... I am still here, blessed to be doing second-generation parties! I can't tell you how many mothers proudly show me photos of the both of us when I entertained at their birthday! I jokingly tell them... "See, I am not only the goodest clown there is, I'm the oldest!" What thrills me the most is that others see the Holy Spirit at work... in me. It doesn't matter whether it is my Clown Ministry at a church, or at a birthday party in a trailer park... His light comes shining through! I wish I had the power to embrace the whole entire world, and make them feel safe and loved, especially the little children! But as Mother Theresa said, "Bring about God's Kingdom in your little corner of the world. If everybody did that we would be in Paradise."

I also continue to enjoy volunteering, and have been the recipient of several awards, including The Franklin Delano Roosevelt Humanitarian Award, The Jerry Louis Muscular Dystrophy Award and last week I was informed I will be receiving the National Leadership Award, and will be invited to meet President Bush. Regularly I am called to entertain at benefits for Senator Bob Mellow, for Toni Gilhooley, who is a very active promoter in political affairs, for WVIA-TV's Appreciation Day... and the like. I also enjoy belonging Business and Professional Women's Club. There I have met many dedicated, talented women, including our president, Milana Williams. And I was introduced as a member of the Disabled American Veterans Woman's Auxiliary, by my neighbor Sonia Baldwin, where I was elected chaplain. Both of these worthy organizations work hard to make our community a better place. Please don't think, "Boy, is this lady conceited, bragging about herself like that!" I did not mention these things to "blow my own horn," because I am fully aware that I cannot do anything without the power of Almighty God. I share this with you to express how God has planned my life, and continues to use me as His instrument to make this world a better place. He is also calling each and every one of you to do the same! Listen... can you hear Him speaking to your heart?

I also want to share my glory with Dennis, because of his unselfishness to share me with the rest of the world. How surprised I am when I meet people out of costume, and they say to me, "Aren't you Jo Jo the Clown? I recognized you by your smile!" In my past this would have never have happened. Now, I am happy and content with myself (except for maybe a little nip and tuck here and there) no matter if I am performing in the spotlight before hundreds of people, or hanging around the house in my baggy, old nightgown. Dennis makes me feel beautiful and loved at all times.

My children Mary Ann, Catherine, Dominic and Danny, have all grown up to be decent, honest, hardworking, respectable, caring people, and each one is close to Almighty God. Tell me; what more can a mother ask for? I am as close to Dennis's daughter Trisha, as if she were born from my very own womb. She is both beautiful inward and out. Her husband, Anthony, is something else. I can't tell you the many, many errors I have made on my computer writing this book, If it wasn't for his help, you wouldn't be reading my story for another few years, and I sincerely thank him. They originally lived in Brooklyn New York; I am pleased that they bought a home in Pennsylvania, and live only a block away!

Dominic's wife Tammy is also like a daughter to me. They only live across town in Carbondale. Tammy and I are so much alike that I tease her that when I was six years old, I gave her up for adoption. She is a fantastic mother, wife and homemaker, and an even more wonderful friend.

Mary Ann and her husband, John live about eighteen miles away in Clarks Summit. John is also a good father and husband. He and Mary Ann teach CCD in their church. Although he thinks of me and Dennis as a friend, I love it when he sometimes refers to us as Mom and Dad. They are expecting their third child around January!

My baby girl Cathy is also married. She and her husband Eric live all the way in West Virginia. Although I miss them very much, I know she is in good hands. Eric is a great guy, who has strong faith, and he is so good for Cathy. Eric affectionately refers to me as "Mama Jo Jo."

Danny is not married yet, but he is in a good relationship with a girl named Mercy. She has a lovely daughter, Megan. We are hoping they will marry soon, only time will tell. He visits often since he only lives in Honesdale, about fifteen miles away.

Our family is growing by leaps and bounds! We are blessed with nine beautiful grandchildren… Tamara, Samantha, Melinda, Brian, Brooke, Paula, Amanda, Johnny and our newest member, baby Isaiah. I am happiest when we are all together for celebrations, Easter egg hunts and holidays. My heart leaps at the sight and sound of one of my grandchildren running up to me with their little arms open wide proclaiming, "Grandma Jo Jo; I love you!" I also have a friendly relationship with Bill and my stepdaughters, Susan and Ann Marie and granddaughter, Sarah. I still refer to them as my children; we have all been through much together. I can't help but to love them dearly.

I have a fantastic relationship with my baby sister, Mary Jane and all our family, especially my cousin, and mentor, Mary (Skripp) Frye.

Dennis and I live in peace and harmony in this lovely, old house on Chestnut Street, with our cat, Rosie, our birds and fish.

Life is very good! All my old heartaches and painful tears are like a bad dream. How I made it through is truly an miracle in my eyes. I don't know why I had to endure so much suffering, however, I like to think is was a learning experience for the work I needed to do in the future.

A tender moment for Joann & Dennis, on their wedding day. Photo taken at "The Party Palace" reception, on November 25, 1995.

Thanksgiving

I think about all the people who have befriended, helped and promoted me throughout my career. Talent agents... Ed Curry, Cosmic Productions, Linda & Keith from Spotlight Entertainment, Harry Meier Talent Agency, Sam Lasante from *Spotlight Talent Showcase*. Also the television and radio stations...WYOU, WNEP, WBRE, WVIA, WOLF, Diocese of Scranton Catholic TV, Warm radio, WCDL, Magic 93. Also newspapers... *The Scranton Times, Wilkes Barre Times Leader, The Villager, The Triboro Banner, The Sunday Dispatch, The Advantage, The Weekly Almanac, The Catholic Light* and the *Carbondale News*. Through their faith in me, they allowed my work to be freely shared, promoted and publicized to the public.

I also think of all my business associates... Damien the Magician. He is a fabulous entertainer, who still makes me cry when he performs the "Linking Ring Illusion." How many gigs have we done together in the past twenty years? Damien not only has promoted and encouraged me, he is a friend whom I know I can always count on.

Then there was Louie Plotkin "Cosmic Louie," he left us all, so suddenly and so young. We were buddies, and I miss him dearly, however his talents will be forever remembered. Neither his magic, nor his stilt walking will leave our hearts and minds for a long time to come.

He is called "Mr. Dunce," Bob Healey, but he is far from dumb. His compassion and caring is beyond reproach. I could never forget one of the first times I met him, we were working at JC Penny in the Viewmont Mall. All I knew how to make were balloon animal dogs and cats. He said, "Here, let me show you how to make a flower." I was touched by this; how many other entertainers would share their trade secrets with you?

Bonsai the Magic Guy... I love him; what a trip, so talented and funny. He, as with Mr. Dunce, was not afraid to share his talents with me. He taught me the fine art of balloon *hat* sculpting.

Rob the Juggler... he can juggle... bowling balls, knives...anything! We are great friends who respect each other's different talents. And the wonderful singing group "The Poets." A group of talented men who never fail to introduce me at all the many, many functions we find ourselves entertaining at... together. They always make me feel extra special.

I also have much respect for many other marvelous entertainers I have worked with... like that young singing group of young ladies called... "The

Pixie Chicks." Although they are not in their teens yet, I have a feeling they are on their way to stardom!

I can't forget all the disc jockeys and bands... like Frankie Carll Productions, Brian K., Dennis the DJ (not my husband), The Fortunes and all of you others... I appreciate your sound systems, timing, and most of all, friendship!

Of course I must mention my three dearest friends who were very instrumental in promoting my Clown Ministry, Sister Eleanor Kalafut, Father Joe Cica, and Ann Murnock. I should also like to thank His Excellency Bishop James Timlin, who allowed me to go forth and spread the "Good News" of our Lord and Savior Jesus Christ.

Then there are all my many sidekicks and assistants...

Jean Collin, "Bashful" is still with me, and has been with me the longest, about seventeen years. I love her strong faith, friendship and the way children are drawn to her kindness and gentleness. She has never let me down, not even once. How many times have I called her to got over to Cal-Ideas to pick me up balloons, and no matter how busy she was she would say... Ok. I must also take this opportunity thank my friends from Cal-Ideas, especially Frank, who always met my clowning needs, including hundreds of long eyelashes, and stayed open after hours, so I could rush in late after a party to pick up balloons!

I also thank "Patches," Cindy Gonsaules, is also still on board; she too is a great friend, not to mention the fact she is my daughter-in-law, Tammy's stepmother. I enjoy her kindness, loyalty and late night visits for a cup of tea.

And I am proud to mention "Bubba," Paula Scirone, she is not only beautiful, talented, fun and great with the kids, what can I say she is my granddaughter. And my two newest cast members... my grandson Brian Juice... Wow! He is following in his father Jasper's, er I mean Dominic's, footsteps! And Marion Stockhower, "Bubblegum," we might change her name because she is so shy; however, both are great assistants, and learning fast!

Another special person I would like to thank is Byrd Pressley, entertainment manager for Caesar's Resorts in the Poconos. He has made "Cassandra" a regular attraction for the guests at Paradise Streams, Cove Haven, Pocono Palace and Brookdale. How delighted I feel each week as I enter the elegant, grandiose resort; all the team make me feel so welcomed, like I am part of a family!

Byrd also has a special gift... a singing voice like an angel. I know he will go far with his new CD... However, we all hope he never leaves us!

There is another person whom I admire. A very talented young man, Frank

Ogozaly, better known as "Frank the Magician." Trained by the well known Damien, he has incentive, the energy of his youth and faith in himself. I believe that he will continue to follow his dreams and go far in this world.

Next, are "Darius the Magician" and "Sir Kevin" who helped run the Party Palace with efficiency, class and timing, while still making it fun.

There have been so many others who shared their talents and walked the path with me to making others happy. You not only helped me in my work, your friendship made my personal life more complete... Katie Blooms, Rainbow, Jasper, Rosie, Chi Chi, Dancer, Happy, Aunt Millie... I simply can't forget Pat Ward, John Graham, and that beautiful belly-dancer Tana... Euliah, Bows, Bubblegum... also Buttons and Jingles... and all you other clowns! It has been many years since I started clowning around, so if I forgot to mention your name, I'm sorry. It is not that I don't appreciate you and I thank you from the bottom of my heart. You are all so wonderful and I am forever grateful for all of you!

A proud Mama and her children. From left to right: first row Catherine, Joann, Mary Ann. Back row Dominic and Danny.

Joann affectionately refers to this photo as her "Motley Crew." Grandchildren: Left to right...Brooke, Brian, Amanda, Paula, Baby Isaish, Tammy, Sammy, Melinda & Johnny.

Chapter 28

The Never Ending Story

Well, my friends, we have arrived at the part of the story, which should read, "The End," however to me, it is just the beginning. I have so much more to share with you, however that's another book! Writing my memoirs has been an inspirational journey back in time, which has filled me with many emotions along the way. My heart has felt satisfaction, regrets, sadness and joy... while taking this walk down memory lane. Most importantly, it has truly been a healing process for me.

I wrote this book, not only to answer the ongoing question people always ask me, "What ever possessed you to become a clown?" I also offer it as a prayer that God will allow my story to be an inspiration to others!

I believe that through my book, someone's life will change for the positive. Hopefully, someone who may be hurting will realize they are very special, and were made in God's own image. That it does not matter what unfortunate circumstances may surround their life... with faith, hope and love in God, others, and especially themselves... they can achieve anything, and satisfy their heart's desires.

If only one person is touched, uplifted, or helped by my life story, then it was worth all the time and effort, and I will be truly blessed!

As for myself, a reporter once asked me, "What do you feel is your greatest success in life?" I replied, "Someday, I will stand before my Maker, and if I could look into His eyes and say... I have used the gifts and talents you have given me wisely, and left the world a little happier, and better place than it was when I first arrived, then I will have obtained my life's greatest success!"

Today I was praying up in the loft. The sky, filled with reds and mauves, made a beautiful, perfect sunset. I was thanking God for all my many, many blessings. Once, I cried tears of pain and sorrow almost each and every day. Now I am filled to the brim with peace, joy and contentment. Sometimes I am so happy I just burst forth with laughter! Maybe someone might think this was a just a little strange, but I know it is the Holy Spirit!

Many times throughout the day I find myself clapping and singing out for joy, "This is the day that the Lord has made... come on everybody sing... let us rejoice and be glad in it!" I think of my dear mother, and the joy I felt when I visited her each day. How I looked forward to her wonderful familiar greeting... "Jo Jo Famous!" I really feel this is a mother's prayer... a mother who is now face to face with God, that keeps me in the limelight and... "Famous!"

The closing of this day reminds me of the days when I was a child... I could almost see my daddy coming home from work in the coal mines, the last of the sun yawning, as it slipped beyond the horizon. I asked out loud, "Lord, why did you shower me with so much joy, and so many blessings? How could you forgive me, and still love me after all my sins and mistakes, especially after all the pain I have caused others throughout my life?" A peace surrounded me; I closed my eyes, and smiled, waiting in the quiet stillness. Then, my Lord and Savior Jesus spoke to my heart and said, "Joann, it's because I truly can't remember them!"

"When I Grow UP"

Copyright

When I was just a child... I used to wonder what I would be... I'd dream about so many things that would become of me.

Maybe, my Prince Charming, would come along, and take me to his mansion on the hill, he'd be Handsome, Rich and loving... all my dreams he would fulfill!

Or... I'd see myself in a little, yellow house, with a rose trellis, and trees of pine... in front there would be a picket fence, in back clothes blowing on the line.

I'd have two perfect children: a little boy and girl...

The boy would have dark wavy hair, the girl a golden curl!

Or... With a black apron upon my head, my hair tied in a bun, Rosary Beads around my neck... yes; I'll become a nun. I'd give my life over to the Lord, and teach little children all day... then at night, down on my knees, I'd bow my head and pray!

Or... Sometimes in front of the mirror, I'd wear Mom's lipstick, and fancy shawl...

Why, I'll grow up to be rich and famous, I'll be a heroine to them all. I'll give big, long speeches; the crowd will stand and cheer...

Yes; I'll do lots of important things, when, I move away from here!

Or... I'd sing into a brush handle, a toy broom for my guitar...

That's what I'll be when I grow up... a "Famous Singing Star"

They'll put me in the movies; I'll see many sights...

I'll wear jewels and furs and fancy gowns... my name will be up in lights

I used to think about so many things I'd do, and be, when I was grown...

Now, all the many years have passed... my, how the time has flown.

And when I reflect about myself, I Thank God, for what I see...

Yes;! I like what I have become... for I've grown up to be

ME! AMEN!!!

Printed in the United States
91552LV00003B/64-81/A